MW01247652

DANGEROUS
INNOCENCE

SOUTHERN LITERARY STUDIES

Scott Romine, Series Editor

DANGEROUS INNOCENCE

WHITE MEN

MASS CULTURE

AND THE

SOUTHERN OUTSIDER'S APPEAL

1960–2020

WILLIAM P. MURRAY

LOUISIANA STATE UNIVERSITY PRESS   BATON ROUGE

Published by Louisiana State University Press
lsupress.org

Copyright © 2024 by Louisiana State University Press

DESIGNER: Barbara Neely Bourgoyne
TYPEFACE: Adobe Text Pro

CATALOGING-IN-PUBLICATION DATA ARE AVAILABLE
AT THE LIBRARY OF CONGRESS.

ISBN 978-08071-8155-3 (cloth)
ISBN 978-0-8071-8212-3 (epub)
ISBN 978-0-8071-8213-0 (pdf)

Contents

Acknowledgments

Any part of this book worth reading has its origins in the countless teachers, family members, and friends who patiently offered advice and helped me along the way. Thank you for your time and wisdom. Much of this project insists on the importance of selfless communities, and the people listed below (along with innumerable others) have modeled that community for me time and time again. I am so lucky to know each of you.

The person deserving the most credit for this book's existence is my brilliant and kind partner: Anne. No words can fully capture the reality of her support and encouragement. Her thoughtful contributions ripple throughout the following pages. While my son Penn is too young to have offered much in the way of advice, he is also part of this book. I love him so much, and in the last chapter, when I write about fathers and sons, it is his face I see. I desperately want him to inhabit a world with more kindness and less cruelty.

Trudier Harris has also deeply impacted my writing and thinking. Those lucky enough to know Dr. Harris understand what a privilege it is to have her as someone willing to talk with you and to read your work. She also gave me the courage to write what I believe to be true, and that is an immeasurable gift. I have been fortunate to have a great many good teachers in my life, but Dr. Harris most fully embodies the kind of professor and mentor I wish I could be.

I come from a large family, and they have all contributed to the ideas and thoughts found in this book. Thank you, Dad, Mom, Haskell, Drew, Babs, Anna, and Sam. I admire and depend on each of you more than you know. Anna, in particular, deserves acknowledgment. She patiently read early versions of this book and offered deeply valuable direction.

For their guidance and encouragement over the years, I would also like to thank a few of the many professors and colleagues who have been so generous with their time and insights: at the University of Mississippi (Colby Kullman and Deborah Barker), at the College of Charleston (Julia Eichelberger and Conseula Francis), at The University of Alabama (James A. Crank, Fred Whiting, Jolene Hubbs, Philip Beidler, Erik Kline, Geoffrey Emerson, and Nathanael Booth), at Baylor University (Ryan Sharp, Sarah Gilbreath Ford, and Richard Russell), at Hendrix College (Hope Coulter), and at Tennessee Wesleyan University (Elizabeth Ruleman and James Schiavoni). There are also too many people within the larger field of Southern Studies to thank by name, but I love being part of this community. You all are incredible people, and each of you has given me so much.

I am also indebted to The National Endowment for the Humanities (NEH). As a graduate student, a grant from the Summer Seminars and Institute Program gave me the time and space to begin writing this book.

Finally, thank you James Long, Scott Romine, Dabian T. Witherspoon, and all those at LSU Press who helped make this book a reality. I truly appreciate your insights and all the effort that goes into producing this series.

DANGEROUS
INNOCENCE

Introduction

Constructing Innocence

Late in 2019, I watched a much-shared clip of Eddie S. Glaude Jr. speaking on an MSNBC political panel. Nicolle Wallace, who was leading the discussion, seemed earnest in her exasperation over President Trump's recent failure to condemn White supremacist violence after a racially motivated shooting in El Paso, Texas.[1] She asks Glaude, "What's next?"—inviting him to join her indignation (MSNBC, "Blaming"). He starts out in a thoughtful tone, saying, "You know, America is not unique in its sins as a country. We are not unique in our evils. Where we may be singular is in our refusal to acknowledge them, and the legends and myths we tell about our inherent, you know, goodness—to hide and cover and conceal so we can maintain a kind of willful ignorance that protects our innocence" (MSNBC, "Blaming"). As his emotion builds, Glaude launches into how "we," referring to pundits like himself and those at the table, protected the Tea Party from being associated with the racism that so clearly helped drive their movement. "The thing is," he continues, "there are communities that have had to bear the brunt of America confronting . . ." He then stops and corrects himself, "White Americans confronting, the dangers of their innocence, and it happens every generation" (MSNBC, "Blaming"). He goes on, recounting some of the suffering that has occurred because of White people's need to protect their perceived innocence, arguing it would be a mistake for viewers and those at the table to place this history of violence on Donald Trump's shoulders alone because that is "too easy." Instead, Glaude, as he slams his hands together, asks that "we" acknowledge that "this is us, and if we are going to get past this, we can't blame it on [Trump]. He

is a manifestation of the ugliness that is in us" (MSNBC, "Blaming").
Visibly shaken, he concludes, "Either we are going to change, Nicolle, or
we will be locked into a cycle that will rob more Black children of their
parents and Black parents of their children" (MSNBC, "Blaming"). Wallace seems to recognize the power of the moment, and she eagerly asks
Glaude, "What else?" To which he replies, "Lord, help us" (MSNBC,
"Blaming"). In the YouTube clip, Chris Hayes's face then pops up on
the screen, telling viewers to hit subscribe and to click on the links for
"lots of other great videos!" (MSNBC, "Blaming").

Later, I located a longer clip of the segment, hoping to see Glaude's
impact on the other panelists. What I found, though, was very little
reflection on what he actually said. Instead, the conversation almost
immediately broadens and flattens to locate racial guilt as belonging to
someone else, not the "we" and "us" Glaude indicts. Sam Stein, who
speaks next, clearly seems uncomfortable. He says, "First of all, that was
beautifully said, but I just want to supplement that a tiny bit" (MSNBC,
"Eddie Glaude"). He then turns to what he calls "a political story, not a
racial or cultural one" (MSNBC, "Eddie Glaude"). The "story" recounts
the failures of the Obama administration to follow through on their report about the Tea Party being racially motivated. As he talks, he turns
what Glaude had framed as a failure of people like those at the table
into a broader sense of failure within political systems. The conversation
then safely turns back to a more generalized sense of racial wrongdoing
and Stein finishes his thought by saying, "So, you know, Eddie is absolutely right, and I think we need to have some hard conversations about
whether our political system is up to the challenges" (MSNBC, "Eddie
Glaude"). Raul Reyes then brings the conversation back to Donald Trump
and how he has failed to treat people with fundamental decency, especially Latinos. Glaude tries to reenter the conversation, perhaps to
correct his fellow panelists. However, Wallace guides the segment fully
back to focusing on the President, cutting away to Philip Rucker and
asking him to further opine on Trump's failure to speak up after the El
Paso Shooting. The scene finally closes with Chris Hayes's face again
popping up and telling viewers to subscribe and click the links for more
"great videos!" (MSNBC, "Eddie Glaude").

I am struck by several things in the longer clip. Most notably, how eagerly the other panelists nod their heads, murmur approvingly, and agree with Glaude. However, the minute he stops talking, they all work to make clear they should not be included in any version of a guilty "us." This shifting of culpability, though, seems to happen regularly when discussions land on racial guilt. The blame for America's racial realities is expertly maneuvered, usually by White people, away from those sitting at the proverbial table and toward others who are really the guilty ones. Whereas Glaude uses "we" and "us," illustrating an understanding that (even as a Black man and a Princeton professor) he is unavoidably included in the problems of Whiteness, the other panelist cannot wait to prove their own innocence through someone else's relative guilt. As Glaude explains, this maneuvering is nothing new, and even in a video entitled "It's Easy to Place it All on Donald Trump's Shoulders. This is Us," there is a near-shameless ability to turn conversations about "us" into denunciations of "them." This book is very much interested in how the United States arrives at such a place, where progressives, like those invited to speak on an MSNBC political panel, are unable or are unwilling to look around and recognize their own participation in the racial violence they ostensibly decry.

There are undoubtedly many reasons White Americans feel entitled to their innocence, and it would take far more than a single monograph to try and articulate the countless strategies enabling centuries of denial. I am convinced, though, the imagined South plays a vital role in constructing White people's views of themselves. I use "imagined South" here and throughout the book in reference to Benedict Anderson's thesis in *Imagined Communities* (1983), which is that "all communities larger than primordial villages of face-to-face contact (and perhaps even these) are imagined" (6). As he argues, modern communities rely on narrative structures that connect disparate individuals into something that can be perceived as a connected whole. Anderson then makes clear that these imagined narratives are capable of compelling incredible acts of violence or love. What produces this power to organize people and compel action is a common sense of reverence attached to sets of ideas or symbols. As he argues, using national anthems as an example, when we "utter the same verses to the same melody" we lose our individual selves in a shared, collective voice (145). He writes, "How selfless this unisonance feels!" (145). Ultimately, Anderson argues it is this sense of losing an isolated identity and sharing a voice or common narrative that lies at the heart of nationalistic power. It seems clear, then, to understand our present condition more fully in the United States, we should work to better recognize common narratives articulating identity. To that end, this book examines how White people use the imagined South (even as it fractures and becomes many souths) to construct a shared voice, proclaiming racial innocence.

In many ways, the imagined South has always played a key role in helping White people in the United States frame racial guilt and innocence.[2] Traditionally, the region performed that role through a sense the South was fundamentally different from a relatively liberal American whole. Jennifer Rae Greeson explains, the North/nation, which produced the vast majority of U.S. literature in the eighteenth and early nineteenth centuries, "spatializes the gap between national ideal and national reality—between our better angels and our frank demons—so that we [White people] may re-present the moral failings of U.S. life to ourselves as matters of geography" (4). This framing of the region as a container for America's "moral failings" persists through much of the twentieth century. Leigh Anne Duck explains in *The Nation's Region* (2006), which covers through the 1930s, that "Southern representations functioned in U.S. discourse . . . as both other and exemplar, providing in their insistent cultural difference, a logic through which U.S. apartheid could be considered separately from the state ideology of liberalism" (27). While the good North/bad South rhetoric softens and mutates at different times in the nation's history, from the eighteenth through much of the twentieth century, a relatively stable imagined South helped White people from outside the region maintain a belief in their own comparatively liberal and progressive identities. Meanwhile, White southern authors, as Fred Hobson articulates, embraced a "rage to explore and explain," seeking "to justify themselves before the critical eye of the world" (9). Hobson then goes on to link the region's obsession with "self-exploration" and "self-explanation" to the South's "peculiar institution" of slavery (9).[3]

As Greeson, Duck, and Hobson articulate, for over 150 years, White Americans understood the South to be a mostly stable, separate region that could contain legacies of racism and slavery away from national narratives of liberalism. This book, though, focuses on what comes next—as White people began adopting the region into a common national narrative. Starting in the 1960s on television, then spreading more widely in the following years, White people began embracing new versions of the South that moved away from its traditional role as a backward and race-obsessed space. John Egerton's *The Americanization of Dixie: The Southernization of America* (1974), along with dozens of other books and articles written during the 1970s and 1980s noticed the region's fading image. They pronounced the South's demise or strategized to help it endure, pointing to technology, globalization, education, urbanization, and continued African American migration as threats to the region's distinctive nature. As this book contends, though, the eventual move past the South as a solidly imagined space does not so much emanate from the reasons listed above, as it does from the civil rights movement's ability to illustrate racism as a national rather than a southern problem. Historian James C. Cobb explains, "Both Southern and northern liberals had presumed that the South could join the American mainstream only by emulating the North's racial model, but by the late 1960s angry and sometimes violent northern protests . . . made it all too apparent that white racism was hardly confined to white Southerners" (217). Put simply, this book argues that once realities of national racial guilt became impossible to ignore, White people needed a different kind of South to confirm White, American innocence. So, they simply reinvented the region's imagined identity to fit those changing needs.

To the surprise of many, then, an identifiable South persists in the late twentieth century as a backdrop for popular narratives. However, the region changes in the White imagination from a reliably stable, racially stagnant South into many "souths," each with its own unique characteristics and versions of history. Remarkably, in the span of a few decades, it became nearly impossible to nail down what exactly someone meant with the label "southern." As Cobb puts it, by the last quarter of the twentieth century, the South was understood as so "thoroughly transformed and so totally discontinuous with its troubled past that it would in reality be not so much a 'New South' as what George Washington Cable referred to as a 'No South,' fully assimilated and essentially indistinguishable from the rest of American society" (Redefining 150). Or, as Scott Romine explains, by the 1980s "if one doesn't subscribe to the South of *Southern Living,* then alternative subscriptions are available" (16). In line with late capitalism's emphasis on choice, individuals could select to which "South" they wanted to subscribe. More than that, the post-Souths from which they could choose seemed to have very little to do with old obsessions over racial violence. Romine goes on to explain that along with the South of *Southern Living,* there is "the South of *The Oxford American,* the multicultural South often circulated in academic journals, the Dirty South playing on XM radio," and "no one is dying— or killing" because of them (16).

Imagining the South as a series of brands, though, did not so much change patterns of who is "dying—or killing," as it changed how White people saw their relationship to that violence. Using an increasingly dominant sense of dissensus and fracture, White people began promoting a view of the region that created distance between individuals and the racial disparities that had long defined southern and Northern/ National communities. Therefore, instead of tortured families unable to escape their communal past, we see White people embracing southern characters who could still be "southern" while maintaining imagined innocence. Much of this book, then, focuses on what I will call White southern outsiders, which are characters who embody this separation from communal guilt. To be clear, though, while this project largely focuses on White men from the South, this is not to suggest one can safely contain guilt to a certain phenotype, sex, or region. Rather, by looking at strategies used to preserve innocence for those who have arguably done the most to enact and protect racial and social hierarchies, I think we arrive at a clearer understanding of how the rest of White America imagines its own freedom from guilt. Given the deadly intertwining of racism and patriarchy in the United States, it should be impossible to construct a White, American man who could somehow remain separated from his inherited positionality. The impossibility of this imagined separation seems especially true if that character is from the South, given the more than 150 years of White Americans using the region as the receptacle for the nation's racial sins. Yet, repeatedly, particularly after the 1970s, White southern men are depicted as being largely free from inherited guilt or communal responsibility, which positions everyone else as even further established in their innocence.

Certainly, outsiders in American literature, film, and TV are nothing new. However, the pairing of this outsiderness with representations of White southern male identity provides a particularly useful window into post-1960s conceptions of racial innocence. One important factor is the changing role of the outsider itself. Before the latter half of the twentieth century, outsiders usually provided insights into a communal identity in which audiences would recognize themselves as participants. In the 1960s and 1970s, though, we see a fundamental change in this equation, which can be witnessed both in narrative texts and how individuals began to imagine their own positionality in relation to their communities.[4] As Bruce Schulman and Robert D. Putnam articulate,[5] by the 1970s, the majority of Americans began to feel distanced and disconnected from one another. There undoubtedly were negative consequences for White people born from this sense of alienation, which is mainly what Schulman and Putnam focus on in their books. However, this distance from a communal identity also gave White Americans, who had long enjoyed the benefits of racist systems, license to start identifying with marginalized outsiders rather than the communities the outsiders critiqued.

In her book *A Nation of Outsiders,* Grace Elizabeth Hale helps explains how White Americans "fell in love" with the image of the outsider. She writes, through this image "they remade themselves. They became outsiders too," and "by the end of the twentieth century, the romance of the outsider had become so pervasive that few scholars questioned how odd and uncanny it was, how historically unprecedented, to understand politically and economically enfranchised people as marginal and alienated" (3). In other words, the post-1960s love affair with the outsider illustrates an unprecedented realignment of imagined identity that allows White people to see themselves as separated from their communities rather than inheritors of a violent colonial reality. The true audacity of this maneuver, though, is that the shedding of communal positionality and embrace of the outsider is imagined as an act of moral bravery and liberation rather than an evasion of inherited guilt. As a result, the White male characters we encounter in this book are mostly held up as heroes and lauded for trading in their old, tainted southernness for a new, better brand of American or (more accurately) post-American identity. In their supposedly admirable forgetting of the past, White southerners then model how White people in the North/nation can also shed any link to their own history, as they embrace an innocent, individualized identity.

While the following pages argue against this repositioning of identity and contend that accepting guilt is a necessary step toward achieving justice, it is not my intention to simply make White people feel worse. Instead, this book maintains that guilt is merely the proper response to the injustice White Americans have created and maintained. The only choices, then, are acknowledging and responding to that guilt or simply trying to ignore it. Certainly, individuals can still combat injustice while denying their role in the systems of violence in which they inevitably participate. However, honestly admitting one's own positionality reframes restorative justice as a project that necessarily involves everyone, regardless of personal feelings or constructed identities. This is not to say intersections of race, gender, and class do not complicate the picture. There is a great deal that separates each person. However, I am convinced that admitting shared complicity and beginning to confront the mythologies protecting fantasies of innocence are important first steps toward achieving a more just and equitable nation. By looking at perhaps the most brazen evasion of guilt (White southern men), I think we begin to better understand the broad umbrella under which a great many other fantasies of innocence exist. I do not think men inhabit some universal identity under which all other identities fit. Rather, this book focuses on what an innocent southern masculinity licenses for those consuming southern texts. The central premise is that if audiences watching TV, for instance, are willing to accept an innocent Andy Taylor or Ben Matlock, then it becomes far easier to accept the Sugarbakers or really any other form of Whiteness as being even further disconnected from inherited guilt.

I suppose literary criticism, like philosophy, is often, as Nietzsche wrote, "namely, the confession of its originator" (15). The ideas behind this book have their origins in my experience as a student at the University of Mississippi. During my second year of undergraduate study, the school erected a monument "honoring James Meredith and those who fought to give all citizens equal educational opportunities in the South" (civil rights). The monument consists of a bronze, life-sized Meredith striding confidently toward a portal with the words "courage," "perseverance," "opportunity," and "knowledge" capping four limestone columns. It is a powerful arrangement and a long overdue reminder of Meredith's bravery in the face of overwhelming resistance. I remember at the dedication feeling proud of my university, as it finally seemed willing to acknowledge a small part of its stained past. At the time, I was only vaguely aware of this past, to be sure, but I still felt it was important the University be clear that it was a school dedicated to universal equality and respect. The monument offered me assurance that we, as an educational institution, were rightly aligned with a post-racial worldview, which was confirmed as speaker after speaker waxed eloquently about Meredith, the monument, and how much "Ole Miss" had changed since the 1962 riots. I basked in the good feelings emanating from the event and left fully assured of my own good, relatively liberal positionality.

During my walk across campus after the speeches ended, I passed another monument, which sat just a few hundred yards away from the newly installed dedication to Meredith. It honors the University's Confederate dead.[6] I wish I could say the Confederate monument's visual rhetoric and implicit support of White supremacy startled or discomforted me on that day, especially considering what I had just witnessed. However, the South (from my perspective in 2006) could live fairly comfortably with both monuments—a kind of recognition there were good people on both sides of the historical racial divide. This is not to say I understood the Confederacy itself as a good thing, or even that I considered the Confederacy to mean anything coherent at all. It seemed entirely possible to me that one could just separate individual soldiers from the institution of slavery many died defending. In my mind, the Confederacy was more closely associated with thousands upon thousands of unique people fighting for any number of personally negotiated reasons, and there had to be good individuals fighting for relatively decent causes, like protecting their families and homes. So, the monument could just be honoring abstract ideals found in those individual soldiers, celebrating something like bravery and sacrifice instead of a war fought to continue enslaving and torturing millions of people.

With all that said, if I am completely honest, I also felt if people wanted to tear the Confederate monument down—that would be fine. I could live without it. The monument seemed largely disconnected from anything specifically relevant to me and my life. In fact, as I progressed in my studies and talented professors made clear the nation's racist past, it felt good, on occasion, to be one of the people who were unhappy with the Confederate monument's presence on campus. When I made it clear in conversation that I felt no allegiance with those who defended the Confederate monument or those who shouted "The South will rise again" at football games, I was able to appreciate the looks of approval I received from my friends. We knew in those moments we were the good kind of White people who understood the Civil War was ancient history located in the bad old days. We possessed the supposed knowledge that it was time to move on and what really mattered was racial blindness and equal treatment for all people, regardless of gender, race, or class. Armed with that knowledge, we were free to construct our own brand of southernness (or not) and could enjoy the University with little concern for the racial realities that actually surrounded us.

Looking back, I think I recognize, first, that my opinions about the Confederate and Meredith monuments are immaterial in comparison to those they more directly impact. Second, and more closely aligned with the purposes of this book, I realize both monuments were able to work as a kind of deflection, helping me understand myself as conveniently disconnected from unpleasant historical legacies. My worldview was (and certainly still is in many ways) guided by the belief I can simply cordon off aspects of my Whiteness I do not need or with which I do not want to be associated. As a student in Mississippi, all this allowed me to believe I stood outside the nation's racial legacies and did not have to really think about the past or inequality as something directly involving me. Sure, I knew racists existed somewhere, and I was vaguely committed to fighting against those racists. For instance, I knew if I were to see one, I should let them know they were wrong and ignorant. As far as I was concerned, though, true racism was something carried out by a few rednecks or old people who muttered racial slurs under their breath and hated people of color. I did not personally know anyone like that, and while I heard a couple racist jokes and knew the fraternities were pretty much segregated, I believed most White people at the University and in the nation more generally were decent, hardworking folks who bore no relation to the angry racists I learned about in my history and literature courses.

Put plainly, I believed people like those who shot at and harassed James Meredith were the problem, and the shiny new Meredith monument reinforced my conviction that we, as a university and as a nation, had long ago defeated and moved past any real power those people might have wielded. The monument was proof in bronze and stone of our moral victory and tangible evidence that the Mississippi and "Ole Miss" of 2006 were places where equality and progress now largely reigned. As Donald Cole (assistant provost and assistant to the chancellor for multicultural affairs) put it, "Although sides were taken, lines were drawn and determinations were anchored, this monument reflects a reconciliation of all those opposing views, emotions and differences" (University). Cole's vaguely worded summation of the past and definitive statement that we lived in a reconciled present pretty much summed up my outlook. Therefore, White people like me were free to lay down what C. Vann Woodward called the "burden of Southern history." We could instead focus on enjoying the supposedly reconciled and equitable world we now inhabited, which was full of competing southern brands—all available for constructing our own individualized identity.

The relationship I entertained with history during college is representative of many White people in the United States, who have invested in the notion that racism is either largely contained in the nation's past or is carried out by a few isolated "bad apples." According to Pew Research in 2016, seventy percent of White people think individual rather than institutional racism is the bigger problem when it comes to discrimination against African Americans. Sixty-eight percent believe being a White person either "hasn't made much difference" in their lives or has made their lives more difficult (Discrimination). These statistics illustrate what Eduardo Bonilla-Silva calls "color-blind racism." He explains, "Social analysts of all stripes agree that most whites no longer subscribe to ['the basic claim that blacks are subhuman']. However, . . . a new powerful ideology has emerged to defend the contemporary racial order: the ideology of color-blind racism" (25). The "new racism," as Bonilla-Silva describes, thrives in the neoliberal, post-truth present, and has its roots in a logic that allows for the mirage of White innocence without interruptions to White power. Put again, even those who claim they believe in equality between the races seem unable or unwilling to admit what George Lipsitz points out: "that whiteness is a matter of interests as well as attitudes" (233). By framing investments in Whiteness as merely a matter of "attitude," White people can focus on individual feelings as being of paramount importance, all while minimizing personal interests in patterns of racial violence embedded in American society. Indeed, if racism is mainly understood as a feeling, then the solution to investments in White supremacy can simply be to stop feeling like a racist.

Part of what makes the post-1960s South such an important case to study is that it illustrates how White people were able to transform the nation's most benighted region into merely one more constructed narrative, governed by individual feelings rather than an inherited reality. Moreover, by using an increasingly ascendent postmodern philosophy, White people could refashion this evasion of historical inheritance as a good thing, reflecting a realistic understanding that all narratives are constructed and unstable. While there is no single consensus on what the signifier "postmodern" means, I find Jeffrey Nealon and Susan Searls Giroux's way of generalizing the term to be helpful. They write, "There seems to be a certain sense of *style* shared by many of the things labeled 'postmodern,' a sense of disjunction or deliberate confusion, irony, playfulness, reflexivity, a kind of cool detachment, a deliberate foregrounding of constructedness, a suspicion concerning neat or easy conclusions" (126). This sense of "deliberate confusion," "detachment," "constructedness," and "suspicion" plays a powerful role in creating distance between White people's history and their imagined identities. According to this brand of postmodernism, the South, Whiteness, patriarchy, and really any facet of society or one's identity could simply be taken apart and rendered open to endless interpretation and, therefore, largely meaningless. As Hale writes, "The romance of the outsider works because it denies at the imaginary level the contradictions between the human fantasy of absolute individual autonomy and the human need for grounding in historical and contemporary social connections. It works because it enables Americans with political and economic power to disavow that power" (308). Indeed, "the romance of the outsider works" because it encourages White people to separate themselves from their historically rooted identity through a simple rebranding effort, which allows for imagined innocence without having to give up the licenses and advantages born from centuries of racial violence.

In writing for an academic press, though, I imagine most readers will likely already acknowledge that systemic racism intrudes into one's individual life and should be dismantled. This book, then, is not meant to convince readers of this truth. Rather, what I hope to address are the strategies White people use to alleviate themselves of the tension between the philosophies they profess and the realities they support. Unfortunately, it seems even among those claiming to be progressive and antiracist, there is a consistent tendency to resist the humility and restorative work that comes from recognizing oneself as personally guilty. James Baldwin writes, when White Americans look into their past, they see "an appallingly oppressive and bloody history, known all over the world. What they see is a disastrous, continuing, present, condition which menaces them, and for which they bear an inescapable responsibility. But since, in the main, they seem to lack the energy to change this condition, they would rather not be reminded of it" (722). Like Baldwin, I believe what largely impedes action is White people's unwillingness to be reminded of their personal complicity in continued racial violence. As bell hooks explains, true progress comes from a change of spirit "that leads beyond resistance to transformation" (297).[7] Or, as Audre Lorde puts it, "the true focus of revolutionary change is" recognizing and fighting against "the piece of the oppressor which is planted deep within each of us" (105). It seems most progressives know the correct language about racism, but their actions betray a spirit unconvinced that they themselves are part of the problem. Instead, there is a tendency for White people to change the subject to someone else's relative guilt, which is ultimately just another way to claim innocence.

Similar to the panelists' response to Glaude or my reaction to the Meredith monument, most White people clamor to associate with narratives that can illustrate they are safely aligned with the righteous. Therefore, despite ready admissions that all Americans are implicated in violent systems of race and power, we see very little reflection on the individual, personal responsibilities born from that guilt. Instead, when confronted with their history, as Baldwin points out, the common response is for White people to just change the subject. He writes, this evasion "can be reduced to a plea: Do not blame me. I was not there. I did not do it. My history has nothing to do with Europe or the slave trade . . . I *also* despise the governors of Southern states and the sheriffs of Southern counties" (723–724). As Baldwin points out, White people should stop relocating guilt as someone else's inheritance and begin looking at themselves to understand the racial violence plaguing America. Admitting guilt, though, does not mean embracing hopelessness. As Ibram X. Kendi explains, "Cynicism is the kryptonite of change" (Hopefulness). However, White people also should not fool themselves into thinking there is a process through which they can simply opt out of the systems they have inherited. This is the fantasy of the outsider, which thrives on the belief that identity is endlessly malleable and unattached to communal inheritances.

This book, then, promotes the position that White people's imagined innocence is a deeply dangerous fantasy, rooted in a strategy of avoidance and scapegoating. Key to this ability to avoid guilt is a perceived divorce from history that severs moral responsibility from one's involvement in the systems of power churning along regardless of individual recognition. Put differently, the following five chapters push back against a way of thinking that was popularized after WWII and embraced more fully in the following decades. Charles Taylor calls this way of thinking "expressive individualism." He writes that after the Second World War "there arises in Western societies a generalized culture of 'authenticity,' or expressive individualism, in which people are encouraged to find their own way, discover their own fulfillment, 'do their own thing'" (300). According to Taylor, this movement toward individualized identity creates an "ethic of authenticity," which encourages an environment of "galloping pluralism on the spiritual plane" (300). In a general sense, there is nothing wrong with "galloping pluralism." However, it should also be clear how this pluralism and personalized "ethic of authenticity" serves as a powerful tool, abetting White people who do not wish to admit the consequences of their history.

Reattaching White outsiders to a communal identity, then, encourages an honest assessment about what Whiteness is and what it means to belong to a nation steeped in inherited commitments to White supremacy. As Ruth Frankenberg explains, "it is not true that a somehow benign notion of 'whiteness' was then made malignant by the march of history." White identity has always been closely linked with racially based violence, which she argues "makes utterly misplaced, entirely falsely premised, the idea of a 'return' to [White] racial innocence" that is "unspoiled by the relations of colonialism" (74). Adding to Frankenberg's argument, Howard Winant writes, "whiteness is a strictly negative category, empty of all content save its distantiation from 'color,' its refusal of 'non-whiteness'" (106).[8] As David Roediger concludes, "it is not merely that whiteness is oppressive and false; it is that whiteness is *nothing* but oppressive and false . . . it is the empty and terrifying attempt to build an identity based on what one isn't and on whom one can hold back" (13). As these authors, along with Nell Irvin Painter in *The History of White People* (2010), Carol Anderson in *White Rage* (2016), and Ibram X Kendi in *Stamped from the Beginning* (2016), demonstrate, Whiteness has always been and continues to be a conceptual blank slate upon which White people manufacture identities capable of sustaining White/colonialist power. Given this history, guilt rather than innocence seems to be the primary characteristic around which White identity should be organized.

Acknowledging guilt, though, does not mean centering White people's feelings or obsessing over their conversion narratives. It also does not mean promoting melancholia, where White individuals are encouraged to wallow in shame and continuously pronounces how badly they feel.[9] Rather, guilt when divorced from shame, as P. S. Greenspan explains, is a particularly powerful form of "moral motivation" (28). What makes guilt more powerful than shame is that guilt is attached to a rooted incident or problem that can and should be addressed. Raffaele Rodogno clarifies, "The focus of evaluation for shame is the global self ('*I* did that horrible thing') as opposed to the specific behavior for guilt ('I *did* that horrible *thing*')" (150). Accordingly, "When experiencing shame, it is not just this or that aspect of the self that one construes negatively: one construes the self as globally bad. When experiencing guilt, what is bad is a particular action; the self is negatively evaluated in connection with that action only and in that sense locally" (150). Therefore, rather than simply a general call to feel badly or to try harder, which produces shame, feeling guilty is linked to a goal for which one should be working, which is most often the restoration of harmed parties.[10] As Tara McPherson explains, drawing from the psychoanalyst Melanie Klein, "guilt is not inherently a negative or destructive emotion." Instead, "guilt can imply the 'never fully exhausted wish to make reparation'" (225). This book, then, focuses on the links between guilt and the need for reparations. Accordingly, reparations should be understood, not as something born from altruism or benevolence, but as merely the action justice requires. Indeed, to be transformed through acknowledged guilt leaves little room for arrogance or pride in one's positionality. It cuts against the presumed superiority of those privileged enough to have access to education, and it should promote a consistent focus on service and restorative action rather than self-centered melancholia or denial.

To that end, this book starts with White southern men on television and traces their evolution as a vehicle of innocence. The first chapter focuses on TV shows from the 1960s–1990s and examines the White southern outsider's rise in the American imaginary. Then, in the second chapter, we see more clearly the consequences of this rise. Through looking at examples from Eudora Welty, Wendell Berry, Walker Percy, and Barry Hannah, we see how well-respected White, southern authors provide a philosophic lens through which White people could separate themselves from the region's guilt. The third chapter then works as a needed interruption to White people's fantasies about their own innocence and a reminder that history, regardless of White people's imaginings, maintains a real and felt presence in the United States. Chester Himes, Ernest Gaines, and Yusef Komunyakaa also make clear that Black Southern identity is not an abject reflection of White violence but has its own rich, vibrant, and too often ignored history. Then, in the fourth chapter, which covers the years after 9/11, we see the White southern outsider's return to community, as he models a new brand of American innocence. This chapter illustrates that while the United States changes a great deal in the more than fifty years this book covers, White people largely remain consistent in embracing logic that protects both their innocence and their power. Finally, the fifth chapter and the conclusion introduce potentially productive ways to approach the nation's history. Jason Aaron's and Ron Garney's *Men of Wrath* (2015), Cormac McCarthy's *The Road* (2006), and Natasha Trethewey's "Native Guard" (2006) establish that in order for White people to truly participate in a radical and organized destruction of racial violence, there first must be a willingness to turn inward and to destroy the outsider's imagined innocence.

1

Desiring Dixie

Television and the Rise of the White, Southern Outsider

I start this book with television because TV is an exceedingly powerful window into popular conceptions of identity. In his 1993 essay "E Unibus Pluram," David Foster Wallace compares television to an "overlit bathroom mirror before which the teenager monitors his biceps and determines his better profile." Or, as he puts it a short while later, "Television, from the surface on down is about desire" (22). Wallace's assertion that TV reflects desire agrees with television's basic economic premise. As Todd Gitlin explains, "High-consumption corporate capitalism implies a certain sensitivity to audience taste, tastes which are never wholly manufactured. [Television shows] are made by guessing at audience desires and tolerances and finding ways to speak to them that perpetuate the going system" (589). In other words, TV shows make money and stay on the air by correctly identifying and then providing people with what they want to see. When networks meet viewers' inclinations, their shows gain loyal fans who return each week to consume both the offered narratives and the accompanying advertisements. Given this need for consistent approval, television shows that remain on air speak almost directly to how White people want to see themselves in relation to their communities.

Television's marrying of high-consumption capitalism and storytelling is not unique, but unlike most films or literary productions, which typically are one-time issues, TV shows must keep selling their product week after week. More than that, television both enters the intimacy of the home, while also linking together a larger viewing audience into a common narrative. Especially in the era where network television dominated what people watched,[1] viewers could tune in to any of the "Big Three" networks and be assured, whether they were watching ABC, CBS, or NBC, millions of other Americans were watching along with them. This sense of common narrative provided a powerful link between individuals, encouraging viewers to see themselves as participating in a national event from the comfort of their own couch. Lisa Hinrichsen, Gina Caison, and Stephanie Rountree explain in the introduction to their collection *Small-Screen Souths* (2017) that "Through its investment in the type of seriality that makes community possible, and by its delivery of the public sphere into the private domestic realm of the home, television has functioned as a medium for fantasies of national cohesion, providing an experience of belonging that generates a complex web of consolation, confirmation, and compensation that intertwines politics with seemingly private personal experience" (4).[2] Put again, the "complex web" television offers can reveal metanarratives linking together national desires across years and even decades. Accordingly, narratives on television provide valuable insights into the stories Americans employ to determine their "better profiles."

More specifically, this chapter demonstrates how constructions of southern men on television, from the 1960s—1990s, helped White Americans abdicate feelings of racial guilt. We start with *The Andy Griffith Show* (1960—1968), in which we see the roots of the White southern outsider—a character whose sense of separation from traditional forms of southern community, in the 1970s through 1990s, would come to dominate depictions of White innocence. By starting in the 1960s, a decade before the outsider's eventual dominance, we see how rural Southern television helped establish a postsouthern foundation upon which subsequent ideations of innocent White men could be built. At first, it might seem odd to consider a series like *The Andy Griffith* Show as "postsouthern." Typically, the term is used in conjunction with the postmodern and focuses on concerns over authenticity—or, more precisely, the impossibility of an authentically southern identity. For instance, Lewis P. Simpson (who coined the term in 1980) frames the "postsouthern" as part of an "existentialist America" increasingly divorced from long-held views on history and place (269). Simpson's framing of the postsouth, as being closely linked to some form of postmodern alienation or existentialism has endured as a powerful lens and lies at the heart of what is often termed "new southern studies."[3] Critics, such as Michael Kreyling, Martyn Bone, and Scott Romine,[4] have all used the concept of the postsouthern to encourage embracing what Houston Baker and Dana Nelson call a "thick" understanding of the South (243).

To be clear, a more postmodern/postsouthern or "thick" understanding of the region does important work divorcing the South from being viewed as a monolithic space defined by something like White, agrarian angst.[5] Yet, this more fractured view of the region also sets up the grounding for a damaging commitment to the post-racial.[6] When we look at the primary framework for the South's distinctiveness in the national imaginary (which has always been its supposedly unique racial backwardness) we see how decades before Simpson articulated the idea that we were "beginning to live in a postsouthern America" (269), there were already widely popular iterations of a racially sanitized postsouth, which would establish the groundwork for the region's more complete separation from its past in the 1970s and 1980s. It is important to link conceptions of the postsouthern to the post-racial because they both hinge on an understanding that the nation has mutated beyond a traditional relationship with its history. In *The Postsouthern Sense of Place in Contemporary Fiction*, Martyn Bone argues the term postsouthern maintains an element of regional specificity that is capable of linking the South to enduring legacies of racial and social violence. In his chapter on Atlanta, he writes, "If 'postsouthern' signifies the postmodern, capitalist redevelopment of 'the South,' it also retains its etymological root: 'Southern.' 'Postsouthern' thus prudently reminds us of the local, historical continuities of racial and economic inequality that remain within [Atlanta]" (169). This argument, though, seems to not fully acknowledge how the term "postsouthern" itself negates "southern." In other words, the word claims to be beyond or past the South as a usefully imagined space rather than retaining "southern" as a still valuable signifier. Indeed, the word almost necessarily signals a movement past or beyond what has rendered the South unique in the national imaginary—which, again, is primarily its racial history.

As Thomas Haddox puts it in his article "Elizabeth Spencer, the White Civil Rights Novel, and the Postsouthern," conceptions of the postsouth have always been more about "recycling rather than reinvention" (579). He explains how White people tend to "recycle" the South as a way to avoid racial reckoning, writing, "just when African Americans begin to challenge, in a highly visible and overtly political way, the hegemonic narratives of the white South, white southerners conclude, whether reluctantly or joyfully, that these narratives are dead or at least evacuated of efficacy" (579). While Haddox uses his conclusion to call into question Michael Kreyling's assertion that "The south is the richest site yet discovered in the U.S. cultural terrain for the study of and participation in the reinvention of culture" (*Inventing* 182), I think this history of "recycling" cast as "reinvention" is key to understanding the South's role in the national imaginary. Put simply, studying southern "reinvention" provides a window into how the imagined region has long-aided White people in manufacturing narratives of their own innocence. Ultimately, both the racially obsessed, isolated South and the integrated postsouth work toward the same goal of "proving" White America's goodness. In 1960s television we see a particularly clear example of how the South is reinvented to offer new fantasies of White racial innocence.

Shows, such as *The Beverly Hillbillies* (1962–1971), *Petticoat Junction* (1963–1970), *Green Acres* (1965–1971), *The Virginian* (1962–1971), and *The Andy Griffith Show* (1960–1968), all depict elements of the region devoid of any real link to racial violence. As Jennifer Rae Greeson in *Our South* (2010) and Leigh Anne Duck in *The Nation's Region* (2010) explain, the South, for the vast majority of its history, functions in the national imaginary as a relatively stable and foreign "other" in which White people could locate racial violence away from the supposedly liberal national whole. As these shows moved past this traditional framing, White people in the 1960s welcomed a new, supposedly postsouthern/post-racial view of the nation that cut against a growing sense of American communal fracture. This attempt to move past race as the South's defining feature appears in all the southern shows in the 1960s but perhaps most clearly in *The Andy Griffith Show*. As Phoebe Bronstein explains, "*Andy Griffith*" discouraged conceptions of the region as racially violent and "remade the rural South as a hospitable space that championed the common white man and small-town values in the face of radical social, political, and technological upheaval" (136).[7]

This "remaking" of the South, though, meant denying racial guilt and imagining the region had embraced what Duck calls "the state ideology of liberalism" (27).

We can gain a better picture of how the nation began adopting the region into the supposedly liberal national whole by looking more closely at how *The Andy Griffith Show* offered viewers a fantasy of an authentic and communal postsouthern South. Undoubtedly, *The Andy Griffith Show* maintains a kind of "Southern" identity, but the series makes a concerted effort to establish Mayberry as firmly American in its values and history. For instance, in Andy Taylor's initial introduction to audiences on *The Danny Thomas Show* (1953–1964), we see how southern difference is cast as only a veneer under which supposedly shared national values reside.[8] The backdoor pilot episode, which aired in 1960, starts with Danny, who is a fast-talking comedian and entertainer from New York City, getting pulled over by Andy, who is Mayberry's sheriff. Danny is pulled over for a traffic violation, and in their encounter, we see all the stereotypes and humor that often accompany a "fish out of water" story about a city slicker in the country. For instance, Danny is angry that he could be ticketed for running a stop sign when there was only a sign and not a road. Andy explains to him the town did not have enough money to build the road and could only afford the sign, inviting viewers to laugh at this example of Southern/rural difference. Initially, though, Danny is exasperated and angry over Mayberry's oddity. He demands to see the Justice of the Peace to rectify the ticket but comedically finds Andy also presides over the courts. Then, Danny decides to go public with his story and reaches out to the *Mayberry Gazette*, only to find Andy is the editor of the newspaper as well (Danny).

In the opening minutes, the episode makes clear that Andy Taylor and the southern town of Mayberry are almost interchangeable. It is never in doubt that Andy, the individual, is deeply imbricated in whatever communal failures or successes Danny encounters. After all, Andy holds almost every position of power in the town, which draws a clear link between Andy's and Mayberry's moral character. At first, it seems the values shared by Andy and his town are foreign and dangerous. It appears that Danny has entered a strange land where supposedly normal American views on law and freedom of the press are not recognized or appreciated. This feeling of lawlessness is heightened when Andy, after glimpsing the large amount of cash Danny carries in his wallet, decides to fine the New Yorker one hundred dollars, instead of the normal five. Danny responds by choosing the alternate jail sentence, and he invites a New York based film crew to come down and expose the injustice he has experienced in Andy's seemingly backward southern town.

If the episode were to end here and the other shows from the era were to follow a similar pattern, I would largely concur with Sarah K. Eskridge's assertion that rural shows of the 1960s made it so "viewers outside of the South could indulge in the televised fantasy that southerners were not like them," and that the shows "reinforce a sense of the South as a world apart from the nation at large" (134).[9] However, as the episode continues, we see Danny and Andy perform a largely traditional regional romance, where characters from the North/nation and the South come together and learn to appreciate cultural similarities and differences. These stories have a long tradition, exemplified by novels such as Caroline Lee Hentz's *The Planters Northern Bride* (1854) or more famously D.W. Griffith's film *Birth of a Nation* (1915). Traditionally, though, the romance revolves around the North/nation coming to recognize value in the South's distinctive racial and social practices. However, in *The Andy Griffith Show* and in the rural shows of the 1960s more generally, White viewers indulged in a different kind of romanticized fantasy. Instead of imaging two distinct regions with different views on culture and race, these shows reinvent White southerners as being maybe superficially different but firmly aligned with the rest of the nation's supposedly liberal values. Indeed, whereas the traditional romance is most often used to justify difference, the shows imagine regional divergence largely existing only at the level of accents, manners, and musical styles.

As the episode continues, Danny begins to recognize these shared values and appreciate Andy and the town he had previously dismissed. Danny starts to change his mind when Andy's son Opie comes into the courthouse mourning the loss of Wilfred, his pet turtle. Lovingly, Andy guides Opie through the realities of life and death, explaining how we all must live with our sorrows, just like he did when Opie's "Maw" passed away. The moment is tender, and it demonstrates the common human experience of pain and loss, as well as Andy's American ruggedness and his ability to endure in the face of suffering. When the camera shifts as they talk, we see Opie and Andy clearly framed by an American flag, which draws attention to the fact that despite Mayberry's differences, the town and its sheriff are still squarely a part of the United States. Andy further demonstrates his morality shortly after this conversation, as he successfully protects an impoverished widow from a greedy creditor. Again, in this scene, he is framed by the American flag. In these back-to-back sequences, the show makes plain that while Andy's ways of doing things may be unfamiliar to Danny, the sheriff embodies the communal values that all "good" Americans supposedly embrace. Witnessing Andy enact these values, Danny starts to have a real change of heart. However, his temper gets the best of him; and he decides to go ahead with the live broadcast from his jail cell.

When the film crew finally arrives, Danny cloaks himself in a blanket and tries to look distraught for the camera. He starts by telling the TV audience what they might expect to hear about a small southern town in the 1960s, that it is a place where an innocent man could unjustly languish in "a cold, damp, dirty cell." However, viewers watching the pilot know that Danny's characterization does not reflect reality. Before Danny can add to his false narrative, Andy steps into the frame and cuts him off. He says, "I'm obliged to point out that, that not only ain't accurate, but that's just downright insulting." Andy then goes on to explain why he levied the high fine against Danny. He delivers a message about how important it is for the rich to pay their fair share and that people in positions of power, like Danny, need to take responsibility for setting a good example. He then closes with a message about how southern towns like Mayberry are misjudged, and Danny and other people from cities need to show respect, even for "rubes and hicks." He explains, "Mr. Williams and a lot of people like him seem to be in a big hurry, and it's a shame. It's a pity because there is a whole lot of fine country to be seen between the city he left from and the city he's going to, and . . . there's a lot of mighty good folks to meet, a lot of wonderful experiences to be had by a fellow that will take the time, you know, to appreciate it."

Following this speech, Danny (literally and symbolically) sets himself free from his jail cell and walks toward Andy. He says, "I'd like to apologize to Andy for being a bellowing city slicker. I'm sorry, Andy. I

had you all wrong." Andy thanks him and says, "I didn't have you wrong
. . . I had an idea that you'd be plumb decent once you got around to
it." With the nation watching, the two men then grasp hands, bringing
together in shared admiration the fast-paced nation/North and the slow
and steady South. Bronstein explains, "the episode suggests, [Mayberry]
is just what Danny and perhaps northern viewers need: the white rural
South as a cure to the rude, speedy, city-slicker life" (132). According to
this logic, if people would just slow down a bit, they would find while
the South may look and sound a bit different, at its heart the region is
just as committed to the same social values as the rest of the nation. The
episode, then, introduces a South that has largely been misunderstood
by "city slickers" who have relied on false TV coverage and fallen prey
to an erroneous view of the region. Indeed, as Bronstein concludes,
Danny's decision to use the news to misleadingly depict Andy and his
community "undercuts civil rights news coverage about the South and
its most violent emblem, the white sheriff" (132). Viewers of the TV
show, then, are encouraged to be skeptical of the news, which supposedly mischaracterizes the South and distracts from a basic American
goodness that allegedly exists just beyond the camera's frame.

By looking briefly through *The Andy Griffith Show*'s first season, we
see example after example of Mayberry "proving" to viewers that the
town is really not that stereotypically southern. Most of the episodes
revolve around moral lessons that could be set anywhere in America
during the 1960s, such as Opie learning about honesty in "The Runaway
Kid" or Andy learning about humility in "Opie's Charity." There is also
a slew of episodes that draw on internationally recognizable stories,
such as an adaptation of *Romeo and Juliet* in "A Feud is a Feud" and *The
Christmas Carol* in "A Christmas Story." Moreover, the show does not
cast Mayberry as a particularly isolated or insular community. Certainly,
there are plenty of episodes where outsiders are revealed to be wrongheaded or dangerous, such as "The Manhunt" (an episode where the
state police belittle Andy's expertise as Mayberry's sheriff) or "Andy
and the Gentleman Crook" (an episode about a thief who comes into
town and fools almost everyone into trusting him). However, many of
these negative encounters happen with other southerners, again shifting
focus away from considerations of regional/racial difference, towards

another traditional American anxiety about the urban and the rural. The season also includes almost an equal number of episodes that depict good or helpful strangers who enter Mayberry and are eventually appreciated because of their differences. For example, in the episode "Stranger in Town," the inhabitants of Mayberry are at first deeply suspicious of a man who knows a great deal about them. However, after he shares that he memorized the information because he admires the town's sense of community, the stranger is welcomed into the fold and celebrated for his good taste. Put simply, the first season (and the show more generally) strives toward a kind of White universality that erases supposedly outdated regional distinctions. As Don Rodney Vaughan puts it in his defense of *The Andy Griffith Show*, "Whether a viewer is in Heidelberg Mississippi, or Heidelberg, Germany, he or she would fit right in Mayberry" (419). Of course, that assumes the viewer is White, which is one of the show's central conceits. It normalizes a brand of Whiteness that supposedly can exist anywhere, bound together by a common and post-racial morality.

There are also several examples in the first season where the show more explicitly rejects a distinctive regional/racial history. For instance, in the episode "The Horse Trader," Andy is tasked with selling a rusty old cannon. First, he tries to sell the artillery piece by connecting it to the Confederacy and Fort Sumter. However, this association makes little impact on the potential buyer. In fact, the association with the South's role in the Civil War does not even really draw out a response from the man. Yet, when Andy claims a crack in the cannon "come from a direct hit whilst Teddy Roosevelt was dragging her up San Juan Hill" (Elinson), the man is immediately interested and offers to buy the cannon at a price well over its worth. The cannon's imagined provenance is one of several examples where the show focuses on shared "American" wars as being the conflicts worth noting and celebrating. Another example can be found a few episodes later in "A Plaque for Mayberry." The action of this episode centers on finding and honoring the last remaining relative of a Revolutionary War hero. When they find the man, he claims to be unworthy and decides Mayberry as a community should actually receive the honor. The episode, then, highlights two of the show's central messages. First, that community, not individuals, should be celebrated; and second, that the southern town of Mayberry is part of a proud national history that can be separated from a stained regional past.

We can perhaps see the clearest example of Mayberry's positioning as part of a postsouthern and united White national identity in a later episode, entitled "Andy Discovers America." In the episode's initial scenes, Andy attempts to stump his deputy Barney Fife with a history question. He asks Barney to tell him about the Emancipation Proclamation. Barney, who had just been bragging about the breadth of his historical knowledge, is unable to recall any information about the proclamation or its connection to freeing enslaved people in the Confederate South. He laughs nervously, claiming everyone knows about that, even Opie. Opie, however, says he has never heard of it either. Now squirming, Barney says, "You tell him, Aunt Bee," to which Andy's elderly aunt replies, "Me? I wasn't there." After fumbling around a bit, Barney finally gives a clearly concocted story about some folks that "needed them some emancipating, so they got themselves a proclamation." The scene ends with laughter and Andy telling Opie, who got the whole conversation started by complaining about his history class, that not everyone needs to know history, as evinced by Barney's and Aunt Bee's apparently acceptable lack of knowledge. Opie then leaves the conversation still ignorant about the Emancipation Proclamation and convinced history is a subject about which he should not be particularly concerned.

Eskridge also looks at this episode, and she suggests the conversation, where the Emancipation Proclamation is left undefined, again demonstrates a sense of division between the North and the South. She writes, "For nonsoutherners" this scene "plays on the ignorant southerner trope: rural southerners are so dumb they do not know basic U.S. history." Whereas, "For Southerners, the characters' failure to recall consequential national history underscores their disregard for federal government" (139). She goes on to contend that this framing of the Emancipation Proclamation also allows the North/nation to view racism as a southern problem and encourages the South "to fantasize about the document's annulment and a return of black Americans to pre-Emancipation Proclamation status" (140). However, if we consider the rest of the episode and put it in conversation with the show's established ethos, I think we can see a different argument emerge. What we see is the episode making explicit what the show had already implied for almost three straight seasons—that the rural South of the 1960s is a space utterly divorced from its traditional racial history. In other words, the show leads White viewers to understand themselves as living in a country where almost everyone (including older people like Aunt Bee and southern law enforcement like Barney) had long ago moved on and forgotten a time when questions of Black freedom were controversial or an important topic of debate. Therefore, instead of illustrating division or difference between the North and the South, the focus on the Emancipation Proclamation promotes a clear fantasy that, regardless of region, the United States shares a common disregard for old divisions and is now joined together as a liberal and healed America.

Put plainly, the conversation and omission of the Emancipation Proclamation's memory works as a defense, justifying the show's selective amnesia. Bronstein's assessment of the conversation is helpful. She argues, "At once, the humor diminishes the relevance of the question, and the lack of an answer evacuates it of political impact and importance: the Emancipation Proclamation becomes just another joke at Barney's expense" (126). However, instead of the "joke" being an example of the show offering a "recognition of civil rights struggles and the racial limits of Mayberry" (139) as Bronstein goes on to suggest, I think it actually works in the opposite direction. Ultimately, the episode positions the lack of knowledge surrounding the Emancipation Proclamation, not as a tacit admission of its own unwillingness to address the subject of race, but as a good thing that demonstrates a necessary forgetting of the nation's divisive past. Accordingly, the episode then presents a correct relationship to American history as being one defined by narratives that (for White people at least) are unifying and inclusive.[10]

The episode promotes its version of history through a common trope often used in *The Andy Griffith Show:* Andy teaching Opie an important moral lesson. Upon hearing his father tease Barney and label history as being inconsequential, Opie decides to lead his male classmates in refusing to do their assigned homework. However, following a visit from Opie's teacher Miss Crump, Andy decides history is important after all and works to get the boys interested in the subject. He entices them by saying history is really about "Indians and redcoats and cannons and guns and muskets and stuff."[11] Opie and his friends become entranced at the promise of such stories, and Andy delights them with a rousing account of the "shot heard clear 'round the world." The boys and Barney listen with glee as he weaves together a highlight reel of the American Revolution that features Paul Revere, plenty of preening redcoats, and a resounding U.S. victory. Andy's account is historically inaccurate, but it does its job. The boys become thoroughly invested in a narrative of American exceptionalism and immediately form a club to celebrate their new national pride, declaring as they leave Andy's office that anyone who is not a member of their new club is a traitor and British.

The episode's message, like much of *The Andy Griffith Show*, is earnest and straightforward: U.S. communities should focus on histories that unite White people, such as killing "Indians and redcoats," not topics that might dredge up old and supposedly almost forgotten intranational divisions, like the Civil War or battles over emancipation. Andy, then, is cast as being right for never answering the question he poses at the beginning of the episode. He is also shown as being wise in directing Opie's interest toward the Revolutionary War. As the show frames it, there are parts of the past that are best forgotten in the interest of uniting Americans against the growing sense of racial and regional fracture illuminated by the civil rights movement. In case this point is missed, the show closes with Barney asking once more for information about the Emancipation Proclamation and Andy again remaining silent. This silence echoes how, throughout its run, the show largely refuses to take on issues of race. In fact, the single named Black character to arrive in Mayberry, Flip Conroy, does not show up until the seventh season, and he only lasts one episode. Moreover, in the episode he unquestioningly and happily coaches a segregated football team comprised of all White players.[12] The only other times Black characters appear in Mayberry, they are in the background walking by the action or standing behind White characters who are speaking.

The reality that a television show in the early 1960s did not feature prominent Black roles is perhaps not much of an oddity. However, the combination of placing the show in the South, ignoring race, and celebrating a shared national history, gives viewers the clear impression that (regardless of how the civil rights movement made it seem) racial violence is rare and isolated. According to the show, southerners were not only unconcerned with questions of Black freedom but were also actively promoting the nation's better values of unity and progress. Correspondingly, if this were true of southern communities (like Mayberry), viewers in the supposedly more progressive North/nation could rest assured their own towns and cities were even further removed from legacies of racial inequity. In other words, by framing Mayberry and its sheriff as being unconcerned with race, the show promotes a kind of racial amnesia. Viewers are then encouraged to minimalize the role racism has played in the United States and instead focus on aspects of community and history that unite White Americans in a metanarrative of national exceptionalism.

In some ways, then, television shows of the era, like *The Andy Griffith Show*, normalized and promoted views of American racial liberalism. They implied that by the 1960s almost all White people, even in the South, were aligned with what James Flanagan calls Mayberry's "pleasant patriarchy and benign whiteness" (308). Given White people's commitment to violence in the 1960s, *The Andy Griffith Show*'s "pleasantness" may have seemed like progress. As Sasha Torres argues, "Television and the civil rights movement, then, through a perhaps unlikely coincidence of interests, formed powerful allies for each other during this period" (6). However, this supposed alliance between TV and the civil rights movement depends on casting racial violence as being an aberration of American character rather than a systemized norm. Andy's goodness, then, is used to supposedly prove America's goodness. Indeed, while programs like *The Andy Griffith Show* perhaps did dissuade some investments in more blatant and violent expressions of White supremacy, they also actively discounted how racism is woven into the fabric of America's past and present. In fact, the shows of the period almost explicitly made the argument that the United States could be defined by a nearly immutable postsouthern racial innocence.

The comforting fantasy of postsouthern communities, like Mayberry, persisted on television until the early 1970s. However, particularly after the assassinations of Martin Luther King Jr. and Robert F. Kennedy, it became increasingly difficult to sell such naiveté, especially to younger audiences. As Bruce J. Schulman points out, by 1969 the nation, led by young people, had developed a "thorough suspicion of the instruments of public life" along with a "profound disillusionment with the corruption and inefficiency of public institutions" (xv). Given this distrust in "public institutions," a character like Andy Taylor, who stood at the center of his town's institutional power, became somewhat of an anathema. TV shows then began to respond to new national desires for a different kind of freedom from the past. First, Andy Griffith left Mayberry in 1968, and his acting career reflects the nation's disillusionment with his brand of southern identity. Despite promises from Universal Studios to turn Griffith "into another Jimmy Stewart" (Visé 190), his movies struggled to find an audience at the box office.[13] The following year after Griffith's departure, Jim Nabors left *The Andy Griffith Show*'s spinoff *Gomer Pyle, U.S.M.C.* (1964–1969). Then, in what became known as the "rural purge,"[14] the cancellations started. First, *Petticoat Junction* was canceled in 1970. Then, the revamped *Andy Griffith Show*, entitled *Mayberry RFD*, along with *Green Acres, The Beverly Hillbillies, Hee-Haw*, and *The Virginian* all were cancelled a year later in 1971. Fred Silverman, the architect of the "purge" who would go on to produce the shows *Matlock* and *In the Heat of the Night*, recognized that valuable younger demographics were no longer attracted to the uncomplicated and harmonious communities depicted in these rural shows.[15] As a result, Silverman's CBS and the other major networks invested in an alternative brand of White innocence that left behind claims of a pure, communal whole and instead promoted southern outsiders, who operated beyond institutional power or were pitted against it.

The two most prominent shows set in the South during the 1970s were *The Waltons* (1972–1981), which takes place during the Great Depression, and the miniseries *Roots* (1977), which focuses on the horrors of slavery. Both shows demonstrate this shift away from national innocence as they frame their protagonists against backdrops of inept or violent American social systems. Unlike *The Andy Griffith Show*, which made a distinct effort to establish a clear connection between "good" individuals and a "good" national community, these shows center their best and most admirable characters as opposing the dominant communal mold. While it is important to note there are many differences between *The Waltons* and *Roots*, the similarities between the two shows demonstrate how White people rejected an image of themselves as part of a shared national body with a common history. Instead, we start seeing an embrace of what Grace Elizabeth Hale calls, "the romance of the outsider" (302), which provides White people with the belief they could simply eject themselves from legacies of guilt and inequity. As she explains, this brand of White identity "celebrates individual will, disavows collective White middle-class power, and imagines relatedness at a symbolic rather than a material level" (302). In other words, White people fell in love with a constructed identity that would allow them an imagined separation from their inherited power and positionality, all without having to give up the material or social inheritances born from that history.

Ultimately, what we see in the 1970s are leading characters who no longer identify with public institutions. Instead, they "prove" White people's innocence through their ability to separate themselves from recognized power, allowing viewers to imagine there is a rich national history that is removed from America's failures. With that said, neither *The Waltons* nor *Roots* take a truly postmodern or relativistic stance toward a shared set of supposed American values. Instead, they take traditional virtues (such as a love of family, a regard for self-reliance, and a celebration of the common person) and locate those attributes outside structures of institutional power. Rather than focusing on someone like Andy, then, who stands at the center of community and is clearly linked to governmental power, White characters like John-Boy in *The Waltons* and Old George in *Roots,* exemplify the idea that there have always been White people who were uninfluenced by the racial and social violence that surrounded them. The characters in the 1970s, therefore, borrow from the unjaded American "innocence" we saw in the 1960s, but what is supposedly good about America is moved from the community to individuals who exists outside traditional frameworks of inherited power. As Daniel T. Rodgers explains, in the 1970s "conceptions of human nature that in the post-World War II era had been thick with context, social circumstance, institutions, and history gave way to conceptions of human nature that stressed choice, agency performance and desire" (3). Accordingly, "Strong metaphors of society were supplanted by weaker ones. Imagined collectives shrank; notions of structure and power thinned out" (3). In other words, after 1969, we start seeing White people moving away from the "contexts" of their identity and increasingly embracing narratives that could free them from any sense of personal, inherited guilt.

The Waltons, then, is not so different from *The Andy Griffith Show* in the morals and social values the two shows project. Yet, the later series reflects a fundamentally different perspective on how individuals should understand their relationship with their larger national identity. For instance, unlike Andy Taylor, John-Boy (the central character in *The Waltons*) lives away from any structured society; he holds no official position; and he does not desire public office when he gets older. Instead, his dream is to be a writer, which is a vocation that wields the power of language rather than institutional power. We can also see the difference between the two shows more clearly by comparing *The Waltons'* pilot episode, "The Foundling" to Andy Taylor's introduction on *The Danny Thomas Show*. "The Foundling" begins with the Walton family finding a young girl on their doorstep who cannot hear and has been abandoned by her own family. Their first instinct is to turn her over to the state, but the Waltons quickly dismiss this idea because, in their view, the state would be unable to properly care for the girl. So the action revolves around the Walton family taking matters into their own hands and convincing the girl's family, who had given her up out of desperation, to take her back. The episode's solution, then, is found in the girl's family taking personal responsibility and trying harder to raise their own child. Like many of the episodes in the following years, the pilot hinges on the supremacy of self-reliance and private, local solutions rather than turning to the government or larger systems of power for answers. Whereas Andy uses his elected position to protect the poor, care for widows, and demand the rich pay their fair share, the introduction to *The Waltons* suggests good Americans solve their own problems and institutional power is almost never to be trusted.

Moreover, by placing this fantasy of self-reliance in the era of the Great Depression and in the South, where the federalized efforts to end poverty were most localized, *The Waltons* encourages an ahistorical outlook that denies the efficacy of those programs. Instead, it determines

White people, or at least relatively decent White people, have always refused outside help and operated independently from the government or any form of concentrated power. As the show frames it, American goodness is a product of good individuals helping one another, whereas actions from the state are either unhelpful or harmful. We see this same framing of historical institutions being dangerous, albeit in a very different context, in the show *Roots*, which follows Alex Haley's family from their enslavement to the author's current success. Certainly, the Black family in *Roots* experiences a far different reality than the Waltons. However, both shows are remarkably similar in their suggestion that even if the nation's institutions fail, every individual (regardless of race or position) can find success through their own individual efforts. The Haley family's rise from slavery, like the Waltons' ability to thrive during the Great Depression, then, is largely framed as consistent with an America that has supposedly always rewarded independence and individual willpower.

White people could watch *The Waltons* or *Roots* and imagine, like these families, they were part of a history separated from society's failures. In watching *Roots*, for instance, they could imagine their ancestors had been like Old George, who is an outsider and largely unmarked by societal investments in White supremacy. Additionally, the decision to cast beloved TV father figures (such as Robert Reed from *The Brady Bunch* and Ralph Waite from *The Waltons*) as villains also provided a larger frame of separation for White viewers. Indeed, casting these men as some of the worst and most violent characters in the show allowed White viewers to see the villains in light of their redemptive later selves. The casting suggests that even if many White people were once implicated in the worst aspects of slavery, they could now be understood as clearly divorced from that past. As Laurie F. Leach puts it, "whites who watched and felt a shock of identification could tell themselves that their part in racial reconciliation was complete" (376). In other words, by framing adored TV fathers as one-time villains, the show could admit the past had been horrific while also insisting White individuals had long ago overcome that past and were now free to enjoy a supposed post-racial present alongside their Black neighbors. Leach goes on to argue White audiences then imagined "the story of Kunta

Kinte and his descendants [as] a form of [the] American immigrant success story," which could be shared among all races (376). As Raphaël Lambert explains, "*Roots,* by overlooking the causes of economic, social, and racial inequality, not only functions as a conciliatory fairytale, but also inscribes the destiny of African Americans in a wider national narrative, which results in playing down the specificity of the black experience" (112).

For White audiences, then, *Roots* frames the South as a location that proves American innocence at the individual level, even as it sheds light on the institutional horror that defined American slavery. As the narrative arc in *Roots* seems to suggest, even the worst instances of systematized state violence had little influence over an individual's ability to create their own narrative outside those frameworks. Couched in that logic, is the implicit argument that progress is realized not through addressing the systemic violence perpetrated by White Americans, but through making room for everyone to celebrate their own narrative, removed from the constraints of an overarching or binding historical structure. Put more simply, the show suggests Americans of all races should frame the nation's violent history as simply the backdrop behind their own individual story of redemption and success. As Schulman explains, "The phenomenal success of *Roots* . . . did not betoken a new respect for African American history or a new ability to empathize with the sufferings and essential human dignity of Black Americans and Africans" (77). Instead, "everyone wanted to celebrate roots, explore identities, cut themselves off from the run-of-the-mill main and emphasize a distinctive heritage" (77). White Americans "looked back— but almost exclusively at themselves" (77). In a similar manner, *The Waltons* discourages reflection on the wide-ranging economic injustice underlying the Great Depression. Rather, the show maintains that the proper response to overwhelming communal failure is to distance oneself from the institutions responsible for that failure and to imagine one's identity as existing separately from whatever damage that system might have caused. Together, then, these shows break from a sense of communal or systemic innocence and instead celebrate outsiders and isolated families who form their own narratives supposedly beyond the corrupt system's reach.

While this move toward individualism led to real expansions in minority expression and a growth in what was accepted as history, there was also an accompanying contraction in how White people understood their positionality within the larger community. Schulman goes on to argue, "Politics always revolves around citizenship—around defining an 'us' against a 'them.' Everyone desires good schools, good housing, roads, and health care for 'us'; few wish to spend their hard-earned dollars on 'them'" (76). As he argues, in the 1970s we see a sharp realignment of who gets to count as an "us." Unlike in *The Andy Griffith Show*, which still made an appeal to an imagined White national community that extends beyond regional lines; shows like *The Waltons* and *Roots* draw relatively tight circles around individual families or small communities that are isolated from the mainstream. This tightening, seen on television, reflects a larger shift in the nation toward abandoning communal definitions of "us." Thomas Borstelmann writes, "Out of the 1970s came a fundamental change in what Americans considered natural or commonsensical. The more communal values of the mid-twentieth century ebbed, particularly the idea that citizens should act collectively, through the mechanisms of government action and taxpayer funding, to reduce the most egregious forms of poverty and extreme economic inequality" (317). Indeed, in the 1970s, we start seeing a brand of American Whiteness emerge that could claim a history of individualism as a basis for separation from any sense of guilt or responsibility for the nation's racial and economic realities.

The Waltons and *Roots* reflect this abandoning of responsibility. However, as we move into the 1980s and for most of the 1990s, we see White people building on this legacy of individualized innocence and claiming freedom not only from the responsibility of an inherited communal history but also from a shared sense of morality that might also compel action. In the 1980s and 1990s, then, we see the White southern outsider reach its full power as a symbol of American innocence. Through the outsider, we also witness a clear example of what Charles Taylor calls "radical anthropocentrism," which focuses on the primacy of the individual subject and "induces us to see our communities, like so much else, in an instrumental perspective . . . making us take an instrumental stance to all facets of our life and surroundings" (59). Particularly, the

TV shows *Matlock* (1986–1995), *The Dukes of Hazzard* (1979–1985), and *In the Heat of the Night* (1988–1995), demonstrate how the South could be instrumentalized to offer separation from inherited narratives that might inhibit personal freedom. Put differently, what we see in these shows is a particularly irresponsible version of the postsouth that aligns with more traditional postmodern understandings of that term. According to this view, the region could be understood as a "postmodern world of dissensus, information overload, and truculent differences," as Scott Romine explains, where "community itself begins to look like a conceptual dinosaur" (210). Ultimately, these three shows reflect a desire for a post-communal brand of southernness that could valorize not only forgetting inherited history but also any sense of larger moral duty for the wellbeing of one's fellow citizens.

In Andy Griffith's return to TV on the show *Matlock,* we can see reflected perhaps the clearest example of White people's growing desire for freedom from history and moral responsibility. Griffith's character, Ben Matlock, offers viewers almost a reverse image of what he embodied as Andy Taylor. Whereas the character Andy demonstrates a deep connection to Mayberry's/America's institutions and values, Ben lives in the placeless suburb of Willow Springs and aligns himself with a national narrative organized around freedom and the pursuit of individual enrichment. Put again, instead of Andy's steady connection to community and grounded morality, which in the 1960s assured the nation that it was not so fractured after all, Ben's amorality and separation from his larger community suggests Americans should embrace their fractured environment and enjoy the freedom to create their own identity. In many ways, Ben inhabits the typical character of the alienated and postmodern outsider, as he lives in the suburbs and does not seem to subscribe to any larger uniting narratives.[16] However, he shares none of this archetype's angst or rootless searching. Rather, Ben maintains the close family ties, self-assurance, and easy sense of humor viewers loved in Andy Taylor's character, all without having to carry the weight of larger communal expectations.

Key to the supposed freedom Ben represents is an understanding of the world as constructed and artificial. Unlike Andy Taylor, Ben's relationship with his community is defined by an unattached irony and unseriousness. In other words, the show fully embraces a postmodern lens of dissensus and fracture, where everything seems framed by a sense of suspicion. For instance, the show's pilot starts by casting doubt on news programs as being actual vehicles of truth. The episode begins with audiences seeing a television within their own TV. Through the series of screens, viewers witness the journalist Steve Emerson questioning a doctor about falsified medical documents and fraudulent payments in the man's practice. At first, the scene is familiar and reminiscent of an exposé on a show like CBS's *60 Minutes*. However, just as viewers might begin to lose sight of the fact they are watching a TV on TV, the shot changes to show the control room. The director's voice breaks in to ask the crew to cut from camera one to camera two. The shift in perspective subtly reminds the audience that when they watch television there are always people out of frame controlling the action.

The camera then pulls back, and viewers are shown a full picture of the interview. Instead of the study audiences had seen through the camera lens, which depicted a cozy room full of thick tomes and leather furniture, they see Steve and the doctor sitting on what appears to be a stage with the books and chairs brought in as props. The change in perspective also shows two other men standing to the side of the stage reading what looks like a script. Then, to fully demonstrate the artificiality of the interaction, the interview abruptly concludes with the doctor storming off the set. Steve acts unsurprised and the director calmly guides him through his polished and witty closing remarks. For *Matlock*'s audiences, who are given a behind-the-scenes window into Steve's performance, there is a clear sense they have just learned that what is passed off as hard-hitting journalism is just another piece of artificial entertainment. Taken as a whole, the opening sequence encourages a kind of postmodern leveling between truth and fiction, where all narratives (including the news) should be understood as mere constructions and not taken all that seriously.

As the camera follows Steve to Atlanta, where he meets his ex-wife Linda Coolidge, the episode further invests in the sense that viewers should be suspicious of appearances and presumed truths. Upon arriving in the city, Linda asks Steve for his assistance investigating a "hot" story about the mob being connected to the government in Georgia at "the highest level" (Diary). Steve begins to help by speaking to an informant, and when he returns, he finds Linda murdered. Since he cannot reveal he was with his confidential source and provide an alibi, the African American Police Lieutenant Frank Daniels charges Steve with killing Linda. Facing murder allegations in a corrupt city, Steve then goes looking for a lawyer, who of course ends up being Ben Matlock. While much of the plot up to this point is fairly predictable for a law drama, the episode's cumulative effect drives home that the world is deeply corrupt and does not align with any organized sense of preconceived order. As the show frames it, the news is fake; the government and the mob work hand in hand; and in the South of the 1980s Black men falsely accuse White men of committing crimes against White women. Put plainly, the world *Matlock* introduces has been turned on its head, leaving viewers searching for some sense of stability or for someone whom they can trust. As David Sirota explains, the 1980s "taught America to worship single, godlike individuals above all else" (37), and the show makes clear the need for "godlike" individuals, like Ben, who appear capable of thriving in a world almost devoid of stable societal structures.

For almost fifteen minutes, though, the pilot leaves viewers lost in this sense of instability. When Ben finally does appear, he seems an unlikely choice. Griffith's familiar face is paired with a suburban/rural environment that suggests a throwback to an earlier age with little relevance to the postmodern disorder viewers just witnessed. The camera introduces Ben first by showing his large plantation style home with green shutters and doors, which is accompanied by a pleasant silence only disturbed by a rooster's distant crow. Viewers finally meet Ben as he feeds his chickens and attends to his morning chores. Upon returning inside, he calls his sleeping daughter Charlene, telling her, "I don't know how it is there in Atlanta, but here in Willow Springs, the sun is shining, the children are playing in the creek, and honest folk are getting ready to go to work" (Diary). If Ben were to remain in this space, it would seem he was simply Andy Taylor reborn, a little older and transplanted to the suburbs. However, in the next scene the show quickly demonstrates Ben's impressive ability to manipulate language and narrative, as viewers watch him use a clever bit of misdirection to convince a jury to drop charges against his client. As the show frames it, Ben inhabits an alternative and bucolic space set outside Atlanta's turmoil and violence, but this does not preclude him from engaging in the larger post-truth and language obsessed culture. In fact, it seems Ben proves that individuals can embrace the role of the outsider while also freely participating in the larger corrupt and rootless society.

What most clearly sets Ben apart from characters, like Andy and John-Boy, is this sense of freedom. He is able to remain separated from both communal responsibility and inherited values, either of which might inhibit his profiting from Atlanta's corrupt capitalistic environment. TV critic Gina Mallet calls this, his "cheerful amorality" (14). Whereas the White southerners in the 1960s and 1970s still clung to a relatively fixed understanding of traditional right and wrong behavior, Ben's character insists on an individual's ability to remain morally fluid and uncontained by any rigid sense of identity or predetermined value system. As Mallet explains, "there isn't anything [Ben] wouldn't do to win a case and a fat fee" (14). According to this construction, Ben's southern identity becomes instrumentalized: he can use it when it is beneficial, or he can discard it if it stands in the way of securing his "fat fee."

The show clearly demonstrates Ben's fluidity as he enters his law office to talk with Steve. First, in the lobby, he meets a Mr. and Mrs. Pearson, who are two elderly neighbors from Willow Springs. Their dog has bitten someone, and they need help in warding off a coming lawsuit. Ben readily acquiesces and gives them legal advice, which is basically to lie and claim their dog does not bite. He then tells his daughter Charlene to write a "strongly worded letter" to "disabuse" the would-be plaintiff "from this fruitless litigation" (Diary). For his services, he charges only fifteen dollars: ten for the letter and five for a leash to keep the dog from biting another person. For viewers, absent the lying, this is what they might expect to see from someone who looks and acts like Andy Taylor. The scene is full of the same kind of earnestness and downhome humor that had defined Griffith's earlier role.

However, when Ben meets with Steve, a starkly different side of his "Southern" character emerges. The conversation starts off in the same folksy vein as the previous one. Ben offers Steve some peanuts he received in exchange for services down in Plains, Georgia. With a twinkle in his eye, he adds, "It's not who you think." Unimpressed by the reference to Jimmy Carter's family (who were also accused of being bumpkins), Steve turns to Harvey Ravenel, who had brought him to the office, and says, "With all due respect to Mr. Matlock, I have some very close friends in New York, and they are excellent defense attorneys." Similar to Danny when he first met Andy, Steve (another well-connected New Yorker) is skeptical that this southerner is capable of doing his job. However, instead of winning Steve over with his folksy charm or an appeal to shared morality, an immediate change comes over Ben's countenance. In a stern voice, he warns Emerson, "I wouldn't do that if I were you." Somewhat shocked, Steve asks why he should not hire a well-practiced New York lawyer. Ben explains, "First off, you got the disposition of the jury to consider. They look at you as a fast-talking TV personality from New York—and you're rich." Steve protests that he is "hardly rich." But Ben cuts him off reminding him, "According to the standards of the folks around here, you're rich." Ben wraps up his pitch, saying Steve being from the North is "another first strike" and that he needs "a local boy" who can put the jury at ease and win them over with his relatability. Harvey then adds that Ben has an impressive record handling trials throughout the United States.

Steve is convinced, but Ben keeps pressing to completely break down the man who will become his client. He tells Steve, "Wait a minute, I said you need someone like me. I didn't say I would take the case." Harvey jumps in and interjects, "Ben, we need you." To which Ben shoots back, "Harvey, I've got my reputation to consider." A defeated Harvey then quietly responds, "Money is no object here." This comment brings them back to what seems to be the point of the whole interchange. Now that Steve and Harvey are utterly subdued, Ben is ready to talk terms. The negotiation is quick and merciless. First, Steve unwisely reveals he has $50,000 in cash and $50,000 in securities and bonds. Ben asks for all $100,000 of it. When Steve protests, Ben evokes the specter of the electric chair, causing Steve to relent and agree to pay the full amount. For viewers, (like how they got to see behind the scenes of Steve's news program) they also get to witness how Ben's folksy southern identity is constructed and ungrounded. However, this realization is not cast as something frightening or as something that should necessarily be resented. Rather, the show suggests that the correct reaction to this reality is to be like Ben, to embrace the opportunities born from dissensus. As Gil Troy explains, the prevailing ethics of the 1980s revolve around "a politics of consumption and the sovereign self" (85), and Ben clearly shows the personal benefits of adopting this dominant worldview. Moreover, Steve does not particularly seem to mind that he has just been coerced to give up his life's savings. He accepts the fee almost as if he had lost a friendly game, and then they all head off together to solve who really killed Linda.

Witnessing Ben's interactions, first with the Pearsons then with Steve, might leave viewers a bit confused. Is Ben the kindly country lawyer who charges fifteen dollars or a bag of peanuts for his services, or is he the well-travelled attorney who uses a malleable southern identity and the threat of the electric chair to maximize his profits? The answer, though, seems largely inconsequential. He is both or neither. In reality, Ben, himself, is an unstable referent, which allows him to freely navigate the postmodern world, juggling multiple identities without relinquishing the benefits of any of them. He is an outsider, who does not have to fill a role in a community or answer to societal expectations. Yet, this does not encumber him from profiting from that society. Again, what Ben demonstrates most fully is a sense of freedom from earlier iterations of morality and responsibility. For instance, whereas Andy also demands a large amount of money from a visiting New Yorker, he does it to prove that wealthy people should set an example and pay their fair share. Ben simply demands the money from Steve because he wants it. This apparent freedom to act selfishly, though, does not dampen Ben's role as the show's unquestioned hero. Indeed, it seems viewers are supposed to respect Ben for his allegiance to profits and his ability to get things done in an irreferential world.

Throughout the first season and in the following years, *Matlock* introduces a wide range of new characters and narrative arcs. However, Ben's "cheerful amorality" and his dedication to earning his "fat fee" remains largely consistent. At least in part, though, he is protected from judgment because the show is filtered through a lens of what Richard Rorty calls "knowingness," which is a mode of narration that relays to readers everyone is in on the joke and understands reality and identity are mere constructions. As Rorty articulates, pervasive artificiality and irony removes the action from any real sense of stakes or authentic feeling (126).[17] Much of the show is governed by prescribed skepticism over truth claims that rebuffs critical interrogation or judgment as misguided because no one is supposed to take the show all that seriously. For instance, early in the episode it appears the private investigator Tyler Hudson (who is a Black man) will be targeted because of his race. The scene takes place in a seedy bar and is initially charged with the kind of racial tension one might expect to find in a southern drama. A large White man aggressively approaches Tyler, clamping a hand down on his shoulder. As it turns out, though, the man appears primarily offended by the fact that Ben (an old man in a suit) and Tyler (who is wearing a sweater that looks like it belongs to Cliff Huxtable) are out of place in the bar. He calls the men "girls" and refuses to let them depart. Then, when he tries to escalate the argument into a fight, Tyler quickly leaves the large man sprawled on the barroom floor.

If the confrontation had been more explicitly about race or if the man had actually been able to hurt Tyler, it might remind viewers of a specific regional/racial legacy. However, even if viewers do recognize intersections between race and the confrontation, which does seem mostly directed at Tyler, the scene's campy feel and the man's inefficacy as an agent of harm suggests they should not be all that concerned about his potential impact. Put again, if the interaction had actually shown a White man hurting a Black man, it would force viewers (at least on some level) to confront the continuing impact of southern racial violence. In turn, this would link Ben's own Whiteness to a damaging regional history. Instead, the conflict in the bar works in the opposite direction, diffusing the tension and offering up the city as a space distanced from effective forms of racial violence. Tyler's nearly effortless humiliation and dismissal of the man drains the interaction of its potential resonance. Then, Ben springs into action and uses the opportunity to pass out his business card in case anyone is not an ex-Marine, like Tyler, and suffers "bodily harm" at the hands of an attacker. Comically, he moves through the bar inviting patrons to call him because their "personal injuries can be worth big money." As the camera pans over the men and women, it also reminds viewers that this is an integrated space. There are as many Black people in the room as there are White people.

Therefore, while the man in the bar is certainly a bigot, his bigotry is positioned as a failure of his individual character rather than something that could indict Ben or other White people.

In fact, almost every individual in the show is cast as a free-floating amalgam of their own making. Only villains, like the "redneck" in the bar, would attach meaning to outward appearances or something like a regional identity. Viewers are positioned, then, to reject any characterization of individuals as necessarily shaped by history or societal expectations. To be clear, though, while on the surface this may seem like a progressive outlook, similar to twenty-first century claims that "all lives matter," this supposed open-mindedness allows White people to exclude specific histories that expose their guilt. As Eduardo Bonilla-Silva explains, "dominant ideology is effective not by establishing uniformity, but by providing the frames to organize difference" (171). According to the show, what is "different," and therefore quickly embarrassed and removed from the action, are the people still judging others based on supposedly superficial characteristics. In other words, even as the show admits there are bigots, it reinforces a narrative that viewers are also bigots if they do not buy into the post-racial and post-historical notion that individuals are free to construct their own identities regardless of any inherited past.

In the episode's conclusion, the show reiterates its position that viewers should understand reality as constructed rather than inherited. Ben proves Steve's innocence moments before he is sentenced to prison. However, instead of any earnest reflection or sincere relief, Ben turns to Charlene and with a twinkle in his eye bemoans there were no TV cameras to catch what they had done. This bit of self-reference and acknowledgment that everything they had just done was, indeed, part of a TV show, fits into the show's larger postmodern ethos. It breaks any illusion that the actors do not know they are on TV. Indeed, it reminds viewers they are only watching a piece of constructed fiction, where everyone is aware that nothing is fully authentic. Much like the framing of Steve's news program, Ben's fluid character, and the scene with Tyler in the bar, the show makes clear that it is almost always a mistake to put faith in anything as being stable, sincere, or true. As Robert L. McLaughlin writes about 1980s television, "In a culture of irony and ridicule no assertion goes unmocked, and if no assertion can be sincerely uttered and heard, nothing can be built" (65). However, instead of lamenting this reality, the show delivers an overwhelming sense viewers should just relax and enjoy the post-referential era that supposedly offers everyone freedom to pursue their own individualized and hopefully profitable identities.

As we saw in the office scene, Ben's relationship to the South fits neatly into that same lens of "knowingness" and unseriousness.[18] It is clear he is a southerner, in that he lives in the South and has access to a folksy persona when it benefits him. However, there is nothing particularly southern (in the traditional, historical sense) about his character. As Mallet puts it, "without that molasses-tone voice and big smile, [Ben] would just be one of the sharks on *L.A. Law*" (14). Ultimately, what defines the southern outsider of the 1980s is not only this license to imagine oneself as existing outside constructions of inherited history (like we saw in the 1960s and 1970s) but also an ability to reduce that history into a mere brand or joke. In the earlier shows, there was still an implicit admission that there are aspects of the United States' past steeped in guilt and that individuals should earnestly strive to overcome (or at least avoid) those elements of U.S. history. For instance, Mayberry's allegiance to "American" wars and Andy's refusal to talk about the Emancipation Proclamation tacitly recognize the dark chapters of the southern past, even as the show insists on selective amnesia and celebrating an alternative history. In the same manner, *The Waltons* and *Roots* acknowledge a widespread failure of American institutions through their focus on the Great Depression and slavery. In those shows, then, to achieve innocence individuals must position themselves outside the reach of historically informed institutions. In the 1980s, though, there is a clear sense that there is no authentic meaning or history beyond one's personal interpretation. Therefore, there is no reason to perceive any part of the past as off-limits or as necessarily unavailable for White people's consumption.

By turning to *The Dukes of Hazzard* and *In the Heat of the Night*, we see the extent to which White people believed they could reimagine and enjoy their history. Whereas *The Andy Griffith Show*, *The Waltons*, *Roots*, and *Matlock* all inhabit "Up South" states or urban spaces, *The Dukes of*

Hazzard takes place in rural Georgia and *In the Heat of the Night* is set in Mississippi. In other words, the two shows inhabit spaces where one would expect to find the worst aspects of racism. Predictably, though, viewers do not encounter unvarnished instances of White supremacy. Instead, the shows depict a South and southern history that is relatively innocuous and safe for consumption. We see this rebranding of the South most clearly in how the shows frame the Confederacy and its icons. As Tara McPherson explains, the battle over the Confederacy's memory is always deeply rooted in efforts for "political domination" (104). However, the "domination" these shows seek, at least on the surface, is one that promotes an ahistorical South and Confederacy where everyone has access to "Dixie's" seemingly harmless brands. To be clear, though, by framing the Confederacy as merely one more available brand to be consumed, the shows suggest even the most openly White supremacist aspects of the nation's past do not actually prove White people, broadly speaking, have ever done anything wrong. Therefore, *The Dukes of Hazzard* and *In the Heat of the Night* conclude that the South's war to protect slavery—an institution that tortured, raped, and murdered countless people—could be made palatable for everyone, regardless of race or region, through a simple rebranding effort.

Indeed, the basic conflict that lies at the heart of *The Dukes of Hazzard*'s weekly plot relies on a long-normalized paradox within the Confederacy's memory, where Robert E. Lee is divorced from the politics for which he fought. Each episode, viewers could watch the Duke family, driving the "General Lee," as they resisted the politically powerful Jefferson Davis Hogg and his ambitions to control the town. The fantasy of enmity between the Confederacy's military (General Lee) and its government (Jefferson Davis) has long allowed White people to separate from feelings of guilt through a simple decoupling of southern soldiers from the commitment to slavery that drove secession. As Michael Fellman explains in his book *The Making of Robert E. Lee* (2000), after the Civil War, White "Southerners had a continuously urgent need for Saint Robert" to perform as a supposedly "shining exemplar of all that was caring and pure and Christian about their rule" (304). This framing of Lee, though, meant that "racial justice [is] shunted aside by national white consensus" (306). *The Dukes of Hazzard*, then, borrows from Lee's nationalized legacy of supposed racial innocence but updates his image to fit the show's postmodern ethos.[19]

Particularly, by melding Lee's legacy to a muscle car, the show suggests Lee can be taken as a mere symbol and divorced from just about everything that had long defined the man's traditional legacy. For most of his time in the national imaginary, Lee has been linked to a rigid sense of morality and honor that would be in direct contradiction to the muscle car's association with excess and individualism. What is important, then, is not that Lee's actual mythology be mapped onto the show as a model for behavior. Rather, *The Dukes of Hazzard* simply uses the innocence long-granted Lee to make a much larger point about individual freedom and the ability to reconstruct brands according to one's personal views. Again, like in *Matlock, The Dukes of Hazzard*'s most potent assertion is not about redeeming a particular history or specific legacy. Rather, it is about affirming the individual's ability to choose their own identity, regardless of facts or inherited truths. As the show frames it, the Confederacy and its icons are not indicative of anything real or stable. They are simply unattached signifiers that gain meaning through the associations they are given by similarly unattached individuals.

We can further see the show's investments in detached meaning by briefly looking at the pilot episode. Viewers are introduced to Hazzard County through a shot of a Confederate battle flag affixed to a police cruiser's bumper. The camera then pulls back to reveal the cruiser is being chased by the General Lee, which has the same flag emblazoned on its roof. As the chase continues, the camera keeps switching back and forth between the cars, drawing attention to the notion that the rebel flag is an appropriate symbol for both the "system" and those who fight against it.[20] In essence, the opening shots introduce what will be reenforced throughout the pilot and much of the show's subsequent episodes, which is that meaning is constructed rather than inherited. As the episode continues, we see this same dedication to unfixed referents applied to the traditional vice of gambling, as the Dukes use stolen slot machines to save an orphanage from destruction. Like the flag, gambling itself is cast as an unstable referent that is either good or bad, depending on the individual with which it is associated. According to the show's logic, it is incorrect to fixate on history or morality as something that exists in a fixed frame, even when we are talking about White supremacy's most overt symbols. Instead, the show embraces the same ahistorical and postsouthern freedom we saw exhibited in *Matlock,* where individuals are encouraged to reject stable definitions and to embrace whatever narratives work for them and their ambitions.

Again, it is this freedom to imagine one's identity as existing beyond structures of inherited power that seems to be at the heart of White people's fantasies about being an outsider. *The Dukes of Hazzard* works as a compelling messenger for this freedom, not only because of its insistence on the meaninglessness of icons, but also because its humor and the Dukes' sense of cool detachment resist any attempt to treat the show's politics as sincere or serious. As a result of this framing, there is a tendency to take *The Dukes of Hazzard*'s rural setting and its juvenile jokes as evidence that it is an unserious harkening to the rural shows of the 1960s. For instance, Zachery Lechner largely dismisses *The Dukes of Hazzard* as a "celebration of Southern rural values" that "has nothing much to say about race or politics" (164). However, just like colorblindness is a form of racism, so too is an apolitical stance toward the Confederacy. Similar to *Matlock,* the show espouses a politics of "consumption and the sovereign self" that denies the very real ways that the nation's history intersects with lived experience. In other words, it is the show's suggestion that Confederate icons can exist without a political or racial context that is damaging. After all, if the icons of a failed slave nation are unfixed and largely meaningless, then there is no aspect of the nation's history that can link White people to the violence they introduced and maintain.

Finally, the show *In the Heat of the Night* illustrates perhaps most clearly the extent to which White people invested in a postmodern/postsouthern version of their own innocence. Like *Matlock* and *The Dukes of Hazzard,* the show flattens history into a mere brand so audiences can imagine they exist outside an inherited racial and social legacy. However, *In the Heat of the Night* does not embrace the same sense of unserious humor to defer interrogation that we saw in the previous shows. Instead, it examines a gritty southern town in Mississippi, aptly called Sparta, which is a setting that invites serious discussions about racial realities. *In the Heat of the Night* also takes its title, central characters, and basic plot from two relatively respected critiques of racism in the United States: John Ball's 1965 novel and Norman Jewison's 1967 Academy Award winning film, all by the same name. Both the novel and the film versions of *In the Heat of the Night* received praise for their depictions of Black excellence in the face of oppressive systems, and the film even enjoyed a somewhat positive review from James Baldwin who wrote the final look shared between the White police chief William Gillespie and the Black detective Virgil Tibbs, was a "fade out kiss" that "spoke of reconciliation, of all things now becoming possible" (521).

While problematic in their own ways, what the novel and film share is the clear sense that a better future could be achieved if White southerners would account for the rotten aspects of their society and embrace Black men and women as important parts of a reconciled whole. However, a little more than two decades after the novel and film first appeared, the TV adaptation largely contends the "reconciliation" about which Baldwin wrote had already been achieved. Therefore, there needed to be a new version of the story that focuses on differences in individual characters rather than a struggle for racial justice. As critic Donna S. Miller explains, "in the film that inspired the series, racial tension was the issue. Here, [in the TV show] the main conflict . . . is style of management. Gillespie is folksy and laid-back; Tibbs insists on doing it by the book" (24). Or, as the show's producer Fred Silverman puts it, "hitting the racial aspects as hard as they did in the movie would be presenting a very unfair picture of this town and the South." Instead, he explains, there would be different tensions, "[Tibbs] is big city versus [Gillespie] small town. One has a very scientific way of looking at things, the other goes with his gut. One practices a very personal kind of law enforcement, the other is very much by the book" (qtd. in Davis). Therefore, while the setting and title suggest viewers would be getting an exposé on the South and still-present racial issues, the show works against those expectations and presents a very different atmosphere—one where racism is largely cast as something no longer important or relevant, at least not as relevant as contrasting personalities and policing styles.

The choice of Carroll O'Connor to play Sparta's police chief Bill Gillespie also works to subvert concerns about still-present racism in southern communities. As in *Matlock,* NBC and Silverman used a familiar face to help frame the show's interpretation of the region. O'Connor was already familiar to audiences as Archie Bunker, the prejudiced yet supposedly lovable man from Queens, NY in Norman Lear's *All in the Family* (1971–1979) and *Archie Bunker's Place* (1979—1983). Like Andy Griffith, O'Connor's persona carried with it a history. However, O'Connor represented something quite different from Griffith's position in the national imaginary. Unlike Andy Taylor, who had represented an age of stable referents and relatively fixed morality, Bunker had embodied a form of 1970s irreverent northern bigotry that made no claims to pure innocence yet still was presented as mostly harmless. Put simply, as both Bunker and then Gillespie, O'Connor played a racist, but he is imagined as the "good" kind of racist, a racist who means no harm and can quickly be convinced to change their perspective when confronted with evidence. In fact, as *In the Heat of the Night* went on, Gillespie's character became increasingly forward thinking and separated himself from any of the racial prejudices he exhibited in the early seasons. As critic John J. O'Connor put it for the *New York Times,* Carroll O'Connor's character became "something of a flaming liberal."[21] For viewers, O'Connor's transformation from Bunker (the good-natured racist) to Gillespie (the reformed racist) suggests that racism might have been a problem in the past. However, even in Mississippi, there is very little real or dangerous racism left to combat. Therefore, most of the show's antagonists are largely driven by placeless and more mundane motivations, such as greed and lust, rather than something rooted in a specific racial or regional history.

Ultimately, *In the Heat of the Night* demonstrates the same allegiance to individuality and ahistoricism we saw in *Matlock* and *The Dukes of Hazzard,* but it takes that ahistoricism a step further. The two-part pilot episode frames racism (where it does exist) as mainly a problem born from attaching meaning to someone's appearance or history, which is a problem it suggests afflicts Black people and progressives just as much as anyone else.[22] In other words, the episodes that introduce Sparta to the watching nation, establish that the "real" problem of race in Mississippi is that both sides are jumping to conclusions and judging one another unfairly. In fact, the worst characters in the pilot and series more generally are those who cling to supposedly outdated notions that race and inherited history should still be considered relevant topics in the 1980s. We see a clear example of the villainy associated with those still thinking about race in the LaPierre family and the self-serving mayor Jim Findlay. The LaPierre patriarch lives in a plantation house, is openly racist, and in the closing moments his family is revealed to be running a pornography ring in Sparta. In his character, we see a relatively clear condemnation of backward-looking conservatism as a perversion of American identity.

Mayor Findlay, on the other hand, serves as an indictment of those on the left, who are also cast as being mistaken for still focusing on race in the 1980s. While Findlay is proven correct in fighting for Tibbs to be added to the police force, he is shown as being misguided as to why Tibbs should receive that spot. As he stands in front of a Confederate monument, Findlay explains to the town council that he is simply doing this because he wants to run for governor someday. To win over the press, he needs a positive record on civil rights. According to this framing, while Findlay may not be as openly dangerous as the LaPierres, their differences are a matter of degree, not kind. Both men are cast as representing two ends of a perverse spectrum, as they both are intent on utilizing a racialized past to further their own interests. Therefore, there is an equivalency drawn between those fighting for equal representation and those actively opposing it. In contrast, the enlightened characters in the show have left the past in the past and recognize only bigots or self-interested politicians still care about race.

Gillespie and Tibbs, then, are cast as admirable largely because of their willingness to put matters of race behind them and to focus on what are imagined as more pressing issues in Mississippi. The pilot establishes this post-racial perspective in an almost painfully obvious way. Early in the episode, Tibbs suspects the police officer V. L. "Bubba" Skinner helped murder a young Black man named Willie Jones who was in police custody when he died. Bubba was supposed to be on watch but said that he left the prison because someone telephoned about an open window in town. Even though Tibbs finds the officer was being truthful about the call and open window, he remains unwilling to believe Bubba is completely innocent. Later, Tibbs jokes with his wife about poisoning

Bubba, and as they laugh about the joke and discuss the day's events, the phone rings. On the other end, a voice claims to have information on Willie's murder. When Tibbs goes to meet the caller, he is ambushed by a group of White men who beat him until they spot an approaching police car. Ominous music plays as the vehicle pulls up to the scene, and the tension steadily builds as the officer steps from his vehicle, draws his gun, and points it at Tibbs's unconscious body. The camera then pans up to show Bubba's stern face looking down at the inert detective.

After revealing Bubba's face, the scene ends with viewers wondering whether or not he will shoot Tibbs. However, following the commercial break, the next thing they see is Bubba coming through the police department doors, carrying Tibbs to safety. Other officers rush to help, and as Bubba turns to leave, Tibbs stops him saying, after a pause, "Thank you" (Pilot Part Two). Humbled, Tibbs then turns to Gillespie and admits, "I feel real bad about Skinner, got him all wrong." The chief looks at his detective and gently admonishes him, as well as viewers who might have also misjudged Bubba. Gillespie says, in a fatherly tone, "Oh well, it happens. I met a Black guy a long time ago. I thought he was the meanest man in the world, until he saved my life," and Tibbs responds sagely, "rash judgments, I take your point" (Pilot Part Two). In this moment, the show makes clear that Tibbs, as a Black man, needs to learn how to see past color and to accept people based on the content of their character rather than the color of their skin, which is a lesson Gillespie apparently learned in his youth.[23]

In case viewers miss this less-than-subtle levelling of history, the pilot's final sequence drives home the show's overarching sense that both Black and White people need to forget racial divisions and focus on the present. Similar to *The Dukes of Hazzard,* the recipe for racial and social healing starts with embracing an individualized history that allows everyone the freedom to choose their own narrative. The closing scene starts with Tibbs hanging a picture, which is hidden from the camera's view. Gillespie hears the hammering and asks about the commotion. Tibbs cryptically responds: "I'm putting up the picture of a famous man, reminds me of other famous men." The camera then reveals a large photograph of Martin Luther King Jr. that will sit behind Tibbs's desk. Gillespie protests, not because he has a problem with King necessarily, but because, as he says, "this is still Mississippi." They quibble back and forth, and as the camera switches from one character to the other, viewers can see King behind Tibbs's shoulder and a large portrait of Robert E. Lee framed by a confederate battle flag over Gillespie's.[24] With a smile on his face, Tibbs brings Lee into the discussion, saying, "Well you put up a hero of yours, and now I got one of mine up" (Pilot Part Two). Gillespie, faced with that logic, cannot argue beyond a few sputtering words of exasperation. The episode then ends with him accepting that the two portraits should be allowed in the office. In the logic of the show, it does not seem to matter that a moral equivalency has just been drawn between Lee, who fought a war to keep people like King enslaved, and King, who fought and died for racial equality. Instead, what apparently matters is that Lee is an important symbol for Gillespie, who is the right kind of White person, so the portrait can stay and remain disconnected from the systems of power Lee fought to uphold. Similar to *The Dukes of Hazzard*'s use of Lee, there is a clear sense that the actual realities of the Confederacy should not matter. Rather, viewers are encouraged to embrace the freedom the show presents, where everyone is entitled to their own heroes and versions of the past.

If nothing else, we should recognize from the TV shows in this chapter White people's audacity in how they reinvented their relationship with history. First, programs like *The Andy Griffith Show* insisted on preserving an image of an innocent and united America, where even the South is free from racial guilt. Then, after the civil rights movement made it nearly impossible to ignore what James Baldwin calls the "ravage and lie" of White history (180), TV representations of the South simply changed the narrative. They imagined the region as a space which proved good White people had always been outsiders, existing beyond their inherited history. By the 1980s, the character of the outsider dominated television, modeling a supposed independence from responsibilities that might inhibit personal freedoms.[25] Indeed, these characters encouraged White people to view their own separation from history as an admirable split from corrupting influences. As we will see in the next chapter, this rebranding of White identity was not limited to the popular culture of television. It also manifested itself in widely respected southern literature that offered White people a similar yet supposedly more nuanced and philosophically grounded way to imagine their own innocence. While the move toward individualism and the embrace of the outsider looks a little different in the trappings of literature, we ultimately see a consistent commitment to protecting White innocence above all else, which makes true healing all but impossible.

2

Switching the Patient

White Southern Doctors and Their Prescriptions

In the previous chapter, we saw how television produced a version of the South capable of reassuring White people that they were separated from racial guilt. First, the rural shows of the 1960s delivered a fantasy that southern communities had long ago embraced a post-racial, liberal American identity. Then, the shows of the 1970s–1990s reacted to growing disillusionment with American institutions and suggested most decent White people had always been outsiders who existed beyond the reach of their failed communities. Television, though, was not acting alone in its use of "the outsider" to alleviate White guilt. As we will see in this chapter, popular and well-respected southern literature from the same period joins forces with TV to present largely the same message: that most White people could look toward "Dixie" and find narratives of their own innocence. By examining how the literature frames racial and social healing, we can better understand not only the southern outsider's role as a powerful symbol of White identity but also how this character reframes approaches to confronting and combatting racial injustice. More specifically, by examining doctor characters alongside conceptions of healing in Eudora Welty's "The Demonstrators" (1966), Wendell Berry's *The Hidden Wound* (1970), Walker Percy's *The Second Coming* (1980), and Barry Hannah's *Ray* (1980), we can more fully grasp how White people used the region, from the 1960s—1990s, to evade responsibility for their history.

The texts in this chapter fit within a larger trend in post-1960s White southern literature—in that they illustrate a movement away from depicting regional identity as inherited and communal. As Fred

Hobson notes, "the decade of the sixties" marks a "watershed in South-ern thought," from which "a new Southern fiction emerged" (7). The "new" fiction promotes a view of the region that has "thrown off the old albatross of segregation" (8). What we find, then, is a similar transition to what we saw on TV, as the region moves away from its role as "the defeated, failed, poor, guilt ridden, tragic part of America" (8). By the 1980s, southern narratives increasingly embraced what Charles Taylor calls "expressive individualism," which is a framing of identity that priv-ileges one's personal feelings and desires over a dialogic understanding of the self, rooted in history and community.[1] Therefore, instead of stories that acknowledge how centuries of investments in White su-premacy necessarily bind White people to legacies of racial violence, White southern authors began delivering characters who identify as outsiders and search for an authentic sense of self beyond the region's influence. As Hobson articulates, we see a shift in southern letters where characters no longer "probe deeply and painfully [their] relationship to [their] homeland" (6). In place of this probing, southern characters began modeling the individual's power to define their own relationship with the southern past. As we will see, this shift (from focusing on the community to focusing on the individual) ultimately leads to the same presumption we saw on TV, which is that White people could use the role of the outsider to find freedom from the nation's guilty past.

It is perhaps unremarkable that White southerners would desire a relationship with history freeing them from racial guilt. However, as we saw in the last chapter, White people throughout the North/nation also enthusiastically consumed narratives depicting absolved southerners.[2] Even as news programs brought racial violence into living rooms across the nation in the 1960s, it seems nothing sold better than characters like Andy Taylor and Atticus Finch—characters who could assure audiences that "good" White people were not to blame for whatever violence occurred in their communities. Indeed, characters like Andy and At-ticus offered national audiences a kind of escape hatch, where almost everyone could claim a related innocence. According to this logic, if White southerners were separated from guilt, then certainly people from less-historically-stained regions could feel confident in their own relative goodness. In the decade of the 1960s, a whole industry arose around selling the South and southern living to individuals across the nation. Books like John Egerton's *The Americanization of Dixie* (1974) and later James Cobb's *The Selling of the South* (1993) and Peter Applebome's *Dixie Rising* (1996) capture the region's rebranding and demonstrate the commoditization of the South from the 1960s–1990s. As they make clear, by the 1970s, most White people were convinced the region had already lost its unique racial identity or was at least headed toward becoming just another detached and placeless brand.

As we saw in the last chapter, though, this shedding of a solidly conceived South corresponds almost precisely with the civil rights movement's illustration that systemic racism extends well beyond the region's borders. It seems when White people were faced with a growing sense of national guilt, they began eagerly embracing southern characters who were freed from their history. Hobson notes, "the literature of shame and guilt" that gained "preeminence" in the mid-twentieth century all but disappears from White southern fiction by the last quarter of the century (11). In place of the traditional guilty South and southerner, audiences welcomed characters who were either saintly, like Andy and Atticus, or were largely dealing with the same post-everything alienation and malaise as the rest of the nation. The "watershed in Southern thought" Hobson identifies, then, demonstrates how White people change the subject, as Baldwin suggests they always do,[3] when Black people make obvious how investments in White supremacy are part of the national character. However, critics rarely acknowledge how the movement past a stable South works as an evasion of White guilt. Instead, there is a sense that the movement away from a stable understanding of the region is largely separated from the preservation of White supremacy it enables. As a result of this framing, the shift toward a postsouthern South is traditionally understood to represent either a crisis in southern authenticity or a largely enlightened recognition that White southern exceptionalism has always been a fantasy.[4] Put plainly, this chapter argues, once again, that when we look more closely at examples from the period, we see how a fractured, postsouthern understanding of the region proves to be a powerful strategy, helping White people maintain fantasies of their own innocence.

To be clear, there are potential benefits to White people recognizing the errors of southern exceptionalism. As Ralph Ellison notes, White southerners, "distorted Negro humanity" in order to construct an enduring "Southern myth" that could defend White people's interests (25). Ellison goes on to identify the fundamental violence bound up in the "distorted" identities born from this brand of traditional southern exceptionalism. Michael Kreyling, Patricia Yeager, Martyn Bone, Leigh Anne Duck, Houston Baker Jr., Dana Nelson, and many others have done excellent work in exposing the violence bound up in viewing the "South" as a singular and solid signifier. Broadly organized under the term "New Southern Studies," their work helps demystify claims of southern authenticity that give White people power to define Black and White experience in the region. However, without losing sight of southern identity's complexity, we should also recognize how an increasingly postsouthern understanding of the region plays into another kind of White-authored mythology—one that blurs links between the self and the history one inherits. In other words, while it is undoubtedly important to remember global contexts and the South's constructed nature, it should also be made clearer that moving past the South as a relatively fixed and inherited space grants White people another tool to imagine themselves innocent and removed from the weight of their history.

Eudora Welty's "The Demonstrators" may seem like an odd place to start a chapter on the dangers presented by postsouthern White innocence.[5] After all, the story directly engages the region's historic and still-present communal failures. Its action follows a White man named Dr. Strickland as he immerses himself in the bloodshed that permeates his hometown of Holden, Mississippi. Welty also makes clear the violence found in the small Delta town is defined by its connections to enslavement and its links to predatory capitalism. At one point, Strickland literally has his hands inside a Black patient's wounds as he tries to stop an unyielding flow of blood. However, despite the story's direct engagement with the open wound of past and present racial violence, it manages to still deliver an argument for why readers should not blame "good" White men like Dr. Strickland for their inaction and inability to bring healing. Instead, the story pivots from focusing on an inherited racial violence (which would compel someone like Dr. Strickland toward restorative justice) to a focus on anxieties about breakdowns in language and shared meaning (which ends up justifying melancholic stasis).

In many ways, "The Demonstrators" reflects Hannah Arendt's concern that society would crumble because individuals were increasingly losing their capacity to understand one another as part of a shared whole. Arendt writes, people gathered around a "table," which represents "the world of shared things" (52), "might suddenly, through some magic trick, see the table vanish from their midst, so that the two persons sitting opposite each other were no longer separated but also would be entirely unrelated to each other by anything tangible" (53). It is this fear of hopeless division and a loss of shared meaning that drives the story's central anxieties. Therefore, Dr. Strickland's primary task is bringing together and healing the fractured, infertile South (or the stricken land) that seems incapable of bearing positive fruits. However, he is rendered powerless and, therefore, innocent because he inhabits a society that no longer possesses the willingness or ability to share a common story. Accordingly, Strickland cannot be blamed since the power to heal exists beyond him and is connected to a larger societal breakdown, where Holden's Black and White citizens no longer share a narrative framework that could organize communal experience.

As Suzan Harrison articulates, "The Demonstrators," at its most basic level, is a text about narrative power. She explains, it "is a story about the power of stories to shape our interaction with the world, about the stories we construct to define national, cultural, and racial identities" (94). Harrison then focuses on the potential benefits born from the realization that "all stories are suspect [and] are never pure, never free from personal and political agendas" (108). In the space of Welty's text, though, the realization that "all stories are suspect" is not liberatory or positive for Holden's inhabitants. Rather, narrative fracture is characterized as potentially devastating for both the town's White and Black characters. It is the lack of a shared, authentic story that leads to the growing division and threatens to tear not only Holden apart, but also Western civilization.[6] In other words, the realization that "all stories are suspect" does not lead to racial or social progress. Instead, this realization leads to a sense of disunity that largely makes it impossible for Strickland to act as a healer for his community. For example, Welty establishes the need for a common narrative in the way she never defines the title's reference to "demonstrators." The opaqueness of the title speaks directly to the story's larger message—in that it illustrates the confusion and inaction caused by competing voices all speaking to their own experiences. Instead of a united voice demonstrating for a common cause or calling in unison for justice, everyone in Holden seems to be demonstrating or lobbying for their own position and version of reality. In the end, the competing voices simply drown one another out, delivering a cacophony of confusion, which keeps Strickland locked in a state of bewildered inaction.

This hopeless division and inability to hear a common voice is most clearly seen in the separation between Black and White characters in the story. As Ebony O. Lumumba points out, in "The Demonstrators" we "are shown the white and black communities of Holden separately and, in the world of the text, this is exactly the way they exist. There is no intermingling of these two disparate communities" (186). Lumumba, like Harrison, goes on to focus on positive elements born from this division, writing about Welty's rejection of traditional White-authored, paternalistic knowledge. While Lumumba is certainly correct that the story's Black characters most likely benefit from Welty not attempting to voice their interior consciousness, what is left out again, though, is how the story positions this lack of knowing, not as something redemptive, but as a threat that will lead to more violence. Indeed, "The Demonstrators" consistently frames the lack of a common narrative as something that shatters any hope for collective action toward racial justice. However, while the story is clear that the town's division has its roots in racist legacies of capitalism and cotton, it is far less clear that the solution or the reconstituted narrative should focus on White people (like Dr. Strickland) admitting guilt and embracing restorative justice. In fact, not only does the story's framing center White men as the best hope for healing the communal narrative, but it also suggests at least part of the blame resides in Black communities that remain inaccessible to the doctor's examination. Therefore, given the resistance by Dr. Strickland's patients, the story wallows in something akin to what Walter Benjamin calls "Left melancholia."[7]

Wendy Brown explains, "What emerges" from this sense of melancholia "is a Left that operates without either a deep and radical critique of the status quo or a compelling alternative to the existing order of things" (463). In other words, when Strickland is faced with the violence that saturates his community alongside his inability to speak across racial lines—he simply becomes immobilized, unable to offer either a "radical critique of the status quo" or a "compelling alternative." As Brown points out, the Left gets "caught in a structure of melancholic attachment to a certain strain of its own dead past . . . whose structure of desire is backward looking and punishing" (464). Therefore, while Strickland, like Holden, is haunted by history, the past itself is an immobilizing presence that offers no narrative through which to understand progress or healing. The South's history only offers a punishing sense of division and fracture, which makes collective action against the forces of capitalism impossible. America's capitalistic interests, represented by the train carrying cotton that divides Holden, ultimately proves to be an immutable force making Strickland's efforts to bring together his community hopeless. Readers are left craving a shared narrative through which Strickland could unite the divided town, but the forces of capitalism and the intractability of both the White and Black sides of Holden make that healing impossible.

While they may seem fundamentally different, "The Demonstrators" and *The Andy Griffith Show,* actually offer a similar diagnosis for what ails America. They both suggest that the fracture caused by the civil rights movement and other societal forces in the 1960s threatens the nation's cultural continuity. Therefore, traditional otherings of the White South needed to cease, and new national narratives needed to be promoted.[8] Where the two narratives depart, and it is a stark departure, is that *The Andy Griffith Show* still imagines White Americans can maintain a sense of historically informed unity. "The Demonstrators," on the other hand, makes the same claim about the need for narrative unity, but it renders that narrative unavailable, suggesting unity is impossible given the breakdown in shared language between the races. There is something liberating for White people, though, in this failure of a binding narrative, in that it shifts focus away from accounting for White-authored violence and towards a fixation on the costs of a divided America. Put again, "The Demonstrators" effectively transfers White people's anxieties from questions about their own participation in racial injustice, to a sense that division is the primary threat facing both Black and White individuals.

Most clearly, we see this need for uniting narratives in the story's brief moments of peace, which almost all revolve around referents linking together Holden's Black and White communities. For instance, Welty writes, "[Strickland] had been carried a cup tonight that might have been his own mother's china or his wife's mother's . . . In that house of murder, comfort had been brought to him at his request. After drinking from it he had all but reeled into a flock of dresses stretched wide-sleeved across the porch of that house" (743). He had recognized the dresses earlier as "[h]is mother's gardening dress, his sister Annie's golf dress, his wife's favorite duster that she liked to wear to the breakfast table" (741). As he reflects on the cup and the dresses, which provide a common referent in this unfamiliar space, he is "faintly rocked by the passing train . . . , and the feeling of well-being persisted. It increased, until he had come to the point of tears" (743). The positive feelings brought about by the shared objects, though, quickly dissipates as Strickland thinks about his daughter's death, his wife's leaving him, and then an encounter he had with a White civil rights worker, who Strickland had invited to dinner. At the table, the doctor confronts the activist about a newspaper account claiming he and some other protestors "were forced at gunpoint to go into the fields at hundred-degree temperature and pick cotton." Strickland accuses the man of lying to the paper because "there isn't any cotton in June." The young man responds, saying, "we are dramatizing your hostility . . . It's a way of reaching people. Don't forget what they *might* have done to us is even worse" (744). Taken aback by the man's stance on the relative nature of truth, Strickland remembers shooting back, "Still—you're not justified in putting a false front on things . . . even for a good cause" (744). The story then jumps to Strickland's present, as he stands in front of the train dividing the town. His thoughts move from the White civil rights worker to another lie. He remembers his wife accusing him: "*You* won't tell Herman Fairbrothers what's the matter with him" (744).

Strickland loses what little hope he has left as he transitions from considering the shared objects he encounters in the African American community, to thinking about his inability to save his daughter or his marriage and the disturbing realization he lives in a world governed by division and falsehoods. He is left, then, standing before the train reminded of his powerlessness, helplessly watching the cotton-carrying locomotive separate Holden. He listens to "the pounding of his heart," which "was like the assault of hope, throwing itself against him without a stop, merciless" (745). By the end of the story, Strickland seems finally to understand that the cotton-filled southern community he has been trying to save has always been built on lies and half-truths, guided by capitalistic greed, division, and violence. In the face of all this, Strickland feels "increasingly tired, so sick, even bored with the bitterness, intractability that divided everybody and everything" (744). He is left in this space of sickness and bitterness, where even hope is likened to an assault on his heart. The melancholic ending leaves readers convinced of the community's guilt and aware of the racial underpinnings that have always linked together cotton and capitalism. However, there is also a pervasive sense that Dr. Strickland is powerless to alter this reality, which suggests he is not to blame for his inaction. After all, what can one individual do against the forces of a locomotive? Again, like *The Andy Griffith Show*, "The Demonstrators" responds to White anxieties in the 1960s by suggesting White people can bring about healing, only if everyone agrees to unite and focus on what binds the nation together, like the generosity symbolized by the cup and the dresses. Bound up in this remembrance, though, is an implied amnesia about White people's guilt that would implicate someone like Dr. Strickland and compel restorative action. Welty seems unable or unwilling to imagine what that accounting would look like, so the story simply ends with a sense of fracture and brokenness, where only the train seems capable of movement.

Moving to Wendell Berry's *The Hidden Wound* (1970), we can see how some of the same strategies centering division and hopelessness were used to protect White innocence in the 1970s. However, whereas "The Demonstrators" suggests a sick community that must be healed, Berry shifts the focus to sick individuals who find healing by escaping their communal inheritances. Similar to what we saw in the last chapter, *The Hidden Wound*, like *The Waltons* and *Roots*, maintains a sincere commitment to shared values while also promoting the role of the White outsider as the true embodiment of American goodness. For most southern literature in the 1970s, outsiders gained their status through an association with the working class and by standing apart or in opposition to more obviously guilty aristocrats. As Fred Hobson observes, "Southern letters" after the 1960s changes from being "principally about the privileged" to literature "by, and treating seriously, the common people," who supposedly had "little past to hold on to [and] little history in which their ancestors had played important parts" (22). This shift in who spoke for the South (from aristocrats to common folks) led to a new sense of imagined regional identity. According to this framing, White southerners could envision their own stories as fitting into broader national narratives of White victimization and individual ascendence rather than being bound to a specific, inherited racial history. The model set by these White outsiders, then, suggested most White people could claim to be victims, aligned with minorities against corrupt institutions that existed beyond their control.[9]

The Hidden Wound is a particularly useful text because it not only illustrates this trend toward individualized White victimization, but also it shows how embracing an identity as a southern outsider did not necessarily depend on any authentic connection to working-class roots. Berry, like a great many White southern writers of the period, was born into a relatively established family, was college educated, and wrote much of his work while employed at a university. Put simply, Berry's writing demonstrates how White outsiderness has always been more of an aesthetic choice than something that could actually be grounded in one's family tree or particular experiences. Again, as we saw on TV in the last chapter, the decade of the 1970s represents a period of transition in dominant philosophies, where White people still invested in a commitment to sincerity and authenticity yet were beginning to embrace postmodern logics that could separate them (as individuals) from specific inherited histories. In *The Hidden Wound*, like much of Berry's work, we see the author earnestly embarking on a quest for truth and meaning that could provide a framework for an alternative version of community. However, like we saw in *The Waltons* and *Roots,* Berry imagines a version of White identity that could mostly be disentangled from larger structures of American power. Whereas Welty still characterizes White identity as being necessarily and inescapably bound up in a dialogic relationship between the self and the larger consequences of the United States' past, Berry embraces the idea that what plagues the nation is something internal and spiritual that can be solved through a realignment of personal perspective.

Readers encounter this sense of localizing the conversation within the self early in Berry's text, as he identifies as a victim of the nation's racial history. He writes he could no longer ignore what he had "known all along to be a wound—a historical wound, prepared centuries ago to come alive in me at my birth" (3). The hereditary disease or internal "wound" that he diagnoses and attempts to heal through the book, is his and presumably his White readers' damaged understanding of race that has been passed down through the generations. He goes on to write, "I want to know, as fully and exactly as I can, what the wound is and how much I am suffering from it. And I want to be cured; I want to be free of the wound myself, and I don't want to pass it on to my children" (4). To search out the source of the wound, Berry probes his relationships, his family's history, and his personal connections to racial imbalances that extend out into the community. In some ways, he then arrives at much the same place as Dr. Strickland. His searching brings him in contact with the links between the South's racial history and the North/nation's all-encompassing logics of predatory capitalism. However, instead of being consumed by the deeply entrenched divisions inherent to American history, Berry seems to move toward a view of overcoming this history through a personal approach. As Joseph R. Wiebe explains, Berry couches healing in the power of "meaningful relationships" and "arduous, uncomfortable friendships" that could turn Black people into real individuals rather than mere abstractions (343). This individualistic way of understanding the region's "wound" as mostly an internal ailment that largely can be healed through a better outlook and having more Black friends, underlies much of the problem in how White liberals approached racial inequity in the 1970s.

Rather than addressing the real structural violence that animates the very fabric of American society, Berry's text positions personal and communal innocence as something that could be achieved through a better perspective and a willingness to include like-minded Black people in a reestablished southern, agrarian identity. As Berry concludes, "A true and appropriate answer to our race problem, as to many others, would be a restoration of our communities—it being understood that a community, properly speaking, cannot exclude or mistreat any of its members" (135). In order to achieve this "restoration" of "our" community, though, he argues individuals must willingly return to a form of socialistic agrarianism that supposedly existed before largescale farming and mechanization destroyed it. What Welty's story seems to grasp, and Berry's text does not, is that this brand of White southern communal innocence never existed because individuals cannot operate freely from their larger communities. For Berry, it seems southern innocence could be located by divorcing oneself from the racist aristocratic South and identifying with "nonracist" White outsiders who lived on small farms and did not directly enslave people.[10] The fantasy of the outsider in the 1970s rests on this belief that individuals, both in the past and present, have always had the ability to disavow as a matter of mere choice the systems and institutions that govern lived experience.

Framing racism as a problem primarily of the mind ultimately provides White people a powerful narrative through which they can fend off institutional efforts to confront systemic racial violence.[11] According to this narrative, governments should not be in the business of trying to fix racial wounds because the problem primarily exists within an individual's thinking. To hand the solution over to the government, then, would mean either a superficial change or submitting to the policing of one's thoughts. Therefore, Berry concludes his book by arguing that the government's efforts in the 1970s to bring about racial equity should immediately stop because "it is impossible to believe that people can be changed fundamentally by government requirement" (135). Instead, he argues, "The only thing a government requirement assures is a prolongation of government supervision" (135). As he puts it earlier in his book, "real healings and renewals in human life occur in individual *lives,* not in the process of adjusting or changing their abstractions or institutions" (104). Ultimately, Berry hopes enough White individuals will volunteer to give up their accrued power and wealth to bring about racial equity, which as he admits means "our predicament is extremely unfavorable" (136). Like Welty, Berry seems unable or unwilling to imagine a fundamentally different version of community that demands action against inherited White power. Yet, they both retain faith in the unifying benefit of common truths and argue for a southern community with at least some grounding in what feels like an authentic history. In other words, in Berry's text, the wound at least feels communal, even if the solution is individualized.

As we move into the 1980s, though, we start seeing White authors promote a purer form of outsiderness and a near complete detachment from inherited histories. Again, like we saw on television, Walker Percy's *The Second Coming* and Barry Hannah's *Ray* embrace a postmodern ideation of the self, where individuals are imagined as almost wholly divorced from grand narratives that could connect White people to their past. Patricia Waugh explains, "Central to the 'postmodern condition' . . . is a recognition and account of the way in which the 'grand narratives' of Western history and, in particular, enlightened modernity, have broken down" (5). She goes on to point out that what separates postmodernism from past instances of "counter-Enlightenment" is that "Postmodernism tends to claim an abandonment of all metanarratives which could legitimize foundations for truth. And more than this, it claims that we neither need them, nor are they any longer desirable" (5). Accordingly, we see White-authored southern narratives in the 1980s moving away from addressing the past as something authentic or meaningful and toward a framing where those insisting on an inherited or relatively stable history are cast as deeply misguided and potentially dangerous. As Waugh puts it, the culture of postmodernism is a reaction to "the terror produced through the instrumental modes of universal reason, the generalizing violence of the concept," which promotes a rejection of not only "truth" but also "truth effect" (5).

In Percy's and Hannah's texts, then, we see the conversation move from a realization that dominant understandings of the White South were false and dangerous, to a view that any sense of a rooted or historically informed identity is similarly fraught. Thus, there is a distinct departure from Welty's and Berry's South, where there remains a sense of enduring historical violence directly impacting lived experience. For instance, the diagnosis in "The Demonstrators" of racial division depends on the idea that Holden and its citizens exist in a continuum dominated by the community's past. In *The Hidden Wound,* the continuum is more localized, but there remains a sense that Berry is directly dealing with a historically informed and still-present racial "wound." However, under the auspices of a progressively ahistorical version of postmodernism, these claims are understood as relying on a rejected appeal to a universalizing metanarrative, which erroneously links individual White people into a common history. According to the postmodern belief that "universal reason" leads to "terror" and "violence," such a desire to link together something as fractured and diverse as Whiteness through a common story is seen as not only wrongheaded but dangerous. As Waugh goes on to explain, drawing from Derrida, Lacan, and Barthes, "History [under the effects of postmodernism] becomes a plurality of 'islands of discourse,' a series of metaphors which cannot be detached from the institutionally produced languages which we bring to bear on it" (6). Indeed, according to the logic of postmodernism that Waugh describes, individuals have no common past even if they wanted one. Instead, history is an "island" of one's own making, an artificial narrative or "metaphor" one creates and uses to understand one's own individual identity. Of course, once again, this framing also excuses White people from feeling compelled toward shared action born from a collective, inherited guilt.

Walker Percy's *The Second Coming* and Barry Hannah's *Ray,* both published in 1980, stylistically are very different texts, with *Ray* leaning much more heavily into a stereotypical, fractured postmodern aesthetic. However, both narratives illustrate relatively clearly how White southern authors began encouraging a brand of postmodern male identity capable of freeing White people from any lingering sense of historically based responsibility. Together, the authors not only push back against framing male southern identity as a byproduct of one's inherited past, but also they suggest White people, who were searching for answers about their own sense of self or society's problems, were doing the right and moral thing when they embraced a view of history as unstable and largely detached from present conditions. Like we saw in the shows *Matlock, The Dukes of Hazzard,* and *In the Heat of the Night,* in the 1980s it became popular to view history as a mere brand that could be manipulated to fit one's own desired sense of self. *The Second Coming* and *Ray* engage in a similar relationship with the past, but they push beyond TV's representation, as they suggest breaking free from inherited positionality is a vital first step toward healing both the self and the society. Whereas the television shows mostly just inhabit a world where history has lost its fixed meaning, the literature provides a philosophic framework that explicitly encourages (at an individual level) destroying the past's power and then building a new, personal identity using whatever pieces of that destroyed history one still finds useful.

Key to this encouraged demolition is a sense that the region had more important things to focus on than supposedly old and exhausted questions about southern racism. For instance, when Zoltán Abádi-Nagy asks Walker Percy if *The Second Coming* could "have been written in the fifties or the sixties," Percy responds simply and clearly, saying, "no" (147). For him, this earlier period was "the Time of Troubles . . . with all manner of polarization in the country, black vs. white, North vs. South, hippie vs. square, liberal vs. conservative, McCarthyism vs. commies, etc." (144). As he told Peggy Castex, his characters, starting in the 1970s "are in a sense post-Southern" (52). He goes on to explain what it means for his White characters to be "post-Southern," saying, "they are not hung up on the black question. As far as they are concerned that is already resolved. Now, we in the South are in the same kind of trouble the rest of the country is in" (52). According to Percy, by the 1970s southerners had moved beyond racial problems and had now begun to grapple with the larger consumerist "suburban" culture, which had already enveloped the rest of the nation (52). As a result of this perceived change in the South, from being "hung up on the black question" to becoming "post-Southern," Percy's *The Second Coming* addresses what he sees to be the dominant issue in the region, which as he explains is soulless suburbanism. In doing this, though, the novel effectively shifts the conversation away from confronting inherited White guilt and toward an imagined need to model a new and healed White identity that could thrive in a postsouthern and irreferential age.

At first, Will Barrett and Allie Huger, who are the primary characters in *The Second Coming*, struggle to live and thrive in their suburban environments. For both characters, this struggle is primarily born from a divided sense of self that is torn between some desire for an authentic identity and the distracting influences of their past and present communities. Early in the novel, Will identifies his need for a better life as he watches a cat "sitting there in the sun with its needs satisfied, for whom one place was the same as any other place as long as it was sunny—no nonsense about old haunted patches of weeds in Mississippi or a brand-new life in a brand-new place in Carolina" (16). The narrator then cuts in, "As for Will Barrett, as for people nowadays—they were never a hundred percent themselves. They occupied a place uneasily and more or less successfully" (16). In this moment, while watching the cat, Will diagnoses his problem: for him, one place is not the same as another and he is not "a hundred percent" himself. He also realizes "to arrive at a diagnosis is already to have anticipated the cure: to restore the ninety-eight percent?" (16). The question mark at the end of the sentence, though, indicates that Will is not yet sure where to find the missing ninety-eight percent. So Percy uses the following pages to uncover how Will, and presumably readers, could find a realized and authentic sense of self in their postmodern/postsouthern age.

Allie Huger similarly experiences an unreconciled sense of self that leaves her deeply alienated from her family and community. However, as David Hugh Werning points out, "The difference between the two is that Allie knows that memory is a tool" (250). Put perhaps more accurately, though, Allie understands that the *absence* of memory is a tool. Whereas Will remembers everything and suffers from both an obsession with his father's suicide (the "haunted patches of weeds in Mississippi") *and* from his current condition in North Carolina (the "brand-new life in a brand-new place"); Allie remembers nothing and is free to build her identity unencumbered by the past. She has undergone a series of shock treatments that have erased her memory and left her almost as a blank slate on which a new (more authentic) identity could be constructed. In this way, Allie has an advantage over Will and can overcome the influences of her environment more quickly.[12] As Percy told Jo Gulledge, "[Allie's] shock [treatment] was good in the sense that it helped her" (308). He goes on to explain how the erasure of memory helped her separate from a singular sense of self, rooted in a problematic conception of human life, which as he puts it, "even schizophrenia is way of doing that" (308). Allie, in other words, demonstrates how embracing Fredric Jameson's version of schizophrenia and leaving behind the enculturated self (even by destroying it) can be a beneficial first step to living in the present as a functioning being.[13] Forgetting, then, is understood as necessary to accessing an authentic self, capable of action. As Allie puts it in her journal, "There is one thing you must not forget, or if you have forgotten be reminded of it here and now . . . It took me (you? us?) all my life to make the discovery. Why so long? And then I (you, we) had to go crazy to do it . . . What was my (your, our) discovery? That I could *act*. I was *free* to act" (40). As the shifts in pronouns suggest, Allie, like Will, has not been fully herself. She, too, recognizes that to move forward as a whole person capable of action means leaving behind the past and repairing herself into a singular "I."

It is this quest for independence and authenticity that drives Will and Allie, as they reject the constrictions placed on them by history and their present reality. Ultimately, the novel suggests that alienated individuals can locate the "missing 98%" of themselves through embracing an identity constructed outside the damaging pressures of their society. Michael Pearson explains, "[Will] senses his true status, that of a pilgrim, and he understands that it will always be his status" (99). The novel makes clear, though, that realizing one's "status" as a detached and wandering "pilgrim" in search of truth also means leaving behind historically informed racial and social inheritances. This need to leave behind the racialized past is illustrated most clearly in Will's reflections on his classmate Ethel Rosenblum. In a recurrent memory he watches her from a small, unclaimed strip of land in Mississippi and imagines speaking to her: "Ethel, why is the world so designed to keep us apart? Is it an unspoken pact? Is it an accursed shyness? Ethel, let's me and you homestead this leftover land here and now, this non-place, this surveyor's interstice. Here's the place for us, the only place not Jew or Gentile, not black or white, not public or private" (8). In this reflection, he offers an understanding that will not be fully realized until the novel's conclusion, when he and Allie build their relationship in a "non-place," a forgotten greenhouse where they can grow, free from societal pressures. It is only through this separation from their inherited identities that they are able to build a new and positive life together—a life which Percy told Robin Leary constitutes his "only unambiguous happy ending" (62).

Like it did for Ben Matlock, the Duke boys, and William Gillespie in the previous chapter, understanding oneself as being free from communal dictates allows Will and Allie to move forward with a new, supposedly post-racial identity. While *The Second Coming* is far more interested in explicating the necessary outsiderness of the individual psyche or spiritual self than the TV shows, Percy similarly asserts the unfixed nature of history and inherited meaning, which encourages White people to eject themselves from troubling communal narratives. Neither Will nor Allie feel any need to account for their own role in the problems they see around them. Instead, the novel implies they and other enlightened White people should shrug off any aspect of their identity that might inhibit their own individual growth or personal sense of authentic freedom. According to Percy's outlook, since "the world is already dead," it makes little sense to try and salvage or revivify the lifeless bodies of the past.[14] Therefore, the only choice really left, given the Baudrillardian hyperreality that has destroyed all meaning, is for individuals to turn inward and to construct a new identity outside their already dead world. Will and Allie's success, then, can be seen as an answer to the sense of division and hopelessness that kept Dr. Strickland from being an effective agent of healing. Through simply shedding connections to both their personal histories and removing themselves from the expectations of their society, Will and Allie suggest the prescription for a healed society is not found in stopping Welty's metaphorical train but in getting out of its way. In other words, conscientious White people should be focused on healing themselves, which can only be achieved through embracing the freedom of the outsider and no longer imagining one's identity as bound to any form of inherited, non-spiritual community.

The characters Dr. Alistair Duk and Dr. Vance Battle, who are the principal doctors in the novel, exemplify the consequences that arise from remaining "in bounds" and trying to heal the system from within a recognized position in society.[15] Kevin D. Majeres explains, "*The Second Coming* has a curiously negative presentation of doctors, pointing out in various ways their follies and ineptitudes in regard to language and communication" (589). First, Dr. Battle, who is Will's primary golfing partner, is a fairly straightforward and simple character. He exemplifies that staying within the confines of society may be the best option for some people. However, such a choice ultimately leads to a shallow and unenlightened existence. Throughout the novel, he does not seem to understand anything is wrong with the world. He sees no need for change or growth, and he goes about his life hearty, healthy, and happy. As Will explains, "Dr. Vance Battle [is] the happiest man he knew, a young husky competent G.P. who liked to get his hands on you, happy as a vet with his fist up a cow, mend bones, take hold of your liver from the front and back, stick a finger up your anus paying no attention to your groans, talking N.C. basketball all the while" (46). Battle is the kind of man who believes the world's problems are on the surface and can be healed through a mere examination or a good medical prescription. His view of humanity, though, reduces his patients to an almost animal-like status. Allie explains, "Unlike Dr. Duk, [Battle] didn't bother to listen, or rather he listened not to your words but your music. He was like a vet, who doesn't have to listen to his patient. There were other ways of getting at you" (248).

Battle's approach to his patients represents the belief that all can be cured without engaging the complex relationship between the spiritual and physical world. Rather than probing the depths of one's interiority, he searches for exterior and nonverbal problems, putting his faith in science as the best hope for curing those around him. His is a worldview devoid of the emotional and psychological turmoil felt by thinking people, like Will and Allie. Therefore, while Battle is happy, he has little to offer those around him in terms of true healing. Tellingly, after Ellis, another doctor, diagnoses Will's "condition" as "Hausmann's Syndrome," which attributes his "inappropriate longings" to "high sensitivity to pH changes" (303), Battle is excited and impressed. He turns to Will, saying, "I can only add one item to Dr. Ellis's diagnosis—incidentally, I concur with him now. I'll make you a press bet that the hydrogen ions will correct your slice . . . the hydrogen ion may even solve the Jewish question" (304). For Battle, almost everything, even his friend's golf game and the nation's larger spiritual crisis, can be fixed with an increase of hydrogen, "the simplest atom" (304). In the end,

Battle is cast as a happy fool, who only sees what is on the surface or can be exposed through a physical examination. He, then, is unable to help heal those like Allie, Will, and presumably readers, who are struggling with questions of language, meaning, and purpose.

Dr. Duk, who is of Pakistani descent, in many ways exists on the other end of the spectrum from Dr. Battle. As Allie points out, he "listens" to his patients and pays attention to the meanings and significances of their words. Yet, despite this ability to discern nuances, he too is unable to bring about any real healing or peace to those around him. Rather, Dr. Duk uses his insights into the human condition to erase his Pakistani identity, which then frees him to embrace a new version of himself guided by Linwood's shallow and capitalistic environment. We see an example of how Dr. Duk manipulates language to achieve his own goals when he meets Allie's parents: Kitty and Walter Huger. As it becomes clear they wish to have Allie classified as "legally incompetent" so they can control her inheritance (117), Duk, "like a prospector whose Geiger counter begins to click," speaks in "a new voice, a deeper richer crisper voice" (120). He says, "But we can agree that no matter what comes to pass, we will bear any burden, pay any price, to do what is best for Allison. Right?" (120). He then convinces them to pay a steep price for the Founder's Cottage in exchange for the diagnosis they seek. As Allie notes, "the meaning of the words went away" (121). All that is left is the marketplace, where language functions as a shallow veneer covering the buying and selling of things.

Because of the erasure of his own Pakistani identity, Dr. Duk understands how beneficial it can be to leave behind a fixed relationship with one's inherited history. After all, his redesigned and post-Pakistani persona allows him to thrive (at least financially) in the brand-new world of Linwood, North Carolina. Using this experience, he then is able to help Allie get halfway to her prescribed destination. However, beyond removing her memory through shock treatments, he is unable to help her construct a new authentic sense of self. This failure seems rooted in his own embrace of the rootless, late capitalistic environment that defines his new postsouthern home. For instance, he says in response to a guttural sound Allie makes (which her parents had interpreted as signaling she wanted to leave the hospital and live with them), "Interesting,

... You thought she said *with view,* meaning room with view. But thought I heard *with you,* meaning praps she might have some reservations about living with you. With you both. With yall" (102). After completing his interpretation, "Dr. Duk smiled, pleased with himself. He could talk Southern" (103). Duk's use of "yall" indicates how he conforms to his environment and tries to speak the language of his surroundings. However, as Allie notes, in an earlier iteration of the conversation, he is not so much speaking "Southern" as adopting an "American" relationship to language that has robbed the world of authentic meaning, all in the pursuit of money and comfort (99).

Together, Drs. Battle and Duk are emblematic of what Percy seems to understand as a failed communal model, where individuals exchanged ninety-eight percent of themselves in order to fit into systems that had excluded the possibility of an authentic spiritual identity. Carl Elliot explains, "Percy's kind of diagnostic exercise is aimed not at physical illness, of course, but at the spiritual pathologies endemic among late-twentieth century westerners" (4). Percy seems skeptical any current system or institution (economic, scientific, historic, religious, or political) could bring about real healing, so he turns to the individual spiritual self that he hopes is capable of existing outside the totalizing influences of late capitalism. As Allie puts it, becoming her true self means shrinking down to the essential self and escaping the fake and artificial modern world. She says, "I can already feel myself coming down to myself. From giant red star Betelgeuse, Dr. Duk's favorite, trying to expand and fan out and take in and please the whole universe (that was me!), a great gaseous fake of a star" (93). Instead of the great gaseous Betelgeuse she "collaps[es] down to white dwarf Sirius, [her] favorite, diamond bright and diamond hard, indestructible" (93). Unlike Duk, who continues to reinvent and lose himself in an ever-expanding attempt to fit into systems and please people, Allie finds herself as a true individual through embracing a "bright" and "indestructible" sense of her authentic self. Will, too, finds himself through shedding conventional expectations and forgetting the past. At the end of the novel, he emerges from a literal cave, reborn and ready to leave behind almost all aspects of his past and present identity. As Alan T. Belsches puts it, "[Will] and Allie are saved . . . because they know that the old ways do not work now and did not work for the Southerners of their parents' generations" (46). In other words, they are "saved" because they both move away from their inherited culture and the sense of self it produced.

Will and Allie's movement outside the "old ways" or their inherited communities, however, largely takes place within their minds and does not materially impact their privileged positions as wealthy White southerners. There is a vague promise the new community they are hoping to build will provide a real, more authentic sense of equality. As L. Jerome Taylor explains, they find their "newfound freedom *from* others on the one hand and [their] freedom *for* them on the other" (173). However, there is little to suggest how exactly their separation from the past makes them more effective agents for communal good. Instead, the novel keeps its focus on internal conversion rather than any external action, especially action taken within inherited systems. Allie explains, she has a growing knowledge of "the supremacy of mental attitude over physical conditions" (344). *The Second Coming* also concludes with the aged priest, who unwittingly brings Will to his final revelation, reminiscing about "a tiny village in Mindanao near Naga-Nag" where the inhabitants "are as poor as any people on earth, yet how kind and gentle and loving they are to each other! And happy!" (359). In Percy's framing, what is truly important is one's mental state and finding spiritual fulfillment. Material conditions, history, systems of power, race—all this pales in comparison to the importance of finding oneself and establishing a sense of being that exists outside the sick environment. It should be clear, though, how ejecting oneself from societal narratives licenses the same imagined post-historical freedom we saw in the last chapter, which tacitly suggests only racists still care about race. Certainly, Percy offers a more philosophically robust defense of White people's innocence, but his movement past inherited guilt still serves the same end, as it protects White people's perceived freedom to reinvent themselves as innocent outsiders.

We see a similar rejection of inherited identity in Barry Hannah's novella *Ray*, which Fred Hobson notes, inhabits "the world of Walker Percy's fiction" (4)—"a postmodern South in which place, community, traditional family, and even class play little part" (36). Like Percy, Hannah promotes the idea that traditional features of southern identity, including race, are no longer important to southerners. Instead, the novella suggests southerners, like the rest of the nation, are trapped in a rootless and fractured America. However, Hannah's Dr. Raymond Forrest (or Ray) goes beyond Will's and Allie's broad rejection of history and its communal dictates. In a manner similar to what we saw on the TV shows *The Dukes of Hazzard* and *In the Heat of the Night,* Ray retains a personal connection to the Confederacy and its icons. Again, this relationship with history is not cast as a wholesale embrace of any inherited or factual account of the past. Rather, history is transformed into a tool or brand that can be used to express a facet of one's desired identity. As Matthew Guinn puts it, "History is for Ray no longer a linear progression but a lateral one; he has relinquished the metanarrative for his own *petite histoire*" (175). The "*petite histoire,*" then, grants Ray license to construct his own version of the past, using whatever parts he finds useful. For Guinn, this relinquishing of the metanarrative opens up an exciting pathway for Hannah to breathe new life into southern literature. He argues, the novella "demonstrates that the past is viable for an artistic vision beyond mythoclasm or emigration—that the mature Southern artist of the postmodern era need not leave the South behind" (178). However, it should be said again that *Ray's* postmodern relationship with history once more encourages White people to see the South as merely a brand that can be used without having to worry too much about the actual realities of southern history and its connections to still-present injustice.

The imagined region and its narratives, then, are instrumentalized and used in what is positioned as a more pressing fight: the struggle to maintain a reconciled sense of self. Michael P. Spikes explains, the novella's central focus is on "Ray bring[ing] unified meaning to his experience by constituting himself as a single narrative consciousness, a unitary narrating and narrated self, which threads together his attitudes and actions" (76). We see this attempt to construct a "unitary" identity in the novella's opening paragraphs. Ray tells himself, "You are a doctor and you are in a hospital in Mobile, except now you are a patient but you're still me. Say what? You say you want to know who I am?" (3). Throughout the narrative, Ray (like Allie and Will) tries to mend his fractured identity and answer the question of who he really is. He works as both doctor and patient, and the few moments of peace or transcendence he experiences take place during his imagined participation as a Confederate soldier in the Civil War. In these constructed memories, he experiences a kind of authentic liminality existing between past and present. It is in these moments he reclaims his personhood, in a "nonplace" where he inhabits an identity free from both the orthodoxies of an older age and the simulated suburbanism of the 1970s and 1980s. Unlike Percy, though, who uses *The Second Coming* to suggest the violent past should largely be forgotten or at least that Will should distance himself from his father's history in Mississippi, Hannah's *Ray* suggests aspects of history can be retained and used to inform one's personal worldview and understanding of self. For Ray, then, the past is productive, as long as it is used to help build an individual's internal, authentic sense of identity.

Accordingly, the history Ray accesses is unfixed from the stable referents of a previous age and bears little resemblance to the actual Civil War fought in the 1860s. As Philip Beidler points out, Hannah (like many other Vietnam-era authors) uses the "transforming power of art" to create "a landscape of consciousness where it might be possible to accommodate experience remembered within a new kind of imaginative cartography endowing it with large configurings of value and signification" (16). Put differently, Hannah uses the "power of art" to map his frustrations with the current age through the lens of an alternative, imagined history. Like the Confederate flag in the *Dukes of Hazzard* or the portrait of Robert E. Lee in *The Heat of the Night,* the Civil War is reimagined in *Ray* to help the doctor establish his identity as a rebel and an outsider fighting a losing battle against a fallen world. For instance, in one of Ray's slippages back in time, he sees himself as part of an outnumbered Confederate battalion preparing to charge the enemy's position. The scene is full of the kind of manly vigor and sincerity Hannah casts as lacking in Ray's present environment. In the action, there is a deep and sweet sorrow as the young men prepare to die. Ray recounts, "The shadow of the valley passes over our eyes, and in the ridge of the mountains we see the white clouds as Christ's open chest. Many of us start weeping and smiling because we will die and we know" (65). The image of these weeping young men charging into "Christ's open chest," using only their sabers because guns "are cowardly" (65), paints a picture of loss and pain that marks the tragedy of war. Hannah then ends the scene with everyone but one Union soldier dead. He writes, "If warriors had known this story, we would have taken the war to the gooks with more dignity" (66). The imagined romance and valor of the Confederate charge, along with the United States' failure to tell "this story," is cast as leading to the ugly, undignified action in Vietnam—the slur driving home Ray's disgust with the degradation brought about by the war in which he fought.

In the end, *Ray*'s imagined and unfixed Civil War and specifically the moment of the Confederate charge work as an illustration through which readers can see what manly nobility supposedly should look like. The image, then, offers a contrast to Vietnam (the war Ray experienced), where it was "so easy to kill" and "so fucking hard to live" (54). This does not mean that Hannah consciously casts Ray as some kind of neo-confederate, who idealizes a war fought to perpetuate African American enslavement. For Hannah (and it seems the vast majority of White people in the U.S. by the 1980s) events from the past fail to exist in any real, shared way. In fact, Hannah rejects the reading of his novella that calls attention to the actual history and context of the Civil War. As he tells John Griffin Jones, "Ray really don't give a damn for history" (9). When Jones confronts him with the many references to the Civil War in *Ray*, Hannah responds, "All right, I just contradicted myself. He cares for a specific battle history. He's always right in the middle of the charge or right before the battle . . . He does not go back to the stately mansions of old, or any year" (9). Unlike William Faulkner's young southerners in *Intruder in the Dust* (1948), who in their charge have "much to lose and all this much to gain: Pennsylvania, Maryland, the world, the golden dome of Washington itself to crown with desperate and unbelievable victory the desperate gamble" (195). For Hannah, "the gamble" of the charge is supposedly not about conquest or gaining societal control. It is just about finding an authentic sense of self in the cavalry's fraternal action. However, Hannah's limited focus on a "specific battle history" allows him an imagined freedom in *Ray* to sidestep any larger discussion about historical legacies and inherited systems bound up in "the stately mansions of old." Instead, the novella shifts focus to an individualized and personal account of the past. As Ray puts it, "You're not sure about your horse. Or the cause. All you know is that you are here" (96). The focus, then, is on finding a sense of authentic being in the "perpetual present" that Fredric Jameson identifies as all that is left in the last quarter of the twentieth century (170). Again, like we saw in the last chapter and in *The Second Coming,* the novella suggests that the answer is not to resist fracture and dissensus but to embrace it and build a version of oneself capable of thriving within that environment. In other words, if a unified history is unavailable, then each individual should construct their own contextualizing narratives that feel real and bring peace or meaning to that individual.

The novella then closes with a final call to fight: "Sabers, gentlemen, sabers!" (113). However, it is not quite clear what Ray is fighting against, other than an overwhelming sense that everything is wrong in the world. Therefore, the call to fight seems to be more about a stance of opposition toward the culture than a specific recipe for resistance. As he explains to Larry McCaffery and Sinda Gregory, "Life is a lot of confusion and pain and death, and the only way to deal with it is to face it with the attitude that there's no place to go but up. 'Sabers up, gentlemen!'" (82). He then concludes, "That's the only solution I know. There's too much depression and confusion and death to allow any real hope. We don't have a fucking chance. But 'Sabers up!' (82). Hannah's diagnosis and prescription are less hopeful than Percy's. However, they agree that readers (or at least discerning readers) should break free from the inherited past and come up with a better narrative. White people then should light out for a mental territory of their own making that supposedly exists beyond their society's influence. Like we saw in the last chapter, though, this also means reducing the Confederacy to a mere tool or brand that can be useful for White people in constructing their sense of self. As Kenneth Seib puts it, *Ray* suggests "Each of us is a Confederate soldier going forth to do battle against overwhelming odds, and ours should be Ray's battle cry at the end of his narrative as we face the deadly enemies of our daily lives: 'Sabers, gentlemen, Sabers'!" (52). However, we should once again recognize how White people's perceived victimhood and claims of alienated identity licenses the reimagining and use of a war fought to protect the enslavement and torture of millions of people. The audacity of such a reimagining should be apparent, but once more we can see how White authors couch this reframing of the Confederacy as a harmless bit of rebranding rather than what it is: a powerful claim that even the worst aspects of White supremacy are not all that damning.

Like Walker Percy, who Barry Hannah calls "maybe" the only "significant Southern philosopher" (Conversations 97), this freedom to reimagine the past is born from a belief that the South was no longer indelibly marked by its historical struggles. Hannah saw the 1970s and looming 1980s as a fundamentally different period with different challenges than the 1960s. In a conversation with John Griffin Jones, which took place the same year *Ray* was published, Hannah characterizes the 1960s as an era when "you could get a pistol pulled on you for wearing tennis shoes . . . If you went to the wrong roadside restaurant, tennis shoes meant 'hippies,' 'Freedom Riders.' I have trembled coming back to my own state [of Mississippi] because my hair was a little long" (14–15). Less than twenty years later, though, he understood the state, and the South more generally, to be entirely transformed. Instead of a place defined by racism and violence, it was now overrun by placid middle-class consumers, whose aspirations were limited to making it into the pages of *Southern Living*. As he explains to Jones, "the middle class, and their dead lives, infest those things [old mansions] all over the South, and I think it is as big a shame as McDonalds. The big dream is to get upper-middle class and purchase one of those big houses" (13). Jones responds, "Right. Get your house in *Southern Living*," and Hannah agrees, "Right. By the time you get your photograph in there . . . you can pretty much figure the people are dead. It's too late. They are awful people!"[16] As Jones and Hannah continue to talk, they speak about their displeasure at having to visit those kinds of homes, and Hannah calls them "Snopeses" because "they didn't make their money in honest ways usually, or dignified ways." Jones finishes the thought for him, "They didn't have the plantation," and Hannah concurs, "No. They're dentists, you know. Or even Northern. They came down here to get 'em a mansion, baby" (13).

This conversation, which takes place between two White men sitting in Clinton, Mississippi, further demonstrates how White people in the 1980s used the South to construct a brand of racial innocence. According to Hannah's and Jones' estimation, they are genuine southerners who see through the artificiality of their era and yearn for something real and authentic. However, there does not seem to be any sense of irony or reflection on what it implies that they think owning a plantation is more "honest" and "dignified" than being a dentist or hailing from the North. Even as they discuss Hannah's fear of returning to Mississippi during the 1960s and their mutual admiration for the Freedom Riders, there is still the lingering sense that those bygone, violent days were somehow preferable to their current, bland environment. It also seems, for Hannah and Jones, the "dignity" of owning a plantation could be congruous with their respect for the Freedom Riders because they are both authentic modes of existence, removed from the artificiality and consumerism they see plaguing their current surroundings. Put plainly, they exhibit almost the inverse of the concerns Welty relays in "The Demonstrators." Whereas Strickland is consumed with the sense of fracture in his community and longs for a common narrative through which to find healing, Jones and Hannah look out at the supposedly placid sameness of the suburban South and long for authentic difference and originality. What remains consistent, though, is the way both the fear of division in the 1960s and the fear of sameness in the 1980s, offer narratives through which most White people could understand themselves as innocent victims, separated from legacies of racial violence.

In *Ray*'s closing pages, we again see how the novella frames the Civil War as an unfixed referent that can be used to fit White people's emotional needs. After Ray experiences the murder of his girlfriend Sister, the near death of his friend Mr. Hooch, numerous failed relationships, and a long separation from his wife Westy, he attempts to move on with his life as a relatively healed person. In the concluding action, Hannah offers some hope for Ray's future as he again slips back into the time of the Civil War. Like before, he is preparing to charge the enemy. Ray describes the scene: "We run counter to them. Looking at the vista, there are cavalrymen of every race and creed. There is the beauty of the horses, with a steam like cumulus rising from their nostrils . . . On myself I have the wool short jacket with every color of the rainbow on the breast" (108). The charge continues, as the men of "every race and creed," wearing the colors of the rainbow,[17] meet the horrors of modern warfare. An air force is deployed against them. The enemy is armed with machine guns. They have heat-seeking bullets, but the charge is undeterred.

Ray recounts the euphoria of the galloping horses as an almost tran-scendent moment: "Their cannon just missed me as my horse started running on water. We are high on our horses and laughing and I can hear the shrill Rebel yell behind me. They are throwing out phosphorus bombs, and . . . [m]y men just laugh and the horses climb the banks. What an open field. We are laughing and screaming the yell" (109). This passage is full of the same sad sweetness and beauty of the earlier charge, and it is perhaps easy for other White people to join Hannah's desire to understand this moment as decoupled from any real or actual history. What is lost in that desire, though, is the way it renders Whiteness invisible. After all, if even the Confederacy can be plucked from the pages of history and reimagined to signify an authentic multicultural/multiracial southern identity, then this effectively destroys history's power to organize and explain lived experience. Indeed, such a divorce from the facts of history makes it impossible to use the past as a referent through which to understand White people's inherited positionality. Instead, the power to define history's role is relocated to the individual's imagination, which is another way of saying it is fractured beyond the possibility of being used to demand justice.

When we put the narratives in this chapter alongside the television shows in the last one, we see how White people across mediums cast themselves as disconnected from inherited responsibility. By turning inward and isolating White male southern identity from its historical relationship to racial violence, television and literature create a powerful myth for national consumption. Together, they suggest it was useless to frame identity through a metanarrative linking individuals to a vio-lent past. Instead, we see a movement toward what Daniel T. Rogers calls an "intellectual construction of reality," which positions truth and meaning as products of the individual mind (3). More than that, what ails the culture (whether it be division or sameness) is positioned as so overwhelming that even if White people wanted to bring about change, they could not hope to succeed. As Robert McLaughlin explains, the culture "that postmodernism has wrought, then, is essentially conser-vative, negating the possibility of change at the same time it despairs of the status quo" (65). Given the ubiquitous "despair" in these texts, efforts to stay and fight from within the culture are cast as hopeless. Therefore, White people who benefit from generations of practiced White supremacy, could begin to see themselves not as perpetrators of unequal and violent systems, but as innocent victims of a nameless and faceless evil. This logic, then, shifts focus away from recognizing any personal responsibility that could lead to restorative action. Indeed, it suggests White people's survival depends on turning inward and focusing on their own healing. Of course, what is left out is how White people continue to profit from the cultural and institutional forces they claim to reject.

Put perhaps more plainly, as White people in the last quarter of the twentieth century saw the violence of White supremacy brought to light beyond the South's border, they turned to a brand of "multiculturalism" or "diversity" that claimed everyone, including White people, should pursue their own individually constructed identity. As Shaylyn Romney Garrett and Robert Putnam point out in their book *The Upswing* (2021), the movement toward focusing on the self over the community is "intimately bound up with white people's reaction to the Civil Rights revolution" (241). They explain White people's embrace of individual expression then led to real stagnation in attempts to address racial inequity. As White people began to promote self-expressed individualism, they also began to reject any form of legislation or governmental action that "demanded a reorganization of power structures, reallocation of resources, reformation of cultural norms, [or] genuine integration" (238). After all, according to the postmodern belief that grand narratives no longer govern identity, any attempt to dismantle inherited systems of power is reframed as government overreach, targeting innocent individuals. Rogers explains that "the terms in which justice and race were being overtly debated had shifted from the historical and social considerations of the early 1970s to a new, more abstract terrain" (136). Whiteness was then cast as "irrelevant," and "Those who pressed the cases against affirmative action in the courts presented themselves not as white or male but as socially unencumbered individuals" (136).

The White male southern outsider powerfully reinforces this dangerous fantasy that Whiteness is no longer relevant to discussions of equity and justice. Again, these characters suggest that even for men from what is imagined to be the nation's most backward region, neither race nor gender plays a foundational role in an individual's lived experience. Rather, each person is tasked with locating and embracing an authentic sense of self that only the individual can find and validate. Predictably, this arrangement leads to a version of identity that leaves behind any grand narrative linking Whiteness to guilt. Moreover, in the next chapter, we see how this postsouthern position both excuses White people and simultaneously seeks to rob Black people of their own rich history in the region. In other words, as White people demanded that history be fractured into individual brands, this performed an attempted erasure not only of collective White guilt but also of Black people's collective contributions and inherited positionality in the United States.

3

Seeing the Lynching Ropes

The Rejection of White Postsouthern Innocence

Almost any discussion of imagined Whiteness in the United States necessarily intersects with conceptions of Blackness. As Toni Morrison
points out in *Playing in the Dark* (1992), "it is not possible" to "speak of
profit economy, labor, progress, . . . almost anything" in White America "without having as a referent, at the heart of the discourse, at the
heart of definition, the presence of Africans and their descendants"
(50). While most of the analysis in this book focuses on White people
constructing versions of the South to frame their own innocence, the
project would be incomplete without addressing how Black people
recognized and resisted the rise of the White southern outsider. Chester
Himes's *Cotton Comes to Harlem* (1964), Ernest Gaines's *A Gathering
of Old Men* (1983), and Yusef Komunyakaa's poem "History Lessons"
(1992), work as representative texts demonstrating how many Black
Americans from the 1960s–1990s employed the South to reframe discussions of race and equity. More than simply opposing claims of White
postsouthern innocence, these authors also use their writing to identify
and to claim a usable version of southern history that more properly
contextualizes both White violence and Black resistance. Himes (who
lived most of his life outside the South), Gaines (a Louisianan living
in California when he wrote *Gathering*), and Komunyakaa (who built
his reputation writing about Vietnam) all use the region to emphasize
how the South's history should not simply be treated as another brand
that can be fractured and reassembled according to individual desires.
Instead, they demonstrate how the region functions as a relatively stable
foundational narrative through which we can better understand how

seemingly opposed racial identities have always existed in a common southern/American frame.

Taken together, the texts in this chapter remind readers how supposedly isolated southern legacies of enslavement, Jim Crow, racial terror, and mass incarceration remain interwoven into the United States' social fabric. As Trudier Harris explains in *The Scary Mason-Dixon Line* (2009), the South (as both a real and imagined space) has always been a vital part of African American literature. She writes for Black authors, the South's "history of repression, violence, and lack calls out to each generation . . . and each generation responds" (206). Their responses consistently illuminate the region's role as a "central shaping force" directly influencing "life and culture" in the United States (206). Or as Imani Perry puts it, if we want to better understand the past's impact on the present, "we have to look South to America" (383). The authors in this chapter recognize the South's role in conceptions of race and show how the region functions as a necessary lens through which to understand both White people's commitment to racial violence and Black people's long resistance to that violence.

Himes, Gaines, and Komunyakaa, then, recenter the region as a space through which we can better understand racial identity in the United States. They reinforce Malcolm X's assertion that "Mississippi is anywhere south of the Canadian border" (417), and they demonstrate the importance of accepting and engaging this reality as a necessary first step toward achieving some semblance of racial justice. Accordingly, there is little room in their texts for the kinds of postsouthern maneuvering we saw in the first two chapters, where White people imagine themselves as separated from the region's more damaging inheritances. Instead, they drive home Morrison's assertion that White people "who invented the hierarchy of 'race' when it was convenient for them ought not to be the ones to explain it away, now that it does not suit their purposes for it to exist" ("Unspeakable" 126). Ultimately, the texts in this chapter refute the fantasy that White people could escape their guilt either by isolating racism below the Mason-Dixon line or by embracing an imagined identity that exists outside the region's racial realities.

At the heart of Himes,' Gaines,' and Komunyakaa's texts, is this refusal to allow a reimagined South that renders race invisible in the United

States. As we saw in the first two chapters, rather than admitting increasingly apparent links between Southern and Northern/National racism, White people invented new narratives capable of excusing themselves from legacies of racial violence. For marginalized people, though, no amount of mere invention or rebranding could erase how the nation's long history of theft and harm impacted daily lived experience. As James Baldwin put it in 1972, when White people consider history, they fail to recognize that "for millions of people, this history . . . has been nothing but an intolerable yoke, a stinking prison, a shrieking grave" ("No Name" 473). What Baldwin explains is that White people in the United States enjoy a perceived distance from the history they have created and from which they continue to profit. This imagined separation feeds the fantasy that individuals can simply choose which historical narratives are important or relevant to their lives. However, as Baldwin makes clear, for many marginalized people, history represents not merely a collection of stories but an inescapable "yoke," a "grave," and a "prison" defining their relationship with their nation.[1] Baldwin goes on to write, "life itself depends on the speediest demolition" of White-authored history and its hold over Black Americans. Yet, he points out this demolition cannot take place until African Americans have gained the ability "to assess" history and to "take from it what they need, and to add to history the monumental fact of their presence" ("No Name" 473). The texts in this chapter demonstrate Baldwin's assertions—in that they seek both to destroy narratives that deny inherited racial violence and to preserve "the monumental fact" of Black people's presence in the United States.

In Chester Himes's *Cotton Comes to Harlem,* we see a particularly clear example of the South's potential in achieving Baldwin's balance between destroying White people's hold over history while preserving Black people's legacies of triumph and resistance. Unsurprisingly, *Cotton Comes to Harlem* also offers a distinct departure from the other 1960s texts we encountered in the first two chapters.[2] Unlike *The Andy Griffith Show,* which embraces a whitewashed Americanized South, or Welty's "The Demonstrators," which suggests hopeless division between Black and White southerners, Himes's novel demonstrates how the South offers a common and potentially productive frame through which to understand nationalized racial violence. As Rosanna Cavallaro explains,

"Without in any way idealizing the slave experience" Himes "recognizes the depth of African Americans' connection to their Southern roots and the degree to which their culture is coextensive with that of Southern whites" (118). This common culture, then, rejects notions that White Americans could somehow separate the South from Black people and their experience in the United States. Indeed, while both *The Andy Griffith Show* and "The Demonstrators" try to separate Black and White experiences, Himes collapses those spheres into a single southern/national reality.

More than that, the text also seems to anticipate and reject post-1970s ideations that one could turn to outsiders, southern or otherwise, as a solution for the United States' centuries-long investments in White supremacy. Even though the novel's protagonists, the detectives Grave Digger Jones and Coffin Ed Johnson, in some ways resemble outsiders—in that they operate at the margins of society and test the limits of the law, the detectives, ultimately, work within their larger community rather than trying to deny its evils or escape its influences. As Himes makes clear, they are not given the luxury of retreat into liminal spaces, like the White men we saw in post-1970s television or Percy's and Hannah's characters in *The Second Coming* and *Ray*. Instead, the detectives navigate a communal pathway forward because it is the only avenue available for slowing the rate of violence that surrounds them.

In the novel's action, then, the South functions as a vital framing device for both resisting various forms of White-authored denial and for illustrating hope in a viable future. To achieve this balance, Himes brings the South's cash crop, cotton, to New York City—the North/nation's beacon of metropolitan and commercial success. Through bringing cotton (both literally and metaphorically) into Harlem, Himes reminds readers that Southern plantations and Northern/National cities have always shared a common, racist commitment to profits over people. As Ibram X. Kendi puts it, "to love capitalism is to end up loving racism . . . They were birthed together" (163). Whereas *The Andy Griffith Show*, largely erases this joint birth and offers a sanitized characterization of small-town America found in the South, *Cotton Comes to Harlem* flips the script and demonstrates how aspects of New York City are distinctively southern—effectively trading the innocence of a nationalized

South for the guilt of a southernized nation. Himes explains, "I could lift scenes straight out of Faulkner and put them in Harlem and all I had to change was the scene" (Conversations 169). By collapsing divisions between North and South, the novel then shifts the discussion away from what Houston Baker Jr. and Dana Nelson identify as an easy and damaging binary: "'North equals good whites, good life for blacks,' while 'South equals bad whites, bad life for blacks'" (233). In place of this binary, Himes uses Harlem to complicate traditional narratives of regional distinction and goes about "laying claim to a culture and to a region that, though fraught with pain and difficulty, provides a major grounding for identity" (6), which Thadious M. Davis argues is a reclamation that is essential for understanding the region's racial legacies.

At a basic level, *Cotton Comes to Harlem*'s plot revolves around two cons, both of which connote the long history of cultural scams promising a better, postsouthern identity for Black people in America. First, the Reverend Deke O'Malley, who is later revealed to be the ex-convict Deke O'Hara, promises the citizens of Harlem that for one thousand dollars they will receive "transportation free, five acres of fertile land in Africa, a mule and a plow and all the seed you need, free" (5). The promise of "free" acreage and a mule repeats the unfulfilled pledge of "forty acres and a mule" after emancipation. When combined with Deke's surname, O'Hara, which echoes the slave-owning protagonist of Margaret Mitchell's *Gone with the Wind* (1936), we see how Deke is simply repackaging an old southern/American ploy recast with new characters. The "reverend," who plans on escaping with the money, is just one more individual using the "intolerable yoke" of American history to lure impoverished people into an untenable agrarian fantasy. Before he can get away with the money, though, he is robbed by a group of White men with "Mississippi voices" (9). While Himes casts Deke O'Hara's short-lived con as problematic, he is only a minor threat compared to the one represented by the White men who take the money from him.

Colonel Robert L. Calhoun, who leads the theft and second con, bears the surname of one of the most avowed secessionists and supporters of slavery: John C. Calhoun. In many ways, Robert Calhoun's con represents a more direct and widespread attempt to erase and destroy Black southern/American identity. His scheme is to use the stolen cash to fund his Back-to-the-Southland movement (BTS), which, as the name suggests, seeks to bring those in Harlem back to the South's physical space. He plans to use the money he stole from Deke to offer a thousand dollars to each Black person willing to serve as a laborer, once again propping up the region's economy. For his scheme to work, though, he must sell an image of the South as a space that celebrates Black cultural production and achievement. In this way, the BTS movement embraces the same kind of post-racial multiculturalism that we saw White people promote in the last two chapters. Its narrative is one that allows for celebrating difference, as long as that celebration does not infringe on constructions of White people's innocence and their ability to earn profits. Therefore, while most of the plot centers on finding the stolen money, the actual stakes are much higher. What the detectives must ultimately work against is a real, continued violence carried out against Black people in the United States.

Calhoun is the brains behind the con, but *Himes* seems to recognize the shifting nature of Whiteness in the 1960s and introduces a more subtle threat that can blend into his surroundings and carry out Calhoun's plans. Himes writes, Calhoun "was clad in a . . . black frock coat and black shoestring tie, and on the ring finger of his long pale hand was a solid gold signet ring with the letters CSA" (57). In 1960s Harlem (or really anywhere in America outside of a KFC), this man would stand out and would be easily identified as an acolyte of the "Old South." His unnamed protégé, though, is a "young blond white man in a seersucker suit, who looked as though he might be an alumnus of Ole Miss" (57). He has no name, wears the clothes of a professional southerner, and Himes associates him with "Ole Miss," a university where in 1962 (two years before the novel's publication) one of the largest and most violent protests against integration took place. The young man's presence in Harlem, as an agent of continued racial inequity, represents the fruits of the rioters' labor. He embodies how each and every year universities turn out new generations of young, educated White men equipped to spread their ancestors' values, using new and more subtle strategies. Like *The Andy Griffith Show*, which shed the Confederate South's overt symbols yet maintained a largely segregated and White supremacist narrative, the young man appears non-threatening and even post-racial as he eagerly carries the torch of exclusion and discrimination into the nation's future.

Accordingly, the nameless protégé and the BTS movement pretend to celebrate African American achievement in the region while simultaneously denying realities undergirding the cultural productions they supposedly promote. In other words, their happy and whitewashed version of Black history, which they use to lure Black men and women back south, belies the actual experiences bound up in the region's history. Readers can see the illusory South that Calhoun and his companion endorse most clearly in the paintings covering the window of the BTS office: "one scene showed these happy darkies at the end of the day celebrating in a clearing in front of ranch-type cabins, dancing the twist, their teeth gleaming in the setting sun, their hips rolling in the playful shadows to the music of a banjo player in a candy-striped suit" (56). Then, "lodged between the larger scenes were smaller paintings identified as ALL GOOD THINGS TO EAT," which include "Chitterling Bred Shoats" and "Pappy's Bar-B-Q and Mammy's Hog Maw Stew" (56). Overlooking it all, is a painting of "a tall white man with a white mane of hair, a white moustache and white goatee, wearing a black frock coat and shoestring tie, his pink face bubbling with brotherly love" (56). These scenes are recognizably dangerous, but most of what they show (food, dancing, music) are central to what Himes goes on to characterize as worth preserving from the Black experience in the South.

The paintings adorning the BTS office, then, illustrate how these potentially powerful cultural productions have been twisted and distorted for the benefit of those like Calhoun and his companion. Himes gives readers another clear example of this manipulation a few pages later when Calhoun seduces the Black Harlemites with "what they could be eating for breakfast if they signed up with him and went back south" (65). In his office, he consumes a large meal consisting of "grits swimming with butter; four fried eggs sunny side up; six fried home-made sausages; six down-home biscuits, each an inch thick, with big slabs of butter stuck between the halves; and a pitcher of sorghum molasses" (65). This may sound like a breakfast as "grotesquely oversized" as the "good things to eat" on the paintings affixed to the building (56).

However, the effect it has on Calhoun's audience is profound. Himes writes, the Black "people, watching the Colonel shovel grits, eggs and sausage into his mouth . . . felt nostalgic. But when they saw him cover all his food with a thick layer of sorghum molasses, many felt absolutely homesick" (65). One onlooker laments, "Baby seeing that scoff makes my stomach feel lak my throat is cut" (65). The reaction to the food is visceral, and the image of the man's throat being cut gives readers a window into the anguish experienced by many Black people who were searching for a rooted identity in the placeless North. Put again, Himes captures the struggle of bearing witness to the cultural theft White people carried out, as they not only forced African Americans from their homes in the region but also had the audacity to then claim ownership over southern food and culture for their own purposes.[3]

As the novel continues, Himes works against this theft by offering a reframing and reclamation of southern culture. We can see an example of how Black southern foodways are reclaimed as Grave Digger Jones and Coffin Ed eat at Mammy Louise's restaurant. After listening to a menu highlighting African American southern cuisine, the two detectives ask for "two double orders of ribs . . . with side dishes of black-eyed peas, rice, okra, [and] collard greens with fresh tomatoes and onions" (101). This meal of traditional, regional staples with roots in Africa rivals the one Calhoun eats. For the detectives, though, the food is a source of sustenance and strength rather than a vehicle for manipulation and violence. As Grave Digger Jones explains to the waitress, the food she brings will help them "think" and gain energy they need to solve the crime (101). Traditional southern fare, then, is turned from a weapon into an element of enablement that can be used against those who wish to oppress Black communities. What seems important is the way in which the food is stripped of its attachment to White romanticism and repositioned into the context of Black ownership. Significantly, it is not as if Mammy Louise's all-night BBQ joint with its neon lights and New York setting is somehow more "authentic" than other instantiations of southern food—at least not in the way authenticity is usually policed and deployed in southern foodways. Rather, the food is simply Mammy Louise's cultural production to do with what she pleases. The profits and framing of that food are rightfully hers. Indeed, this sense of ownership and agency is what moves the food from a symbol of White racial violence to a source of sustenance and empowerment.

Himes also offers a similar recuperation of music and dance as he reclaims these cultural productions from the White people who wish to pervert them. According to the images on the BTS window, Black southerners are depicted as "happy darkies" who are "playing the Banjo" and "dancing the twist" as they pick cotton (56). The pictures connote African American music and dance as being associated with happy labor, which is an inaccuracy at least as old as Frederick Douglass.[4] In contrast to this imagined narrative of happy captivity, Himes places the power of southern blues, jazz, and dance back into the hands of its original producers. We can see the results of this cultural ownership in an interaction between the character Iris O'Malley and a White policeman, who has been tasked to surveil her. The dynamics between Iris and the officer (as defined by the greater society) are clear: she is Black, female, and largely without political agency; he is White, male, and a member of law enforcement, which affords him a great deal of cultural authority. Iris, however, is able to subvert that inequality, at least partially, through the power of dance and blues music. Himes writes, "She went over to the small record player against the wall and put on a slow sexy blues number and stood for a moment waving her body tantalizingly, snapping her fingers" (71). The policeman almost immediately succumbs to her seduction, and as Patricia Kane and Doris Y. Wilkinson explain, Iris, in her resistance, is "a black woman who refuses to accept defeat and transcends the potentially crippling identity her situation invites" (103). Himes weaves music and dance into this moment of transcendence as a diegetic reminder of how these cultural expressions speak to a rich African American history rooted in the South. In fact, Blues music is heard throughout the novel, along with jazz,[5] in order to illuminate the fertile past that came before Harlem. The music informs readers that the characters are part of a history and a culture with deep artistic and musical ties extending far beyond "spirituals" and "a banjo." As Amiri Baraka points out, "Early Blues" was a vital "expression of [Black people's] individuality within the superstructure of American society" (Jones 66). By the scene's end, Iris uses this expression alongside the power bound up in her physical body to help her claim freedom. Meanwhile, the White policeman is left naked with a brown bag over his head, essentially robbing him of the constructed authority born from both his white face and his badge.

Iris's subversion of culturally prescribed power dynamics and eventual freedom again remind readers that when removed from claims of White ownership, southern cultural productions can be used to root and empower Black American identity. However, while reclaiming food, music, and dance is important, the novel ultimately centers around cotton, as a negotiated artifact of memory and capital. In the space of the story, the stolen cash is literally hidden inside a cotton bale, drawing an unsubtle link between agrarian fantasies and capitalistic realities.[6] The paintings outside the BTS movement's office are again instructive in showing how White people sought to deny this connection between cotton and the unyielding pursuit of profits. Throughout the image depicting the "Southland" are "conk haired black cotton-pickers, clad in overalls that resembled Italian suits, delicately lifting enormous snow-white balls of cotton from rose-colored cotton bolls that looked for all the world like great cones of ice cream" (56). The painting's characterization of enslavement and sharecropping as part of an idyllic and pastoral scene dominates what onlookers see, but there is also a "small notice in one lower corner, which reads, *Wanted, a bale of cotton*" (57). This smaller poster, which goes "unnoticed" (57), is focused on finding the cash hidden within the lost bale of cotton. In the juxtaposition between what is seen and what is left unseen, Himes makes clear that loud proclamations about happy laborers have always worked to distract from White people's real obsessions with securing money and power.

Like he does with southern food, music, and dance, Himes goes on to return cotton's symbolic power to Black southerners. He does this primarily through illustrating the importance of understanding cotton as a kind of cultural touchstone. The character Uncle Bud, who still recalls his time in the South, demonstrates the power found in honestly remembering the region's history. When he comes across the missing bale, he recognizes White people have always hidden their profits beneath the crop's white façade. He likens the bale's smell to the "sweat" of Black Americans, and it is through this association between labor and stolen capital that he is able to find the money that rightfully belongs to people like him (63). His understanding of cotton in its proper context is akin to what Trudier Harris writes about in her memoir *Summer Snow* (2003). In her book, she explains cotton symbolizes the historic toils of a people striving for a better future. While distance from cotton meant progress, it also meant a possible detachment from understanding what many Black people experience in the United States (22). Put again, when the labor associated with cotton is forgotten, there is a dangerous loss of perspective that not only minimizes sacrifices made by previous generations but also allows White people to seize narrative power through rewritten histories. Because Uncle Bud or Cotton Bud, as he calls himself when he moves to Africa, intimately understands cotton, he is able to ignore false promises recognize the crop for what it has always been—a hiding place for violently secured profits. By adopting "cotton" as part of his name, he then illustrates an ownership over this history, which allows him to prosper in a new life on a new continent.

Like Welty in "The Demonstrators," Himes uses cotton as a central symbol of racial division in the United States. However, his use of the crop differs from hers in two important ways: first, while both authors seem to understand cotton's damaging and continued presence, Welty seems to struggle imagining any solution to this problem or even conceptualizing how Black and White southerners could see cotton in a common frame. Himes, on the other hand, uses his novel's conclusion, where Calhoun is forced to pay back the missing money out of his own pocket, to indicate there is a necessary reimbursement or reparation that should take place for what the nation has stolen from Black people. While both authors convey the region's history has a role in current communal failings, only Himes sees his way toward a starting point that actually begins addressing the problem. The second difference, which is related to the first, is there is a discernably dissimilar sense of the stakes in how their characters interact with cotton's legacies. Welty's Strickland appears, on some level, to recognize ignoring cotton will lead to an irreversible fracture in towns like Holden. However, the cost of that fracture is still largely felt in the realm of a philosophical division rather than any actual threat to his own security or safety. Indeed, there are no indications that Dr. Strickland or his office, which sits atop the bank building, are truly endangered by the division in his community. On the other hand, Grave Digger Jones and Coffin Ed cannot afford to retreat into the realm of mere conjecture and speculation. As they tell the junkyard operator Mr. Goodman, "We're cops, not philosophers. And we just want to find out what is missing from your junkyard and we can't wait until Monday morning because by then someone else might be killed" (107). The detectives, unlike Strickland, cannot wallow in melancholy while pondering and struggling with the philosophical meaning of cotton. Rather, they must be relentless in their pursuit of restorative justice because each minute they delay means another dead person.

As we move on to Gaines's *A Gathering of Old Men,* which is set in the 1970s but published in the 1980s, we can better see how Himes's emphasis on knowing and responding to southern/national history, as a matter of life and death, survives White people's growing idealization of the individual outsider.[7] Perhaps no author has covered the necessary relationship between race, southern history, and community more fully than Ernest Gaines. In part because of his focus on history and community, though, Gaines is often read as being a writer focused on rejecting change and still-clinging to an older, traditional version of the agrarian South. For instance, Fred Hobson characterizes Gaines, saying, "Indeed, it would be difficult to find in contemporary Southern letters any writer who is more traditional" (92). He then goes on to champion Gaines as the rightful heir to traditional southern literature and as "the quintessential Southern *agrarian,* in that he had a closer acquaintance with the soil—a deeper intimacy with it because of working it, than most of the upper-case Agrarians ever had" (101). Or, as Jeffrey J. Folks argues, "[Gaines] has appropriated a highly developed Southern literary tradition that suggests conventional responses to mechanization" (33).[8] However, reading Gaines's fiction as "appropriating" themes White southerners had long obsessed over (such as the fear of increased mechanization and a fading agrarian way of life) does not fully acknowledge the revolutionary power of his work. It is important, then, not to conflate Gaines's promotion of a communal history with "traditional" White-authored lamentations over a disappearing agrarian South. Put again, I think it would be a mistake to read his work as expressing the same nostalgia for small farms or working the land that Wendell Berry conveys in *The Hidden Wound*.

At the same time, it would be equally misleading to suggest Gaines's work fully abandons a more traditional attachment to grand historical narratives. Instead, we see a relationship with history that echoes how bell hooks' frames the usefulness and limits of postmodernity. She explains how postmodern rejections of "essentialism" and the legitimization of "difference and Otherness" allows for a broadening in what counts as an accepted and valuable narrative or identity (129). She argues, therefore, it is dangerous to reject completely the postmodern rupture that has unsettled racial binaries—as "The critique of essentialism encouraged by postmodernists thought is useful for African Americans concerned with reformulating outmoded notions of identity" that have promoted a "constricting notion of blackness" (132). She goes on to point out, the usefulness of postmodernism arises from "critiques of essentialism which challenge norms of universality and static over-determined identity" (132). hooks then concludes that postmodern critiques of essentialism "can open up new possibilities for the construction of self and the assertion of agency" (133). However, she is careful to point out while there are positives emerging from the fact "many other groups now share with black folks a sense of deep alienation, despair, uncertainty, loss of sense of grounding" born from the death of grand narratives, the sense of loss felt by White people is not the same thing as having "shared circumstances" (131).

It is this difference of "circumstances" that helps explain the contrast between what we saw in the last two chapters and how the authors in this chapter treat postmodern/postsouthern identity. In the 1980s, as we witnessed, White authors could propose embracing liminal spaces as a solution to White violence because their inherited positionality allowed them the fantasy that they could shed their past and construct new detached identities. Whereas, for those who have suffered from centuries of White violence, it is not an option to find peace through merely imagining oneself as an outsider or building one's own personal relationship with history. In *Gathering*, Gaines directly engages this difference and illustrates how Black people's freedom to write their history is only a small part of what needs to happen for justice to be realized in the United States. The novel, which uses alternating speakers to explain why any of the Black characters might have killed a White foreman named Beau Boutan, affirms the postmodern shift toward destabilizing "essentialism" or hegemonic understandings of the past. However, through the novel's use of television and its anticlimactic ending, we can recognize how merely destabilizing or adding to history does not diminish racial imbalances in the United States. Put again, without ignoring benefits gained from polyvocality, *Gathering* casts doubt on any hopeful reclamation that could occur through merely adding more voices or brands to the American cultural milieu.

Much has already been written about how Gaines uses the text's multiple narrators to challenge conceptions of a singular history, so I will not belabor that point. Both Terrance Tucker's "(Re)Claiming Legacy in the Post-Civil Rights South" and Keith Clark's "Re-(W)righting Black Male Subjectivity" cover how the novel wrestles back narratological power through the narrators telling their stories and standing up to the White people in Bayonne. However, both scholars also view the men's ability to voice their own histories as a foundational act having the potential to lay new groundwork for future growth. As Tucker puts it, *Gathering* is a "multi-vocal tale which centers on the storytelling in which the men engage, creating space from which they can lay the groundwork for a resistant, progressive black community" (115). Clark adds that the men's voices work as means of "speaking one's self into existence and, concomitantly, renegotiating the conditions of one's subject status" (202). As he suggests later, this act of telling has the potential power "to interrupt a history of social—and self-erasure through collective, communal action" (205). Without diminishing the significance of the old men's ability to speak themselves "into existence," I believe *Gathering* is actually not very hopeful about the future impact of their voices. Instead, the story only concludes after demonstrating the limits of reclaiming narratives in a postmodern environment. It is true the story's climax, where Fix decides not to lynch Mathu and the men stand up to White vigilantes, signals a sort of individual and collective victory. However, the novel ultimately suggests their victory is fleeting, so long as large swaths of the public (including those who inhabit courts and enforce laws) still do not understand the nation's enduring commitment to White supremacy and racial violence.

Particularly, Gaines uses television to illustrate how the White community resists systemic change and instead invests in an easy post-racial narrative that promises peace without justice. Television's quiet intrusion into the novel hardly garners attention, yet it works in the background to soothe and alleviate White racial guilt. We see this soothing influence primarily through the character Thomas Vincent Sullivan, who is also called Sully or just T.V. and describes himself as "a television nut. A vidiot" (112). It is mostly through his perspective readers gain their understanding of the relationship between the White fullback Gilbert "Salt" Boutan (called Gil) and the African American halfback Calvin "Pepper" Harrison (called Cal). Gil, who is also Beau Boutan's brother, and Cal make up Louisiana State University's or LSU's rushing attack. Their play on the football field receives national attention, and T.V. casts the backfield of "Salt and Pepper" as the consummate symbol of equality and racial harmony. T.V. tells readers, "Both were good powerful runners, and excellent blockers. Gil blocked for Cal on sweeps around end, and Cal returned the favor when Gil went up the middle. It drove the defense crazy because both Gil and Cal carried the ball about the same number times in a game and the defensive team didn't know which to look out for" (112). However, this image of complete racial harmony, where the two men block for each other and share carries equally is somewhat destabilized in the next line. T.V. almost dismissively adds, "Besides that, you had 'Sugar' Washington at quarterback" (112).[9]

As LSU's quarterback, Sugar is the team's de facto leader. He is the member of the team who guides the offense and decides who carries the ball. While Gil and Cal may be the most popular members of the team, or at least the ones on which T.V. focuses, Sugar is still in command. Not too subtly, Gaines links the quarterback's name and position to the region's cash crop and the labor dynamics enforced for its production. Therefore, while the rushing duo offer an image of racial harmony and equality, they are still playing a game controlled by a symbol of White people's capitalistic interests. It does not matter that Gil and Cal are the center of attention. Sugar's position as the one who leads the offense is unthreatened. As the quarterback, he can sit back and direct the offense, while Gil (who is poor and Cajun) and Cal (who is Black) run the ball and bear the brunt of the game's violence. T.V. and the rest of the novel's White characters see this arrangement as proclaiming post-racial harmony, but Gaines appears to be signaling for readers to be wary of T.V.'s comforting fantasy. Instead, they are again reminded to look for the subtle ways White people are profiting off newly packaged, supposedly equitable versions of American society.

The White characters further demonstrate their desire for television's post-racial narrative through their focus on a symbolic matchup between LSU and the University of Mississippi, also called Ole Miss. In the 1980s, with its Rebel flags and Colonel Reb mascot, Ole Miss represented a connection to an increasingly out-of-vogue antebellum South. Similar to a good television show, then, the two teams are matched against one another as forces of good and evil. T.V., who is the third-string quarterback for LSU, cannot wait for the showdown. However, Gil's reaction to Beau's death temporarily interrupts T.V.'s focus on the upcoming game. "Out of the blue, he [Gil] looked at Cal like he suddenly hated him" (113). T.V is flabbergasted, reminding him, "Gil, that's Cal" (114). Later, when T.V. drives Gil back to Bayonne, T.V. listens as Gil illustrates his prejudice by grouping together all Black people as "them" (115). Reflecting on the racial resentment Gil apparently harbors, T.V. thinks to himself, "So that's why he [Gil] went against Cal like that. Whether he had anything to do with it or not, he was guilty because of his color. Jesus Christ." T.V. then imagines speaking to Gil, "Jesus Christ, man. The two of you work on that field together as well as any two people I've ever seen in my life work together, and because of this—Jesus H. Christ. Come on Gil . . . you're made of better stuff than that" (115). Gil picks up on his friend's judgment and says, "You don't know my folks Sully. So little you know about me" (115).

Without putting too fine a point on it, Gil in this scene turns to T.V., who is a representation of television or at least a product of watching a great deal of it, and tells him that he knows very little about the complexities and depths of American racism. For T.V., the narrative was supposed to be simple, like on television, where someone like Gil would almost by default be ejected from legacies of history and positioned as a post-racial hero. Just like we saw in the *post-1970s television in the first chapter,* "good" White people were supposed to be completely un-concerned with matters of race and instead focused on defeating some outside source of corruption or evil. According to the logic found on television, the battle lines are clear and the winner predetermined, like in a game between LSU and Ole Miss. What T.V. finds, though, is that the nation and the region are bound up in complex attachments to his-toric systems of White supremacy. While Gaines lauds the importance of Gil's and Cal's relationship in an interview with Elsa Saeta and Izora Skinner—where he says "They're the ones living in the present and they're the ones who must make this America work. We've got to block for each other and do all kinds of things to get to the goal" (250)—he demonstrates in the novel that Gil's and Cal's positive relationship ac-tually ends very closely to the sidelines of the football field. Put again, when the action moves beyond what could be watched on television, we see how quickly White people abandon truly "blocking" for one another and how they are working toward very different goals than the novel's Black characters.

Gil's and Cal's relationship as it is presented on television, then, can be understood as one more narrative, like the BTS window, offering a fantasy of multicultural/multiracial unity while serving primarily to protect White people's interests. Similarly, Gil's bid to shed his Cajun identity and become an All-American fullback for LSU again demon-strates how television helps White people pursue their own ambitions. As he explains to his father, the image of him and Cal playing together is a key part of his ability to thrive as a national symbol. He says, "Papa, I want to be an All-American at LSU. I have a good chance—Cal and me. The first time ever, black and white, in the Deep South. I can't make it without Cal, Papa. I depend on him" (138). On one level, Gil depends on Cal's ability to block for him, but almost more importantly, he depends on the interracial image that will be shown throughout the nation. It is the fact they are playing in "the Deep South" that demonstrates the post-racial fantasy to the rest of the United States and makes him a particularly attractive candidate for being named an All-American. He pushes back against Fix's desire to go out and lynch Mathu (who is the primary suspect in Beau's killing) because he knows that his father engaging in such an action will ruin his national appeal as a symbol of interracial harmony. As Valerie Melissa Babb puts it, "[Gil] has come to cherish his position in the public eye as an all-American and wants no racial vendetta to besmirch it" (127). In other words, he is not concerned with Mathu's life, which is at stake. Instead, Gil is preoccupied with how the larger, watching audience will perceive their actions. He tells his father, "I couldn't make All-American, Papa . . . the Yankee press would destroy me" (138). Put simply, while the interracial image has constructive power to shape a better future, especially for White people like the Boutans, it does little to address the systemic devaluing of Black people's lives beyond perhaps discouraging the most overt acts of racial violence, which Fix represents.[10]

Salt and Pepper's projected unity, then, means something quite different for the novel's Black characters. They do not talk about the upcoming match between Ole Miss and LSU and appear unconcerned with the game's outcome. Instead, they seem to recognize they are destined to lose no matter who wins the game and are uninterested in embracing the post-racial fantasy an LSU victory would suggest. As Sheriff Mapes demonstrates in a conversation with the novel's Black men, the new post-racial image found on television does not offer any real victory over White people who have carried out centuries of murder and racial terror. Mapes asks, "Which do you want? Salt and Pepper to play together, or you want God to keep Fix the way he was thirty years ago so you would have a chance to shoot him?" (171). In this question, he encapsulates the conundrum at the center of postmodern ahistoricism. On one hand, it is good that Gil and Cal are playing with one another and that images of post-racial harmony rein in those like Fix who wish to continue enacting overt segregationist violence. On the other hand, this post-racial image also keeps any true confrontation from happening, which suspends the necessary reflection and action that must take place in order to rectify the nation's violent history. For Mapes, this question, about whether the old men want to confront Fix or see Salt and Pepper play, brings him glee. As Albert Jackson or "Rooster" puts it, "I had never seen a happier white man in all my born days. Looked like he was ready to kiss the first person who come up" (171). The sheriff is happy because neither narrative threatens his position of power. He can let them choose either the violent racist past Fix represents or the post-racial fantasy offered by Salt and Pepper's role on television. Both narratives allow for his continued privilege because both fail to acknowledge the positionality of White men, like him, who can remain largely invisible while benefitting from the nation's long investments in White supremacy.

Gathering's final chapter drives home its rejection of empty, postmodern multiculturalism. The closing scene, which takes place in a courtroom, illustrates the absurdity of projected unity without justice.[11] During the trial, there is an almost comical arrangement of Klansmen, Nazis, NAACP members, and Black militants, who are all gathered in the same room to watch the action. The courtroom erupts into a cacophony of peoples and types all expressing their own individual views. Everyone is laughing and shouting, and nothing seems serious. For instance, the hugely symbolic game between LSU and Ole Miss is dismissed in just two sentences. Gaines writes, "By the way LSU beat Ole Miss, twenty-one to thirteen. Both Gil and Cal had over a hundred yards each" (212). There is no real change brought about by Ole Miss's symbolic defeat or the two running together. Charlie, a young Black man, is still dead; and Gil is back sitting with his family in the courtroom. Also, presiding over all the empty laughter and bedlam is Judge Ford Reynolds. Like Sugar Washington, whose name also signals a marriage between the North/nation and the South, Judge Reynolds remains above the chaos taking place in his courtroom.[12] His power and control are never threatened, and he gets to watch the comedy unfold beneath him without any sense of personal stakes. Put plainly, in this final scene, the gravity of the old men's stand against Fix is lost. All we are left with is a White man presiding over a multitude of voices full of sound and fury but signifying nothing.

In the end, Gathering's conclusion demonstrates while the old men's stand might represent some gains, it does little to shake the foundations of systemic injustice. As Gaines pointed out to Mary Ellen Doyle, "Fix's kind of vigilante vengeance is dying out, but there will be the new Luke Will type. The Luke Wills [who drive much of the novel's violence] are in the police department. Fix is seventy or eighty and can't shoot straight, but Luke will do it for him" (169). Gaines's image of police doing Fix's bidding is made even more frightening by the judge's final ruling. The old men are not sentenced to prison, nor are they violently punished for their actions, as one might expect in a story capturing southern justice. Instead, the judge takes away "their privilege of carrying any kind of firing arm, rifle, shot-gun, or pistol" (213). Their disarmament suggests a new tactic for those, like Judge Reynolds, who are invested in maintaining White supremacy. Rather than overt acts of violence and intimidation, he promotes a more subtle kind of control—hidden in the power of the police state and disguised behind narratives of freedom and choice. As we saw in the last two chapters, by the 1980s, White people were mostly ready to move on from Fix's brand of blatant racism. In place of this, though, there grew a sense that everyone could simply possess their own story and individualized history. Indeed, Gaines seems to recognize that this form of postmodern multiculturalism works to disarm Black people and rob them of their ability to forcefully demand justice.

Finally, Yusef Komunyakaa's poem "History Lessons" builds on the sense that embracing a postsouthern identity is a White person's fantasy, unavailable to most people of color. In the short, forty-one-line poem, Komunyakaa demonstrates not only a rebuttal against forms of post-history that were well established by 1992, when *Magic City* the collection containing "History Lessons" was published, but he also helps illustrate how the South's long-fractured image works to hide still-present systemic violence. What he writes anticipates Tara McPherson's assertions, in *Reconstructing Dixie* (2003), where she points out the South's sense of division is rooted in a failure to acknowledge and amend what she calls "lenticular logic." McPherson uses the example of a postcard to illustrate what she means by the lenticular. The card contains two images and when it is tilted one way it reveals a serene image of a plantation's big house, but when the card is tilted the other way, the face of an enslaved person becomes visible. McPherson's argument is that individuals, too often, experience the South along this divide. For many White people, when they see and experience the region it reveals a heritage of antebellum wealth, postbellum loss, or countless other available brands of innocent White identity. However, this sense of an innocent South denies the other side of the card that shows racial violence permeating the region and larger nation.

McPherson goes on to suggest the correct frame through which we should see the region is not the division of the lenticular but one where "black and white" are held "within a single Southern frame" (115). Borrowing from Minnie Bruce Pratt, McPherson argues "the metaphor of overlapping circles is a powerful conceptual tool, one that shatters the fixed binary logic of a lenticular vision, exploding rigid separatist modalities and refusing partition." (247). Much of what McPherson writes here rings true. It seems apparent that White Americans should abandon their fantasies and move "toward a model that values difference and strives toward accountability" (247). However, Komunyakaa shows that locating this discussion largely in the realm of philosophy or moral responsibility divorces the conversation from many Black Americans' lived experience. Studying and understanding the South and how it mutates and continues to exert influence over individuals, then, changes from a matter of conjecture or debate to a matter of survival. Again, the stakes are different when White and Black people are discussing the importance of knowing and accounting for history. As Komunyakaa demonstrates, life itself depends on knowing and seeing clearly how White and Black versions of the past intersect in the present.

At its most basic level, the poem "History Lessons" focuses on a mother and her son walking through a southern town, as she uses the lens of history to help him see his environment more clearly. The lesson starts at the courthouse, and the boy recounts, "squinting up at leafy sunlight, I stepped back/ & shaded my eyes, but couldn't see what she pointed to" (1–2). In many ways, the rest of the poem is largely concerned with helping him see what is hidden in front of this building where justice is supposed to occur. Often literally, courthouses stand at the center of American communities. As we saw in *The Andy Griffith Show*, the courthouse works as the symbol of "law and order," binding the people to some larger sense of national unity. The mother, though, points out that the courthouse lawn, which had looked to her son like a "pool table" (4), was really "a stage for half the town" to gather and watch a brutal lynching (5). Because the boy "couldn't see the piece of blonde rope" (7), he cannot understand how this serene space hides such violence. To remedy his lack of vision, he "stepped closer to [his mother], to where we were almost/ in each other's arms, & then [he] spotted the flayed/ Tassel of wind-whipped hemp knotted around a limb" (8–10). As he draws closer to his mother (both symbolically and in the space of the poem), the boy begins to see the hidden lynching rope. Komunyakaa marks the "blonde rope" with charged words like "flayed" and "whipped," and through this imagery, he illustrates how for Black Americans the courthouse works as a very different symbol than what we saw in *The Andy Griffith Show* or *Matlock*. Whereas these shows presented the courthouse as a space associated with American innocence, the poem illustrates the importance of reckoning with a different perspective— one that acknowledges not only White people's crimes but also the long legacy of denying and hiding from those crimes.

The boy's lesson, then, revolves around him learning to see that what looks innocent and safe is often a "stage" for systems supporting violent White supremacy. After seeing the rope and recognizing its symbolic importance, the boy and his mother leave to share a meal. Over breakfast, she helps him understand why the lesson about the courthouse is so important. She tells him "How a white woman in The Terrace/ Said that she shot a man who tried to rape her" and how the White men of Bogalusa went out and found a Black boxer to kill for the crime. She explains, "they tarred & feathered him & dragged the corpse/ Behind a Model T through the Mill Quarters" (21–22). Following the details of the murder, she informs him that in reality the rapist had been a White man in blackface. Through this story, she establishes not only the horrific theft of a Black man's life, dragged behind a Model T, a symbol of American capitalism; but also, she touches on how White people stole and mocked aspects of Blackness itself through the legacy of blackface and minstrelsy. American capitalism and American popular culture, then, are brought into the poem and married to the Boxer's murder as potent reminders of how systems of national wealth and entertainment are interconnected with the region's racial violence.

The mother tells the story about the boxer over a meal, and in some ways, the food they share ("coffee & chicory with lots of milk,/ Hoecakes, bacon, & gooseberry jam") briefly interrupts the violence that fills the rest of Komunyakaa's poem. Similar to *Cotton Comes to Harlem and Gathering*, "History Lesson" introduces a quiet reminder to readers that despite pain and turmoil born from America's commitment to racial violence, there is a strong Black community born from this shared experience. The communal relationship surrounding the meal is worth acknowledging and celebrating. It helps demonstrate the important truth that abject suffering does not define Black identity in the United States. However, in the end, its ability to interrupt the violence saturating their environment is short-lived. Indeed, the meal does not offer a fundamentally different or separate narrative because it still exists in the context of a larger society that does not recognize or value their lives.

When they leave the restaurant, this reality is brought to life as the boy receives his final lesson. Upon stepping outside, a White man leaning against his van accosts the mother, telling her, "Emmett Till had begged for it/ With his damn wolf whistle" (32–33). The boy recalls, "hot words/ Swarmed out of my mouth like African bees/ & my fists were cocked" (35–37). The mother, upon hearing these "African" words, pulls him close and whispers in his ear, "*Son, you ain't gonna live long*" (41). These whispered words are the culmination of what she has been trying to teach her son. The mother does not show him the lynching rope and tell him about the boxer's murder simply to arouse anger or to reopen old wounds. Rather, the boy must absorb this history to survive in a society that will not allow him to fully protest his condition or openly express his rage. Even given the financial inversion that takes place in the poem, where the White man is now doing the mother's laundry,[13] the son is still not safe from White people and their commitments to an established racial hierarchy. Like the man who was lynched in front of the courthouse, the boxer who was murdered, and Emmett Till, he too, risks an early death if he does not learn to navigate White people's demands for a version of history that denies access to Black people's justified anger.

For the son, then, there is no option to forget aspects of the past that are not useful to him or to embrace an ahistoric sense of self. Instead, the very real threats to his life mean he must move closer to his mother and the community she represents. In their collective strength, they find the power to move on and to resist the culture that threatens them. However, the need to step closer to his mother also illuminates the limits of the White outsider fantasy. Put again, unlike the post-1970s White characters we encountered in the last two chapters, the son cannot move through the world inhabiting a liminal, postsouthern space that he individually crafts. Instead, he must immerse himself in a painful southern history that illustrates national commitments to White supremacy. As his mother teaches him, White people are committed to their positions of power and will not allow him to disrupt their myths of innocence. If he were to react to his environment as Barry Hannah suggests, "Sabers up!" and "Straight ahead. Hit 'em high. Let's go get 'em again" (82), like the boxer or Emmitt Till, he will not live long. It is this fundamentally different relationship to history and inherited positionality that underlies the contrast in "circumstances" that bell hooks identifies. As she makes clear, while both Black and White people might find themselves in a place alienated from traditional national narratives, for Black people this does not mean they have the same freedom to forget the past and to construct new post-racial/postsouthern identities.

As White people abandoned their sense of history and embraced individualism it probably felt like progress and a difficult rejection of their ancestors' worldviews. This perceived distance from the past, however, also produced a false and unearned fantasy of separation from the licenses and privileges born from generations of more overt theft and murder. As Robert Putnam, Shaylyn Romney Garrett, and others, like Bruce Schulman and Thomas Borstelmann, have made clear, the nation's movement toward individualism worked as a kind of trade, where White people abandoned their sense of community to gain imagined racial freedom. Put again, when the civil rights movement forced White people to face the reality that American communities were deeply steeped in racism and inequity, instead of acknowledging this truth, most White people traded their connections to an established community for an individual sense of their own innocence. What Himes, Gaines, and Komunyakaa demonstrate, though, is that this trade is rooted in a false premise—one that suggests it is possible to leave behind a history that has formed the nation's material and social conditions. As James Baldwin puts it, "each of us, however unconsciously, can't but be the vehicle of the history which has produced us" ("One Black Man" 765). For much of the last quarter of the twentieth century, White people united around the idea that Baldwin was wrong and that new post-racial and post-historical identities could be achieved simply through embracing alternative brands and imagining oneself as separated from inherited systems and values.

However, as the nation entered the twenty-first century, this imagined trade of giving up community for innocence would be challenged. The fall of the Twin Towers and the rise of global terror led to a renewed desire for an innocent and communal American identity. Armed with a shared sense of national goodness, White people could then see themselves as unified with all patriotic Americans, working together against an encroaching and alien evil that threatened the United States' future. What we really see in the next chapter, though, is how little was learned from Black authors, like Himes, Gaines, and Komunyakaa. As Gaines anticipates, postmodern multiculturalism and an increased ability for Black people to tell their stories did not fundamentally change White people's commitment to protecting their own interests. Instead, after 9/11 the strategy simply changes once again to meet White people's desires. In this next chapter, we see that strategy exemplified, as White southern outsiders reverse course and triumphantly return to a sense of shared community—licensed to reassert power by whatever means necessary.

4

Searching for Innocence

The Age of Terror and the Outsider's Return to Community

Following the 2001 attacks on the World Trade Center and Pentagon, White people began increasingly investing in narratives that offered a new brand of southern, male innocence. Instead of using dissensus and fracture to declare separation from racial guilt, the texts in this chapter illustrate a model of southernness that invites outsiders back into communities built around shared values. The male outsider's return to communal identity, which we will see in this chapter and in the next one, is part of a larger cultural and philosophical realignment after 9/11, which is often organized under the terms post-postmodernism or metamodernism. As Linda Hutcheon bluntly declares, a year after 9/11, "The postmodern moment has passed" (181). Marjorie Perloff goes on to explain that 9/11 represents a "turning point," and when the attack on the World Trade Center is compounded with the rise of "ISIS and other political upheavals," authors found it "increasingly difficult" to present "simulacra and multiple truths, . . . the absurdity of master narratives and the refusal of all categorical imperatives" as relevant or applicable to the realities of daily life.[1] Put differently, after 9/11, postmodernity and its freedom from "master narratives" no longer felt liberating or safe in the face of what seemed like pressing threats from foreign and domestic enemies. Therefore, instead of postmodern stories rejecting not only "truth" but also "truth effect" (Waugh 5), we see narratives where White people move from a place of alienation into a sense of healed community that is supposedly built on common experiences and shared truths.

Similar to postmodernism, there is no agreed upon or single definition for what comes after it. However, at its most basic level, post-
postmodern or metamodern texts encourage embracing shared meaning
as a powerful tool capable of organizing collective identity. Jeffrey Nealon
defines this movement past postmodernism as an embrace of "the effects of truth," which takes place even without a wholesale belief that
truth exists or can be defined in any stable way (162). Post-postmodern
texts, then, seek to reassert shared narratives as "crucial, or at least
useful, equipment" for living in a violent and unsettling present (170).
Robert L. McLaughlin adds, we can understand the "sea change" away
from postmodernism "as being inspired by desire to reconnect language
to the social sphere to reenergize literature's social mission, its ability
to intervene in the social world, to have an impact on actual people
and the actual social institutions in which they live their lives" (55).
This is not to say postmodern artists were uninterested in impacting
lived experience or social institutions. Rather, what seems to change
after 9/11 is an increased desire for progress within a shared "social
sphere." Instead of achieving gains through the outsider's rejection of
shared truth or communal answers, metamodern texts often work in
the opposite direction. They promote sincerity instead of irony and
community instead of fracture. Jeffrey Nealon adds that, for readers,
a postmodern obsession with "meaning" is replaced with a focus on
"usage" (148). The shift in focus from "what does it mean?" to "What
does it do?" then encourages a stronger "power of the false" that can
again position literature as a vital resource for those attempting to build
more stable and unified communities (159).

Depictions of a unified American identity show up across genres
and mediums after 9/11, but the clearest example is perhaps found in
country music. In the weeks and months after the September attacks,
airwaves were filled with songs like Toby Keith's "Courtesy of the Red
White and Blue" and Alan Jackson's "Where Were You (When the World
Stopped Turning)"—songs that sought to define the United States as a
place where the flag and faith meant something stable and real. It does
not take much analysis to see how country music after 9/11 reflects
a narrow version of American identity. As Andrew Boulton explains,
"America's enemy is defined, in country music, both as a place in the

world, out there, separate from America, and in more human terms as groups of individuals and a set of values, differentiated from Americans and American values" (377–78). Of course, this framing of "the enemy" as those who disagree with "American values" is only possible if there is such a thing as a shared set of national beliefs, which is something it seems Americans were eager to believe after 9/11. Moreover, according to country music, these values not only exist but are tightly defined around a traditional Christian faith, a confidence in long-established American exceptionalism, and a dominant military.

This chapter, though, is interested in a different kind of post-9/11 Southern White identity—one that, at least on the surface, admits to American guilt. The television show *The Walking Dead* (2010–2022), Ron Rash's short story "Dead Confederates" (2008),[2] and Pat Conroy's novel *South of Broad* (2009) all acknowledge that racism and violence have long plagued the United States. More than that, they also present a shared commitment to diversity and inclusion as being necessary for any form of healed American community. However, they also demonstrate how little was learned from authors, like the ones we encountered in the last chapter, who made clear that healing requires a reckoning with White people's collective history. In other words, while the TV show, short story, and novel all concede the nation's violent past and encourage a better future, they simultaneously refuse to admit how that past directly informs their White protagonists' identities. Indeed, they draw on the outsider's supposed divorce from institutions to imagine their White characters have little to do with the still-existent violence they encounter and help defeat. The texts in this chapter, then, ignore the inherited realities of Whiteness and marry a postmodern separation from history to a post-postmodern insistence on community and shared beliefs.

The television series *The Walking Dead* offers a relatively clear example of how White people frame this brand of post-postmodern or metamodern southern community. The show, which shares its name with the comic series on which it is based,[3] is set in the wake of a zombie apocalypse that has consumed much of humanity and destroyed all of America's government. The show, then, is set in a post-American setting, where characters are striving to survive and create new, viable communities. At the center of the rebuilding effort, stands Rick Grimes, a White southern policeman who at the beginning of the series is cast as an outsider, emotionally alienated from his wife and disillusioned with his job. Early in the pilot episode, he is shot. When he awakens, he finds zombies have destroyed his previous life, giving him a real chance to break away from the ennui and isolation that dominate the show's opening scenes. Despite his fear and the violence surrounding him, the changes in condition fill Rick with a new sense of purpose. As Katherine Sugg explains, "the zombie apocalypse speculates about possible ways in which masculine agency in liberal modernity might be reimagined and/or reinvigorated" (793). In other words, the presence of an alien and encroaching threat gives Rick's life meaning, as it necessitates the construction of a new, better sense of self and community.

Much of the recent academic work on the TV version of *The Walking Dead* focuses on Rick's efforts to reinvigorate different brands of historically informed, masculine identity. For instance, Katherine Sugg links the show to the "Hollywood western" (796), as she argues it offers a *"return* to social norms of gender and racial difference" (795). Or, as Stephen Olbrys Gencarella suggests, "the show" is akin to "a popular guide to the fascist life" (127). More closely related to the topic of this book, Matthew Dischinger demonstrates how *The Walking Dead* employs patterns of southern violence that "require viewers to imagine a setting in which regional stereotypes are maintained after the literal collapse of both the nation and the region" (260).[4] However, while this scholarship does important work in outlining some of the many ways the show fails to deliver a truly progressive or equitable vision for American community, it also tends to cast the show's failure as being bound up in a kind of conservative allegiance to the past. In other words, it sees the problem as being one of looking backward and seeking to reestablish a damaging U.S. colonial, regional, or patriarchal order. What largely fails to be acknowledged, though, is the show's somewhat clear insistence that it is rejecting previous versions of White-authored American community and trying to establish something different and better. This is not to say it succeeds in modeling something new or redemptive, yet through its failure we witness a new kind of imagined White innocence—one that suggests multicultural/multiracial communities can thrive if Americans would only embrace the freedom offered by the White outsider. In other words, what *The Walking Dead* articulates most clearly is a belief that successful communities can be built around the outsider's liberating divorce from history.

We see the show's attempt to reject older frames of White identity particularly clearly in Rick's relationship with the American cowboy. Like Sugg, Cynthia Miller also notices Rick's association with the Hollywood Cowboy. She suggests the show ultimately embraces the cowboy mythos, arguing zombie-infested Georgia becomes a proving ground for Rick's "cowboy masculinity" (4). Miller writes, he negotiates a wasteland where "Western narratives of good versus evil [are] replaced by those of the living versus the undead" (4). While she is right about the framing of "good versus evil," the show is doing something quite different than simply remanufacturing the traditional cowboy character, which is an archetype deeply tied to fantasies of American individualism. If Rick were truly representing this myth, he would be able to rely on his own skills and strengths, as he rescues the environment from a threatening evil, akin to how the lone cowboy supposedly conquered the West. This, though, is not how things work out for Rick. Instead, his association with the cowboy is marked by failure and a realization that he needs a community to survive. We see this illustrated in the pilot episode's closing action when Rick travels into Atlanta, searching for his missing wife and son. As Rick approaches the city, there is an iconic shot of him riding a horse into Georgia's defunct capital wearing a cowboy-styled police hat. Almost immediately, though, the show works against the mythology the hat and horse evoke. Instead of Rick finding his family and triumphantly rescuing them, the zombies notice his intrusion and begin closing in around him. Rick reassures the horse, saying, "It's just a few. Nothing we can't handle" (Darabont, "Days"), but as they round a corner, they find a sea of the walking dead blocking both their way forward and their retreat. The zombies then quickly pull Rick's horse to the ground, and as he scrambles away, he loses his hat.

Viewers then see Rick as he really is, without his horse or his hat: just a frail White man, who is alone and scared. With nowhere else to go, Rick dives beneath a tank and manages to crawl into its belly. He is momentarily safe; however, after a quick look outside, he begins to recognize the sheer numbers organized against him. Rick then holds a gun to his head, preparing to end his life. Before he can pull the trigger, though, the tank's radio starts to sputter. A voice comes crackling through, saying, "Dumbass—yeah, you in the tank. Cozy in there?" (Darabont, "Days"). As the voice reaches Rick, it brings him (and viewers) a wave of relief. Finally, the peppy tune of Wang Chung's "Space Junk" begins playing in the background, signaling a break in the episode's tension. Hope, then, is reintroduced, not through a would-be cowboy's heroism, but through the potential for community and shared action. Put plainly, Rick's rescue (which is carried out by a multiracial group of survivors) signals the need to move past fantasies of lone White colonizers riding in to save the day. Indeed, Rick's short-lived attempt to repossess the cowboy's supposed power ends in utter failure and near suicide. He only survives because a diverse community works to free him from his predicament.

What we see in Rick's rescue is echoed throughout the show, where working together and in concert with one another almost always leads to better results than acting alone. When the group does go astray, it is typically because some character selfishly tries to leave the group or revivify some dead aspect of the past—like the farmer Hershel Greene, who keeps his zombified friends in a barn in case they ever find a way to bring them back to life. In fact, the show's political vision seems to rest almost entirely on the idea that we should reject old allegiances and organizing principles, so we can build something new out of the world's ashes. However, it is in this very hope for a brand-new post-everything community that we see the show's limits as a model for a healed America. Put again, while *The Walking Dead* clearly condemns U.S. commitments to capitalism, racism, sexism, and a host of other societal ills, it largely does this through framing these issues as something easily disconnected from present-day Whiteness, or at least Rick's version of White identity. Similar to how *The Andy Griffith Show* promotes the idea that moving forward means forgetting divisive, supposedly outdated issues; *The Walking Dead* also encourages a sense that communal healing is best realized through collective amnesia.

Rick, though, is not simply Andy reborn in a grittier, more violent environment. Whereas Andy works to reassure audiences that America's identity is still rooted in a righteous and longstanding pattern of social solidarity, led by White men; Rick reflects the desires of audiences relatively at home with the United States' shortcomings and the failures bound up in its long adherence to White male leadership. The view of masculine leadership that Rick helps discourage, though, is largely separated from his individual identity as a product of history. Instead, like Will, Allie, and Ray, he is mostly cast as a well-meaning isolated individual, who is just trying to survive in an irreferential world still-suffering from the racism, violence and sexism carried out by other, worse people. Rick's perceived separation from a historically informed identity, then, allows him to be understood as both a critique of Whiteness and the answer to that critique. In other words, the show imagines that while traditional brands of White identity (like the cowboy) might be a problem, it is a problem that most decent White people can easily leave behind if they have not already done so. As a White man, a southerner, a police officer, a bad husband, and a lonely, isolated individual, Rick becomes a chief witness, helping the rest of society realize they too can forget damaging identities or their status as an outsider and unite around an improved version of community.

To drive home its message of leaving behind damaging versions of American identity (like the cowboy), the camera cuts from Rick and his multicultural/multiracial saviors to a White man named Merle, who is on the roof of a nearby building taking potshots at zombies. Here, (encapsulated in Merle's character) is the clearest embodiment of the lingering southern stereotypes Dischinger identifies. Standing in his cutoff vest with a rifle in his hands, Merle embodies the consummate gun-toting redneck who has long symbolized southern disruptions to a supposedly otherwise liberal American identity. His shooting from the roof is attracting more of the walking dead, so several members of the group race up the stairs to ask him to keep quiet. When they reach the roof, Morales, a Latino man, yells at him to stop shooting. Merle responds by laughing maniacally and continuing to fire his rifle. He then turns toward the group, saying, "Hey, you ought to be more polite to a man with a gun. Huh?" T-Dog, a Black man, joins Morales, in asking Merle to put down his rifle. To which, Merle responds, "Hey, bad enough I got this taco bender on my ass all day; now I'm going to take orders from you? I don't think so, bro. That'll be the day." T-Dog steps closer and asks, "That'll be the day? You got something you want to tell me?" Merle answers, "I'll tell you the day, Mr. Yo." He goes on, while flashing a mock gang signal, "It's the day I take orders from a ni**er" (Darabont, "Guts"). A fight breaks out, but Merle makes quick work of T-Dog, hitting him with the butt of his rifle and beating him mercilessly to the ground.

The violent beating T-Dog receives stands in stark contrast to the encounter in *Matlock,* where Tyler Hudson is able to stand up for himself and dismiss the White man who accuses him of dressing like a wimp. Instead, T-Dog, like Rick, needs a community to rescue him. However, no one on the roof seems willing to step in and take on the threat. Merle turns to the group saying, "Alright, we gonna have ourselves a little pow-wow, huh, talk about who's in charge. I vote me." The group reluctantly votes for Merle to be in charge, even though he has just managed to insult Latinos, African Americans, and American Indians. However, as Merle relishes his new appointment, Rick walks up behind him, hits him in the head with a pistol, and handcuffs him to a pipe. In this action, we see the intervention of a White ally asserting himself squarely on the side of minorities, who are being threatened by an obvious sym-bol of southern racism. If Rick were not also a southerner, it might be easy to see this scene as reanimating a traditional good North/bad South mythology. However, he is a southerner, which like Andy Taylor, demonstrates a version of American identity that includes the region. To make even clearer the point that old divisions no longer matter, while unloading Merle's gun, draining the phallic symbol of its power, Rick ex-plains how things have changed in the new world. He says, "Look here, Merle. Things are different now. There are no 'ni**ers' anymore. No dumb as shit inbred white trash fools either, only dark meat and white meat. There's us and the dead. We survive this by pulling together not apart" (Darabont, "Guts"). Merle remains unconvinced, spitting back, "Screw you man." So Rick demonstrates the cost of not adhering to this new community's values. He leaves Merle handcuffed to the pipe to die a lonely death as the group escapes from Atlanta without him.

The scene's post-racial/postsouthern message is fairly obvious. It is driven home not only in the overt message that those like Merle, who preserve racially defined notions of "us" and "them," have no place in the new world order, but it is also evinced through Rick's use of the n-word, placing it alongside "white trash," as if those words are coequal in their power and historical resonance. As Helen K. Ho puts it, "Rick clarifies for the viewers and the survivors witnessing this altercation, the post apocalypse is postracial" (62). Again, though, I do not think it is "cowboy masculinity" that is on display as she suggests (63). At this point in the show, Rick has already rejected the role of the cowboy and is now embracing a different (perhaps no-less-toxic) version of White masculinity. He saves the day cast not as an isolated colonizer but as a supposed champion of a diverse coalition working toward inclusion and mutual survival. Put plainly, *The Walking Dead*'s answer to building a more sustainable future revolves around previously alienated White men leaving their isolation and establishing new, better communities, organized around their own supposedly clear sense of good and evil. As Angela Tenga and Jonathan Bassett argue, "*The Walking Dead* voices the concerns of a nation living in fear of its demise and a generation engaged in a daily struggle to manage the terror caused . . . by anticipation of a possible world that, bereft of institutionalized authority, forces individuals to confront the terrifying reality of moral uncertainty" (1296). Therefore, instead of "moral uncertainty," Rick delivers a clear binary: us and the dead, which makes the choice to join the post-racial "living" exceedingly easy. There is some irony, though, in Rick being the messenger of this supposedly new post-racial binary. After all, he is part of the group that would benefit most from ceasing to consider race as a powerful organizing force. Nevertheless, the show earnestly frames its version of progress along the lines that we should leave discussions of race in the past and focus on "real" problems that demand the nation's collective attention. Accordingly, every American should shed any negative brands to which they might subscribe, such as the racist or the cowboy, and instead embrace a communal worldview, where everyone is given a fresh start and seen as an equal.

In some ways, then, the show's message is progressive, in that it frames Rick's western cowboy persona and Merle's southern racism as defunct identities that are no longer welcome in American communities. Yet, as the show condemns the historic West and South, it performs a relatively predictable maneuver, dating back to at least Crèvecoeur[5]—in that it isolates the violence associated with these histories away from an innocent White American identity that supposedly represents the nation's true character. The solution the show suggests, then, is rooted in embracing Rick's seemingly unattached, post-racial identity, which is imagined as having always been representative of "real" America. Of course, leaving behind the cowboy does not inhibit Rick's ability to lead, and Merle is absurdly villainous and offensive. It is exceedingly easy for most White people to disassociate from these brands, especially from Merle, who represents the poor and violent South. After all, what he represents is not important to Whiteness or the systems maintaining White power. As Kristine Taylor argues, there has long been a recognition amongst empowered White people that they could shed blame by focusing on "poor whites' primitiveness" (59). She explains, "By crafting white trash as repositories of racial backwardness and violence, political moderates produced fertile ground for the renewal of racial innocence," which allowed "racial violence and domination in other forms, particularly those designed by moderates themselves" (65). In other words, what we see in *The Walking Dead* is an updated version of an old strategy, where the show casts aside versions of western and southern identity that have already been rejected by most White Americans. Explicit racial violence like Merle carries out (or Fix in Gaines's *A Gathering of Old Men*) has almost always been easy to vilify and to use as a foil against supposedly decent White folks. Similar to Gaines's Sugar Washington and Ford Reynolds, though, Rick acts under the auspices of multiculturalism and a dedication to equality but only in a way that conceals his own inherited position and secures the material and social benefits of those inheritances.

What Gaines recognizes in *A Gathering of Old Men* and is ignored in *The Walking Dead,* is how White identity mutates and can thrive even when ostensibly promoting something that looks like universal equality. Rick embodies this kind of surface level inclusion, where through defending a diverse vision of community he establishes a fantasy of White innocence. Put again, he accomplishes his innocence through a kind of disappearing act in which White people are positioned as mere members of a larger American community, no different from any other group. In fact, the most important facet of *The Walking Dead*'s prescribed new communal order is this adherence to a post-historical and post-racial multiculturalism. The show's villains are almost always those with inflexible views on identity and personal expression. For instance, the Governor and Negan, two of the show's primary antagonists, are similar to Merle. They, too, are White men who enact a worldview where if you do not agree with their outdated and hierarchical views, then you face severe and swift punishments. Ultimately, what sets these "bad" men and their communities apart from Rick's "good" alternative is their commitment to maintaining restrictive views on self-expression and identity.

Rick's community, then, offers the freedom of shedding the past and reinventing oneself as a part of an accepting and diverse community that has room for everyone but the bigot. This privileging of self-determination makes the group more unwieldy and at times vulnerable to attack. However, it is also the ability to "be yourself" that makes them the show's preferred community. The primary evil represented both by the zombies and the show's principal villains is conformity or a forced sameness. Rick's group, then, offers an enlightened alternative where everyone is free to independently define themselves, as long as they allow others to do the same.

Their actions are plenty violent and at times cruel, but they are almost always understood to be justified because they are protecting and perfecting what is cast as most important to healthy communities: tolerance and freedom. Moreover, since their goodness is couched in what liberal Americans have always claimed to be the United States' best feature (its welcoming of diverse peoples into one nation), Rick and his group are understood to be protecting a model version of Americanness. Almost any act of violence, then, is justified as long as it is rooted in defending that ideal. Whether or not this version of America's collective identity actually ever existed is beside the point. What matters is that "good" people, living in a threatened world, forget old divisions and form communities capable of fighting against any force that threatens this freedom.

The group's desire to exclude bigots and to organize against common enemies certainly sets up a foundation for a better community than the one Merle represents. However, Rick's rooftop philosophy of "us and the dead" ultimately promotes the same kind of "colorblind racism" about which Eduardo Bonilla-Silva writes, which encourages forgetting or, more accurately, ignoring racially informed systems of power. By expelling Merle, the only character who insists on seeing race, the show actively precludes explanations for differences other than the one Rick offers. Accordingly, Merle's silencing functions not only as proof of Rick's liberal credentials but also as an affirmation of the view that only bigots remain focused on racial difference. As Bonilla-Silva puts it, "By framing race-related issues in the language of liberalism," which promotes freedom to choose one's own identity, White people "can appear 'reasonable' and even 'moral,' while opposing almost all practical approaches to deal with de facto racial inequality" (28). As it usually does for White people, the group's "liberal," post-racial views work out well for Rick. After the conflict on the roof and Merle's dismissal, he becomes the group's largely unquestioned leader and continues in that role through most of the series. Rick, then, achieves a kind of invisibility that allows him to protect an imagined innocence while also reaping the fruits of generational violence and privilege.

In shifting to Ron Rash's "Dead Confederates," we see a similar prescription for unity and equality that again narrows who is guilty and broadens who is considered innocent. However, whereas *The Walking Dead* inhabits a post-American fantasy, Rash's story reaches into history and directly engages one of America's darkest expressions of White supremacy: the Confederacy. Like *The Dukes of Hazzard, In the Heat of the Night,* and *Ray,* "Dead Confederates" evokes the Confederacy and its icons to frame the South's current moment. But while the texts in the previous chapters suggest Confederate icons are only defined by individual intentions, the short story strives to draw from an authentic narrative from which modern southerners can understand their own rooted positionality. In some ways, then, the story is more akin to *The Andy Griffith Show* than the more recent post-1980s texts. Like the version of history Andy offers Opie ("Indians and redcoats and cannons and guns and muskets and stuff"), "Dead Confederates" draws from real events and speaks to an American past that can unify the North/nation and the South. More than that, the short story seems willing to confront the hard subjects that *The Andy Griffith Show* avoids, as it directly condemns not only the historic Confederacy but also its present manifestations.

As Zachary Vernon explains, Rash employs the Civil War in his fiction not only to prevent amnesia about the region's past, but also to shape how readers view their present (24). In Rash's Civil War writing, we see a particular interest in revisiting the Shelton Laurel Massacre—an event in which Confederate soldiers in Madison County, North Carolina murdered civilian Union sympathizers.[6] There is a personal connection to the massacre for Rash, as the unit that committed the atrocity included a member of his family. However, as Vernon points out, Rash has also identified other ancestors fighting for the Union, who were working to defeat the Confederate murderers. Rash draws from this split family history to deliver a sense of internal White southern division that pitches not only brother against brother but also divides the self into warring factions with differing allegiances. In "Dead Confederates," we see this sense of division in the White South and southerner, as two characters literally dig up Confederate graves and reckon with the buried past they uncover. However, while the story appears to be in many ways a gritty, direct rebuttal of the ahistoric iconography we saw in the 1980s, it actually performs a similar function for White readers, in that it liberates them from accounting for a guilty past. Put again, despite its metamodern commitment to "truth effect," the story suggests individuals are free to find and align themselves with whichever history supports the identity they want to embrace. Indeed, it becomes clear not only that White southerners have this freedom to pick a better past, but also that it is in everyone's best interest to bury damning history and to separate from any link to the Confederacy.

The story's rejection of the Confederacy, as a proper framing for White southern identity, can most clearly be seen through the character Wesley Davidson. Rash opens the story with his unnamed narrator telling readers, "I never cared for Wesley Davidson when he was alive and seeing him beside me laid out dead didn't much change that . . . [T]he hard truth is had you known Wesley you'd probably feel the same. You might do what I done—shovel dirt on him with not so much as a mumble of a prayer" (45). As the narrator continues, readers learn why they should despise Wesley and wish him buried and forgotten. Like Merle, Wesley seems to have completely missed any hint of modern aesthetics or cultural sensitivity. His truck has "a big rebel flag decal covering the back window;" he wears "a CSA belt buckle" and a "gray CSA cap," while sporting a "rebel flag tattoo" (46). As if his association with the Confederacy is not clear enough, he also hatches a plan to dig up a few Confederate officers and to sell the artifacts they find at a Civil War convention. However, again, like Merle, Wesley is not so much a direct representation of a broad historic Confederacy as he is an embodiment of a certain brand of White southern identity that is linked to a certain version of the Confederacy. The brand Wesley represents is rooted in the version of the South defined by consumption and greed—similar to Boss Hogg in *The Dukes of Hazzard* or the LaPierre family in *In the Heat of the Night*. He is an obese and lazy man who watches others do all the work as he scarfs down "three Hardee's sausage biscuits" each morning (47). Wesley got his job because of nepotism, and his desire to dig up the Confederate bodies is also connected to his love of money and desire for profits. In this dedication to self-advancement and opulence, Wesley represents a supposedly isolated segment of Southern identity: a historic White aristocracy that can help locate guilt far away from most White people and their histories.

Moreover, Wesley's relationship with the aristocracy also serves to rebrand the Confederate cause as distanced from widespread racial violence and more closely associated with enduring tensions between the rich and poor. In fact, the short story's only explicit mention of race serves to demonstrate how the characters' environment exists largely beyond questions of racial equity. The narrator (who works on a road crew) references Wesley's affinity for Confederate icons, explaining, "[T]here's no black guys on our crew, only a handful in the whole county, but you're still not supposed to wear that kind of thing" (46). With this one sentence, which takes place in the story's third paragraph, the narrator not only claims a South, like *The Andy Griffith Show,* that is mostly devoid of Black people, but he also makes clear that he, too, is past questions of race and opposed to Wesley's insensitivity. Put simply, the story attempts to interrogate the lasting impact of the Confederacy, a government formed almost solely to preserve slavery, without the interrupting presence of Black people. We see why this exclusion is so important as the story continues and offers competing brands of White southern identity. Without Black characters, who might connect Wesley and the narrator by race, the story can focus on carving out versions of Whiteness that remain innocent. Indeed, by focusing on class, which separates the narrator from Wesley's guilt, rather than race, which would link them together, the story can fracture Whiteness into any number of innocent or guilty variants. There are certainly productive ways to consider class divisions in the United States and in the South. However, the story's evocation of the Confederacy while sidestepping discussions of race, speaks to the same historical omissions we have already encountered, where most White people are invited to understand themselves as separated from legacies of inherited racial violence. According to this framing, Wesley represents a narrow slice of White regional identity, and, like Merle, he can be easily left behind while everyone else embraces a past, present, and future separated from his guilt.

The most powerful symbol of this separation from Wesley's guilt appears in the form of the graveyard's caretaker, who catches Wesley and the narrator digging up the dead Confederates. As Wesley makes excuses, going on about his "great-great-granddaddy" who "fought Confederate," the old man interrupts, saying, "My folks sided Union . . . Lots of people don't bother to know that anymore, but there was as many in these mountains fought Union as Confederate" (62–63). In aligning himself with White southerners, who "fought Union," the caretaker offers a brand of identity rooted in an authentic southern history that supposedly sidesteps the racist/classist legacies that Wesley embodies. He also suggests there are "lots of people," as many as not, that are like his family and separated from the Confederate past. To be clear, while it is factually accurate that many White southerners did not want to secede and that some did fight for the Union, there is also a false narrative tacitly accompanying the old man's revelation. Like the perceived innocence Mayberry achieves by forgetting the Civil War and aligning with the American Revolution, "fighting Union" is cast as an innocent alternative to Wesley's obviously dangerous connection to the Confederacy. Put differently, Wesley and the old man represent two ends of a spectrum: Wesley signifies the South's most damaging histories and allegiances while the caretaker offers a brand that taps into national fantasies of unity and goodness. The story, then, performs largely the same function as *The Andy Griffith Show*'s pilot episode, in that it invites the vast majority of White people into a single and supposedly innocent U.S. mythology.

If the caretaker and Wesley represent two poles of White southern identity, the narrator gives readers a middle ground. We see this made clear after the caretaker lets the theft continue because he figured the Confederate soldier's "soul's a lot deeper" than his body, "all the way to hell" (63). After opening up the coffin, though, Wesley dies from the exertion. The narrator and the caretaker then decide to simply bury Wesley's body in the open grave and forget the whole night occurred. The caretaker wants nothing to do with the Confederate artifacts, but the narrator decides to go ahead and sell the soldier's sword and belt buckle. The decision to profit from the dead body causes him bad dreams from time to time. However, this occasional disturbance pales in comparison to his ability to pay hospital bills and to give the extra profits to his mother. As he explains, "I give what's left to Momma. That makes what I done feel less worrisome" (74). While it might be better if the narrator joined the caretaker in completely leaving behind the Confederacy, readers can hardly blame him for his relatively minor links to this past. As he goes on to explain, "I think about something else too, how both them graves had big fancy tombstones of cut marble, meaning those dead Confederates hadn't known much wanting of money in their lives. Now that they was dead there was some fairness in letting Momma have something of what they'd left behind" (74). In other words, the narrator's reasoning for taking the money largely rests on the idea that he, and poor White people like him, have been given a bad deal. Therefore, they should not be blamed if they occasionally partake in the violent systems that dominate their environment. While parts of this logic are undoubtedly true, in that people like him and his family are indeed victims of unfair capitalistic systems, the story seems to want this truth recognized while actively rejecting intersections with race.

Again, according to this framing, racial guilt can be contained and isolated away from mainstream White identity. Unlike *The Walking*

Dead, though, which blames poor White people like Merle, the story turns in the other direction and focuses on a narrow slice of villainous wealthy individuals who should be considered responsible for what ails the region and nation. As the story continues, the narrator goes on to make it more explicit that the guilty parties should be organized by class, not race. He reflects on his father who "worked himself to death before he was sixty," and how his mother had to learn "that fifty years of working first light to bedtime can't get you enough ahead to afford an operation and a two-week stay in a hospital" (49). He adds, "I'm pondering where's the fair in that when there's men who do no more than hit a ball good or throw one through a hoop and they live in mansions" (49). The narrator goes on to talk about "doctors and bankers from Charlotte and Raleigh" who have second homes that "cost a million dollars" (49–50). However, he qualifies the statement about doctors and bankers, saying, "You could argue they worked hard for those homes, but no harder than Momma and Daddy worked" (50). To be clear, not all professional athletes are people of color just like not all doctors and bankers are White, but by framing one of the few professions where people of color are well-represented as the most egregious example of problematic wealth disparity, the narrator clearly suggests a post-racial view where class is the best lens through which to understand current divisions. Like Rick Grimes, he seems to see the world in a clear binary of "us" and "them," where to move forward Americans must forget old racial divisions and confront the nation's "real" problems. The deeply sympathetic narrator, then, offers an invitation for readers to join him in a common enmity towards those (other people) who can be blamed for the nation's unfair practices.

In the end, "Dead Confederates," like *The Walking Dead,* suggests White people, even White men in the South, should avoid race as an organizing lens through which to understand their relationship with the larger nation. Instead, both texts encourage focusing on what are presented as more pressing and important concerns around which individuals should coalesce. On the surface, again, this movement appears to be inclusive and progressive. And, in some ways, it is a rejection of the racial essentialism that has long-defined power dynamics in the region and nation. However, it should be repeated that the desire to move past race conveniently erases how most White people benefit from and work to protect investments in White supremacy. Instead of confronting the myriad ways legacies of White-authored racial violence have intersected with constructions of class and gender in American life, the narratives position racial violence as something isolated and carried out by obvious bigots. Characters like Merle and Wesley, then, serve to carry the nation's racial sins while excusing most White people from seeing their own guilty reflection in the nation's past and present. In fact, it is hard to imagine almost anyone would see themselves represented by Merle and Wesley. Instead, most likely, White audiences would see themselves in Rick Grimes or the caretaker, who wash their hands of guilt and declare themselves champions of a new, post-racial community.

This logic of White innocence is extended even further in Pat Conroy's *South of Broad*. Like the other texts in this chapter, Conroy's novel promotes a view that most southerners have long ago abandoned any real connection to racial violence, and now it is time for previously alienated White outsiders to re-enter and reclaim control of their communities. Using the same tactics of marrying a fractured, postmodern view of the past with a metamodern appreciation for unified action in the present, the novel offers a version of Whiteness that needs neither zombies nor an explicit disavowal of the Confederacy to prove one's individual innocence. Put again, Conroy's novel illustrates how the same logic that protects Rick Grimes and Rash's unnamed characters can be applied even to relatively well-off and socially secure White people. Also, like the other texts, at least on the surface, *South of Broad* uses a celebration of diversity and inclusion to excuse and anonymize Whiteness. The novel's protagonist Leo King, who is White and middle/upper class, stands at the center of the novel's redemptive, multicultural/multiracial community. As Amy Watts explains, "he is perhaps not the [group's] leader but [he is] certainly the glue" holding everything together (80). He is joined by Trevor Poe (who is gay and also White), Sheba Poe (his flamboyant twin sister, who later becomes a movie star), Starla and Niles Whitehead (poor White characters, who come to Charleston from the mountains), Betty Roberts and Ike Jefferson (who are the novel's primary Black characters), and finally, Chad Rutledge and Molly Huger (who are White, aristocratic Charlestonians). Similar to *The Walking*

Dead, South of Broad uses a diverse cast, glued together by a White man to introduce a healed sense of southern/American community.

Unlike *The Walking Dead,* though, *South of Broad* is not merely interested in offering a future that exists beyond or outside the nation's history. Instead, similar to "Dead Confederates," the novel introduces and defends a relatively innocent past that can then provide the basis for a viable present and projected future. The narrative jumps back and forth between 1969 and 1989–90, following Leo and his group as they work to take on the AIDS epidemic, racial tension, suicide, child abuse in the Catholic Church, and seemingly every other societal ill in the nation during those years. At the center of the projected violence and healing, stands the city of Charleston—a contested space that must be won and remade into a hospitable locale for shared community. Similar to how "Dead Confederates" carves out an innocent Civil War narrative for White readers, *South of Broad* transforms Charleston from a space of White southern treachery and rebellion into a place that models the best of American multiculturalism and collective action. Leo explains his relationship with the city, saying, "My soul is peninsula-shaped and sun-hardened and river swollen. The high tides of this city flood my consciousness each day . . . Deep in my bones, I knew early that I was one of those incorrigible creatures known as Charlestonians" (1). His devotion to the city is physical and spiritual. Charleston is a part of his "soul," his "consciousness," and the "bones" of his body. Almost literally, Leo's virtue, which we see throughout the novel, is intertwined with the city's own beauty and goodness. Like some kind of Fisher King, Leo is linked to the land, and to heal his kingdom he has to form a rooted, diverse community that can confront America's historic and present ills.

At the prologue's end, Leo establishes that to restore Charleston he must form a group that could save his city. He writes that in 1969 he "had built an impregnable castle of solitude," and to move forward "that castle [must come] down no matter how serious the collateral damage or who might get hurt" (5). Leo, here, outlines the basic premise that the novel then defends, which is that White outsiders need to return and rebuild a healed version of American community. Much of the novel then centers on how Leo gathers and employs allies to wrest back their environment from those who would pervert it. Starting their redemptive effort in

1969, also frames the group as the clear inheritors of the civil rights movement. The novel then suggests that to carry on the Movement's work, Leo must overcome his initial sense of alienation and build a larger, more diverse community that could unite Charleston's disparate parts. Like Percy's or Hannah's characters, Leo feels alone and isolated in a world that does not make sense and has little room for progressive White southerners. However, instead of using that sense of alienation to validate an individual ethic of outsiderness, *South of Broad* suggests a communal model, similar to what we saw in both *The Walking Dead* and "Dead Confederates." Put again, it is understood to be Leo's moral responsibility, "no matter how serious the collateral damage," to seize back power and to rebuild a viable, diverse community that extends outward rather than inward.

For Leo to be understood as the proper agent for building a healed community, though, requires a rewriting of history that grants him the outsider's innocence. *South of Broad*'s maneuvering of the nation's past to grant Leo this status is perhaps most clearly seen in his high school's experience with integration. To start the process of adding Black students to the fictional Peninsula High, Leo's mother (who is the school's principal) hires Coach Jefferson, a Black man, to lead the football team. She then asks Leo to help by befriending Ike, the coach's son. Things do not get off to a good start. The two meet early one morning, and when Leo asks, "Did you bring your father's workout plan with you?" Ike shoots back, "Seem to have forgotten it, white boy" (60). Confused that his new teammate is focusing on race, Leo says, "I knew integration was going to be a pain in the ass, Ike, . . . I really did. But I thought I was going to have to worry about my redneck boys a lot more than the black kids." Ike responds, "Sorry to disappoint you, white boy" (60). The argument continues and Leo calls Ike "Dr. George Washington Carver" and eventually threatens to call him "a name with a long tradition in the South that rhymes with Roy Rogers's horse [Trigger]" (60), but Ike appears to give as good as he gets. He calls Leo "White boy" and "Strom Thurmond"—all while refusing to workout with his teammate (60). In their interaction, we can recognize almost the same leveling Rick performs, where Black people and White people are placed alongside each other as being similarly guilty for racial division. We can almost hear Rick's equation of "white trash" and the n-word in Leo's threat to use that same word because Ike calls him "Strom Thurmond." In both texts, then, audiences are encouraged to understand racial division as primarily grounded in childish and outdated beliefs, which both races must relinquish for healing to occur.

As the interaction between Leo and Ike continues, the novel goes on to further position racial division as a matter of misunderstanding or a lack of personal relationships. To prove the point, in less than a page, the two young men have taken off chasing one another, smiling, and laughing as they sprint down the field. After the workout, Ike tells Leo that his mistrust of White people comes from his uncle being shot by a police officer, to which Leo basically tells him that not all White people should be blamed (63). By the end of their interaction, they are fast friends. In fact, the only thing that obstructed their brotherly camaraderie was Ike's initial and supposedly unfair resentment of Leo, as a "white boy." However, once Ike puts down his guard a bit, Leo can prove his goodness and they can put their division behind them.[7] As Leo reflects on their first interaction, he tells readers, "It was Ike who first called it 'carrying the cross.' That is what integration felt like for everyone after *Brown v. Board of Education* when boys like me and Ike and men and women like my parents and Coach Jefferson were put to the noble task of making it work" (61–62). Of course, Leo's characterization of integration is almost laughable. For instance, it leaves out why Peninsula High and his mother apparently took fifteen years to comply with the Supreme Court's 1954 decision. However, in the space of the story, his characterization is coupled with a scene of sincere friendship, which delivers the "effect of truth," even if readers know that it does not mirror what really happened in the 1960s.

As the school year officially starts, the novel builds on this sense that problems with integration were largely due to a few reticent individuals rather than anything larger or systemic. Similar to what we saw in *The Walking Dead* and in "Dead Confederates," *South of Broad* introduces a character (like Merle and Wesley) who can embody the region's problem while also giving the White protagonist a chance to prove his relative innocence. On the first day of school, as Leo watches the "breezeway," where the "hoods and rednecks and no-goodniks of both sexes gathered" (305), he notices Peninsula High's most notorious villain. Leo explains, Wilson "Wormy" Ledbetter "was the *Tyrannosaurus rex* of the classic Southern redneck" (306). He then clarifies, "Wormy was also racist, peerless in his hatred of black people" (306). Leo immediately moves to confront Wormy, asking him why he did not sign up for football that year. Wormy tells him, "I ain't playing for no ni**er coach" (306). When Leo presses him, he reiterates, "Don't you understand plain English . . . I ain't playing for no ni**er" (307). The Black students in the breezeway hear the language and start to react. As tempers rise, Leo cuts in: "I can handle this . . . My fellow students! My name is Toad [Leo's nickname], the good-hearted white boy. Stand back and watch me kick Wormy's cracker ass" (307). Leo says this as a joke, but it pretty much predicts exactly what is about to happen.

Before Leo can act, though, his multicultural/multiracial community cuts in to confront the would-be bully. First, Trevor approaches and slaps him, and when Wormy pushes him away, Sheba comes in and adds another slap. After Wormy escapes Sheba, Starla, and Betty jump on him, which as Leo explains, "made it racial again" (309). Finally, Niles comes up and tells Wormy, "You ever touch my sister [Starla] again, I'll slit your throat" (310). In this series of confrontations, we can see the disparate elements of the region coming together, united against a single enemy: the racist redneck. The scene then culminates with Leo stepping back in and finishing the fight. He says, "Let me take it from here Niles . . . You get back in line" (310). Wormy tries to punch Leo, but Leo "was not the same boy that Wormy had beaten up the previous year." (310). Instead, because of his working out with Ike, Leo defeats the much larger Wormy with a single punch "that seemed driven by the Lord himself" (311). Like Merle's disarming and Wesley's burial, Wormy's fall suggests that it is relatively easy to remove the region's cancerous elements. As these texts suggest, all that it really takes is good White people and their minority allies standing up together and defending their communities against a few clearly identifiable racists. Moreover, *South of Broad* joins the other texts in suggesting that White men are the best agents for bringing about and leading this newly formed community because it reflects their own supposed detachment from problematic histories.

The novel's views are illustrated in even starker terms as Wormy quickly realizes the error of his ways, forgets he hates Black people, and embraces a role on the football team. Unlike Ernest Gaines's *A Gathering of Old Men,* Conroy's *South of Broad* positions football as a powerful symbol of American unity that reaches back into the 1960s and extends well beyond the sidelines. Peninsula High's first match, which is against the "awesome and storied" Green Wave from Summerville, punctuates football's power to bring healing and achieve change (315). Yet, with Wormy newly installed on the team, the novel switches its focus to another problem. It again proposes that Black people, too, must learn to let go of the past. Before the game, Coach Jefferson addresses his players, saying, "I want to talk about integration. Just one time. After that, no one on this team is going to mention it again" (317). Jefferson goes on to admit how it hurt his feelings that those like Wormy did not want to play for him, so he had been especially hard on the White players in practice. He says, "I tried to break your spirit. I couldn't do it, and I gave it my best shot," but "Now what I have left is a team. I think it's a team with character and mental toughness" (318). As the drama builds, he continues, "Look around you. Look at your teammates. If you see black faces or white faces, you get the fuck off my team. No white. No black. No more. The time for that is over. We walk the world as a team, and we're going to have fun kicking a little ass this year" (318).

The players erupt, and the subsequent game demonstrates the uniting power of his words. Ike and Leo start at linebacker and direct the stifling defense. Wormy and Niles captain the offense, with Chad kicking field goals and extra points while their female classmates cheer them on. They all work together, consistently shutting down their superior opponent. However, at the end of the game, the score is tied: "14–14 with a minute left" (321). On the final play, as we know they will, Peninsula High scores the winning touchdown in spectacular fashion. The whole team unites to move the ball across the goal, again illustrating the power of communal action. With the game over, the fans rush the field. Leo describes the scene, saying, "I watched in amazement as my mother and father . . . helped an out-of-control mob of football fans pull the goalposts to the earth. I howled with laughter when I watched Betty Roberts kiss Wormy Ledbetter on the cheek in her sheer exuberance . . .

History was changing all around me" (322–23). This lighthearted and romantic version of the 1960s seems a far cry from the period Chester Himes describes in *Cotton Comes to Harlem,* but it speaks directly to the way history, after postmodernism, is made malleable and unfixed. Like the post-1975 TV shows and literature we discussed in the first two chapters, *South of Broad* imagines its own personal version of innocent history. The major difference is to what end this history is employed. While the White southern outsider in the last quarter of the twentieth century gave audiences the ability to imagine themselves as existing beyond shared communities, the narrative offered by *South of Broad* bids White people to return to an imagined post-racial narrative that feels authentic and is based on unity and progress. In this narrative, both Black and White people are tired of talking about race and are more than ready to move on together against a shared, easily identifiable foe.

According to the novel's logic, most decent White people have either always been fighting for justice or were converted shortly after integration. Therefore, any insistence on linking individuals to a racist past is deeply misguided and unfair. We see this logic brought to life again and perhaps more clearly when Leo departs Charleston for San Francisco in search of Trevor, who has gone missing after contracting AIDS. While in California, Leo checks out Trevor's old apartment, now inhabited by a lawyer from Minnesota named Anna Cole. Anna is suspicious when he shows up at her door. So Leo tries to calm her, saying, "Ma'am . . . My good friend Trevor Poe used to live here, and I'm with a bunch of friends who're looking for him" (237). She shoots back, "What's with the 'ma'am' shit?" (238). He tries to explain, "I'm Southern . . . It's instilled in us at birth. Sorry if it offends you" (238). This does not sit well with Anna. She replies, "Look, George Wallace, or whatever your damn name is, I'm on edge here" (238). Leo responds by calling her "Garrison Keillor." When she expresses displeasure at being stereotyped, he tells her, "We George Wallaces tend to stereotype ice fisherman from Duluth who stereotype us" (238). Similar to Leo's interaction with Ike, though, the encounter quickly deescalates once they have a chance to talk for a bit. Soon, Anna apologizes and lets him search the apartment for information that might reveal Trevor's whereabouts. However, Leo remains frustrated. He asks Anna to tell him everything she knows about

South Carolina. All she can produce is a tentative, "Didn't you start the Civil War or something," and then she mentions knowing about "the Research Triangle" (244). When Leo tells her the Research Triangle is in North Carolina, Anna becomes exasperated and tells him, "It's all the same thing to me. I've never given a shit about the South" (244).

Leo is deeply bothered by Anna's views on his home state and the larger region. After leaving the apartment, he reflects on what it means to be a southerner. He says, only after leaving the South "did I learn that the Southerner represents a disfigurement in the national psyche, a wart or carbuncle that requires either a lengthy explanation or cosmetic surgery" (246). He then goes on to share an article he had written "about the reasons people seemed to hate the South" (246). The list of ten causes for hate is interesting in many ways, but it centers on a strong feeling of resentment that he, Leo King as an individual, would be associated with the region's negative reputation. He writes in a sarcastic, cutting way that "Some dopes still blame me for the Civil War, though I remember killing only three Yankees at Antietam" (246). He adds dryly, "Many black people I have met outside the South blame me personally for Jim Crow Laws, segregation, the need for the civil rights movement, the death of Martin Luther King, the existence of the Ku Klux Klan, all lynchings, and the scourge of slavery" (246). The list goes on, but it keeps coming back to how the larger nation paints southerners, like him, in a supposedly unfair light. In the story's logic, Leo (like Rick or the caretaker) is one of the good ones—who represents the best hope for healed community in the United States. How dare someone accuse him of being linked to an inherited racist past just because the color of his skin or the place of his birth. Indeed, Leo feels entitled to being defined only by the southern narratives or brands which he feels to be true and authentic to his own sense of self. Of course, these end up being narratives that erase any link to the region's violent history and his own inherited privilege.

The novel finally ends by making its message almost literal. Hurricane Hugo sweeps through Charleston erasing much of the city's physical history. Through this devastation, readers then see the possibility for a new, better future that reflects Leo and his group's image. As Leo ponders all that has happened, he gets philosophical. He thinks, "We have been touched by the fury of storms and the wrath of an angry, implacable God. But that is what it means to be human, born to nakedness and tenderness and nightmare in the eggshell fragility of mortality and flesh" (510). However, this condition does not diminish his community's power to impact and shape lived experience. He continues: "The immensity of the Milky Way settles over the city, and the earthworms rule beneath the teeming gardens in their eyeless world. I am standing with my best friends in the world in complete awe of the loveliness of the South" (510). While an angry God and incomprehensible realities might exist above and below the earth, Leo rests in the fact that he and his friends have the power to thrive in a lovely South, made beautiful through the hurricane's erasure and their collective ability to transcend it all. As Catherine Seltzer puts it, the hurricane demonstrates how "Charleston will make new histories where it cannot salvage the old, and the sort of snobbishness and latent racism that had defined its value system will have to give way to a system more reflective of its creators" (115). The "creators" Seltzer references are "painters and carpenters" (482), who literally built Charleston. The new history, then, depends on a rebranding of the South that aligns with outsiders and working-class folks who supposedly have little interest in upholding structures of White supremacy and inequity.

A few pages later, the novel reaffirms this emphasis on a new Charleston that could model rebirth and healing. Leo and his friends are visited by a porpoise, which Leo explains "has always been a sign of renewal and of the charged magical life of the Low Country" (511). *South of Broad* closes with this image of regeneration and magic, where the 1990's South is positioned as a lovely and transformed space. This sense of beauty and renewal, though, depends on a postmodern understanding of history that is married to a metamodern commitment to "truth effect." In other words, the novel suggests postmodernism's individualized and unfixed relationship with history is a necessary good, providing a needed erasure that is essential for organizing new and collective narratives around freedom and self-expression. According to this framework, all we need to do is embrace the hurricane's cleansing power. Similar to the zombie apocalypse or Wesley's burial, there is a promise of something new and better if Americans would just submerge or ignore history and embrace a sanitized organizing narrative—one that supposedly has room for everybody but the bigot.

To be clear, though, by washing away the past, the novel also erases the historic frameworks that explain present inequities. Similar to the other White male characters in this chapter, Leo shows how White people could arrive in the twenty-first century deeply believing in their own innocence. More than that, the characters in this chapter model a supposed moral duty to come back into community and to organize it around their own liberal, post-racial image. Ultimately, instead of promoting the hard, introspective work of dealing with one's own personal role in communal systems of injustice, like Himes, Komunyakaa, and Gaines suggest is necessary, *South of Broad* and the other metamodern narratives in this chapter reify notions that equitable community can be achieved through an effective rebranding campaign and doing away with a few race-obsessed rotten apples. What the next chapter demonstrates, though, are metamodern narratives that take a different approach. The authors seem willing to show how the barrel itself is rotten. By starting with that realization, they then work to acknowledge and amend still festering wounds in the national body.

5

Building on New Foundations
The Search for Something Different

Jason Aaron and Ron Garney's comic *Men of Wrath* (2015) and Cormac McCarthy's novel *The Road* (2009) offer examples of metamodern literature that use the "effect of truth" to illustrate White people's indelible connection to inherited racial violence.[1] Using what Mary K. Holland calls, "literature's return to belief and earnestness" (200), they present inherited and maintained violence as being inseparable from twenty-first-century White American identity. They then illustrate a moral responsibility born from this violence as something that cannot and should not be forgotten or explained away. Whereas the texts in the last chapter clung to an easily earned innocence for relatively progressive White people, *Men of Wrath* and *The Road* work to uncover how the mythology of the White outsider obfuscates deeply embedded links to White supremacy. Put again, the focus on guilt in this chapter reflects what Christina Sharpe so effectively demonstrates in her book *In the Wake* (2016). As she explains, we in America are all still unavoidably consumed by slavery's violent legacies, which are an "overwhelming force" inescapably shaping understandings of self and community (Sharpe 15). While White people in the United States almost certainly do not experience the slave ship's presence or "wake" in the same way as Black Americans, the texts in this chapter offer a useful reminder that the ship leaving the wake is not a ghost ship. It is instead largely captained and maintained by those choosing to ignore or deny their own personal relationship to violent White supremacy.

Men of Wrath and *The Road*, then, offer a small bit of recognition that White people, too, are defined by the slave ship's presence. Indeed, the texts contend White people should address how they have created and profited from a society that demands other people's exposure and suffering. The narratives make clear, to ignore that reality should be impossible. As Sharpe explains, it is akin to ignoring the weather. She writes, "The weather is the total climate; and that climate is antiblack. And while the air of freedom might linger around the ship, it does not reach into the hold, or attend the bodies in the hold" (Sharpe 104). As we have seen throughout this book, White people's longstanding pattern is to try and ignore the anti-Black weather while clinging to the "air of freedom" that "might linger around the ship." *Men of Wrath* and *The Road* are far from perfect texts, but they offer some correction to the White-authored narratives of innocence we have already encountered. In other words, the authors seem ready to admit what should be obvious: that the weather impacts all of us and always has. For White people to do what Sharpe calls "wake work," then, means acknowledging and resisting the horror and omnipresence of their inherited identity, even as such work necessitates destroying the ship upon which most White people have almost assuredly built their lives.

To be clear, there is immeasurable work that must be done to dismantle centuries of adherence to White supremacy and then to enact restorative justice. These texts do not have easy or complete answers for how to achieve this goal. However, they do offer a place to start. By presenting a more honest accounting of the South and its continued legacies in the United States, they demonstrate how the region's supposed unique backwardness is rooted deeply within ideations of even progressive Northern/National Whiteness. As we have seen in the other chapters, though, interrogating the South to explain the nation's racial realities is not new. Yet, these texts offer us an important alternative to the White-authored narratives we have already covered. Instead of continuing to allow most White people to see themselves as personally distanced from violence, *Men of Wrath* and *The Road* use the region to suggest a clean separation from White racial terror is impossible. This marrying of violence to one's individual identity then frames America's crimes as a personal issue that cannot be denied or amended through merely adopting a better southern brand. In other words, whereas most White-authored southern literature written after 1960 locates the region's guilt as an aberration or an alien entity that can be, and most often is, rejected by "good" White people, the texts in this chapter indicate that the opposite is true. They suggest the reality is that most White people are not only inescapably linked to what George Lipsitz terms "possessive investments in whiteness" (2), but also that they will do whatever it takes to protect those investments. The only real option for progress, then, is presented through a kind of self-annihilation that destroys the structures and beliefs surrounding traditional understandings of American innocence.

Before moving to the White-authored narratives in this chapter, though, it is important to acknowledge that Black authors, along with other minority writers and artists, have long recognized a need to annihilate traditional understandings of White/American innocence. In the third chapter, we explored how Chester Himes, Ernest Gaines, and Yusef Komunyakaa all use the South to push back against notions that individuals or the United States as a whole could heal without first accounting for the nation's history. Their work participates in a long and ongoing tradition of Black authors using the region to demonstrate White supremacy's damaging national presence at both a personal and systemic level. The reality is while White authors largely vacillate between projecting communal and individual versions of innocence, Black writers, for the most part, remain consistent in their call to problematize these evasions of inherited history and identity. Recently, authors such as Colson Whitehead, in his novel *Underground Railroad* (2016), Kiese Laymon, in his novel *Long Division* (2013), and Jesmyn Ward, in her novel *Sing Unburied Sing* (2017), to name a few of many examples, have employed the South to remind twenty-first century readers how systemic racial injustice intersects with an inherited American identity. Put again, what the White authors in this chapter demonstrate is not something new, but a long overdue echo of much older calls for justice. While we may acknowledge their efforts as positive steps toward accounting for the nation's past, we also should not act like these stories exist in a vacuum, unaided by the countless minority voices who have long been calling for restorative action informed by an honest accounting of history.

Men of Wrath and *The Road*, then, do not uniquely possess racial wisdom, nor do they have some special claim over how to heal communities in the United States. However, there is some value in interrogating the limits and possibilities of White voices to express their own positionality within the landscape of American racial consciousness. Too often, those who have been harmed by unjust systems are then charged with the labor of elucidating why their nation should value and protect them. Audre Lorde explains, there is real damage when it is assumed to be "the responsibility of the oppressed to teach the oppressors their mistakes" (95). As she points out, this expectation most often allows "oppressors [to] maintain their position and evade responsibility for their actions" (95). Indeed, White people exact "a constant drain of energy," which Lorde argues would "be better used" elsewhere (95). Part of contending with Whiteness and its continued impact means moving away from a model that demands Black people explain to White people the damage done by commitments to racial violence. This is not so White people can fall back into old patterns of supposed authoritative knowledge, but it should promote the kind of reflexivity that can grapple with personal connections to systemic problems. As James Baldwin puts it, "one wishes that Americans—White Americans—would read for their own sakes," the record of history "and stop defending themselves against it. Only then will they be enabled to change their lives" (321). The texts in this chapter encourage this kind of inward reflection, which is born from the intimate knowledge of a mirror. They track what it means for White people to read history for themselves, as Baldwin suggests they should, and to recognize the horror staring back at them is their own reflection.

The texts in this chapter also engage White people's guilt without using an imagined Blackness as a means of escape or denial. This is important because White authors so frequently use the authority of Black characters to frame innocence.[2] For instance, in the last chapter, we saw how Coach Jefferson reaffirms Leo's commitment to colorblindness, as he declares, "If you see black faces or white faces, you get the fuck off my team" (318). Not only do characters like Coach Jefferson give White authors a false power to declare the conditions of innocence, but they also tend to promote a view that Whiteness and its attendant violence only exists in the view of a disapproving Black gaze. This assessment fails to acknowledge that the inequity linked to Whiteness is a problem that endures beyond Black people's reaction to it. Put differently, the European invention of Whiteness that links color to human worth underlies the very fabric of enduring inequity in the nation. It permeates throughout systems of capital and power defining America's past and present. As legal scholar Thomas Ross puts it, "any person who is part of the culture has been taught the lesson of racism" (31). He explains, while we may try to unlearn our teaching at a conscious level, "none of us can slough off altogether the lesson at the unconscious level" (31). This reality, he argues, makes fantasies of "innocence" a "powerful and very dangerous idea" (31). To grapple with the true nature of Whiteness, then, means wrestling with a guilt that resides deep within relationships that organize daily living. Indeed, it means confronting a personal responsibility that should motivate a reordering of priorities for both the self and the larger society, regardless of who is watching.[3]

It is perhaps understandable why White people are uncomfortable with this kind of framing. After all, it is much easier to consume what is packaged and sold in many diversity workshops, which suggest racial reconciliation or at least personal innocence can be achieved through "waking up" to problematic vocabularies and being nicer to one another. This view of diversity and inclusion, though, where one is either asleep or awake, erroneously suggests relatively superficial changes, like achieving consciousness, can account for injustices deeply embedded in almost every facet of daily living. This is the logic we saw in the last chapter, where characters like Rick or Leo could prove their innocence through confronting obvious instances of racism and then move on as racially absolved heroes. This view of racial innocence, achieved through better vocabularies and rejecting obvious racism, also grants a kind of perverse superiority and security to White people who have access to the newest language and who rarely encounter the kind of violence represented by Merle, Wesley, and Wormy. To be clear, there are obvious benefits to adopting more thoughtful and considerate language, and we should not diminish gains brought about by increased attention to how words wield power. Yet, similar to the other brands of Whiteness we have encountered in this book, what often gets left out is the extent of the problem and our nearness to it, which tends to minimize the necessary metaphoric violence that must occur to even relatively liberal understandings of self and society. Ultimately, what sets the characters in this chapter apart from the other White men we have encountered is their willingness to turn the critical lens inward and to admit a deeply embedded personal guilt that demands the death of their own organizing narratives.

Men of Wrath's and *The Road*'s reflective power partially comes from the fact that both texts are clearly linked to their author's lives. As a result of this link, there is a narrowing of focus that shifts attention away from someone else's guilt and toward personal involvement in the violence the texts capture. McCarthy dedicates *The Road* to his son John Francis, and in an interview with the *Wall Street Journal,* he calls his son a co-author because of how much of their relationship he puts into the novel.[4] Jason Aaron also brings himself into *Men of Wrath,* as he connects the novel's unredeemed protagonists to his own family's lineage. In the preface, Aaron writes about his great, great-grandfather who killed a man over some sheep. Sammie (this man's son and Aaron's great-grandfather) also meets a violent end after contracting rabies. Aaron then uses these bits of family history to suggest an inherited violence that has been passed down to him and readers alike. He writes, "Whatever was passed down to me from Ira Aaron, down through his doomed son Sammie, down through generations of Alabama farmers and coal miners and rebels and preachers and the occasional murderer, I'm now passing on to you . . . Thanks for joining the family" (3). The family, of which the reader is now a part, consists of "the culmination of a long bloody cycle of Southern violence, one that's been passed down from father to son over the course of a century" (3). The reader, then, regardless of who they are, has been named as part of a southern family, marked by the region's supposedly unique commitment to racial and social violence. Moreover, as Aaron adds a bit later, the violence "will only end when everyone dies" (3). Put plainly, this is not a group in which one would most likely want to be included. It is soaked in a history of blood and theft that will only end in some form of complete annihilation. Aaron, though, neither gives himself nor readers much of a choice about entering into this ill-fated family. As he presents it, by engaging with the text, readers are being introduced to their already existent family—a family from which they might be estranged but, nonetheless, are part of the readers' identity.

By situating himself and his readers as being part of a familial cycle of violence, Aaron makes clear that we inherit rather than choose our connection to the cycles of bloodshed the text depicts.[5] This framing needs added nuance, yet it is a useful reminder of the extent to which our identities and lives are related to exterior and often violent legacies. Aaron and Garney go on to demonstrate how the familial history, into which readers are born, revolves around physical and mental domination. They frame this violence as being passed down from "father to son," and the promised destruction born from this violence suggests an urgent need to disrupt the family's cyclical inheritance. The novel's graphic form also accentuates the violence being passed down, as the pictures make visible and explicit what is only imagined in traditional literature. Drawings depicting bloodshed, fire, and destruction dominate the pages. Their cumulative effect is a bit overwhelming. No cape-wearing heroes save the day or alleviate the impact of cruel men. Instead, Garney draws most people in the text as helping perpetuate cycles of murder and mayhem. Readers are presented image after image calling attention to the realities of White patriarchal violence in the United States. Similar to *The Walking Dead, Men of Wrath* seems to almost relish showing things that are hard to stomach. For instance, one of the first images readers encounter is a man who has been stabbed and staggers away with blood spurting from his neck. Next, we see a man with rabies murdering his family, who is only stopped by his son who shoots him point blank in the head. These scenes make readers yearn for someone capable of stepping in and stopping the violence, but there is no voice crackling through a radio or Leo King to offer reassurance for a better future. Instead, for most of the graphic novel, readers are greeted with page after page of selfishness, cruelty, and death—with the Rath family, which is the reader's family, standing near the center of it all.

Over the course of the story, Aaron focuses on three generations of Raths: Ira, his son Ruben, and Ruben's child, who is unborn for most of the narrative. Through each generation, readers can recognize and engage with different possibilities for dealing with inherited violence. First, Ira, who is the family's patriarch and named after Aaron's ancestor, fully embraces his role as a broker of death and destruction. He lives in a bulletproof house lined with guns and works as an assassin for the Polks, a local crime family. When Aaron introduces Ira, he is in the process of executing a young husband and wife. The couple's murder is ugly. They are led into a swamp and gunned down in cold blood while they beg for their lives, but it gets worse. Ira returns to their car, where he finds a baby. Without hesitation, he throws the screaming infant into the water to be eaten by alligators. Unlike *The Walking Dead*'s opening scene— where Rick shoots a young zombified girl—Ira's violence toward a child does not make us pity or mourn the White male protagonist's plight, nor does it revolve around the killing of an alien other that threatens an innocent good. Rather, it demonstrates one of the graphic novel's central conceits, which is that White men stand at the heart of an inherited willingness to trade human life for profit. Ira's inclination to murder just about anyone for money is further demonstrated a few pages later when the Polks hire him to kill his own son. Ira seems utterly unphased by the order and simply proceeds about his business. Without a second thought, he tracks down Ruben's girlfriend Lizzie and tells his son she will die unless he comes to a church in rural Alabama.

In the following interaction between father and son, readers witness the basic pillars of traditional American community (family, faith, and the rule of law) all come crashing down. First, there is the obvious familial breakdown, which we see in Ira's attempt to murder his own child. Then, we see the space of the church violated, as Ira threatens Ruben during the church's Sunday service. Instead of helping their threatened neighbor, the members of the congregation either look away or glare at them for talking in church. As the preacher drones on, speaking emptily about honoring veterans and those who have sacrificed themselves for a greater good, the churchgoers ironically stand idle, watching Ira don a mask and then try to gun down his son. It is only after stray bullets begin impacting their own safety that the church members begin to react and to acknowledge the violence taking place around them. After Ira kills a couple congregants trying to hit Ruben, someone finally calls the police. The law, however, also fails to intervene on behalf of those threatened by violence. As we learn later, the town's sheriff is in the Polks' employ and has been told to avoid disrupting Ira's work. What readers witness, then, is a scene where almost every facet of community has failed because of an intense selfishness. What remains is an environment where everyone turns on one another and those who have access to guns grab them as they try to protect their individual interests.

The preacher conforms to this model of forceful protection and joins in on the action. He finds his own rifle and moves into the adjacent cemetery, where Ira is still attempting to kill Ruben. As the preacher draws his sights on Ira, he says, "Wasn't always a preacher. Not in Phu Bai in '68" (59). Unimpressed, Ira turns and shoots the preacher in the throat. Here, in the cemetery, we begin to more fully grasp the dog-eat-dog world in which the Raths thrive. Adding one more man with a gun, even if he is a preacher and a veteran, does not seem to offer much hope for a viable future. Rather, the graphic novel illustrates Martin Luther King Jr.'s claim that "the ultimate weakness of violence is that it is a descending spiral, begetting the very thing it seeks to destroy" (62). As King concludes, "Returning violence for violence multiplies violence, adding deeper darkness to a night already devoid of stars" (62). Ruben, who up to this point has been a rather mild-mannered character, further demonstrates the descending spiral. He takes advantage of his father being distracted by the preacher and pistol whips Ira in the back of the head. Then, as the old man lies on the ground, Ruben hits him again and delivers a vicious kick to his father's face. Blood spews from Ira's mouth. He coughs weakly, and Ruben yells, "Stay the fuck away from my family!" (64). To which, Ira responds, "I am your fuckin' family" (64). As Ruben leaves his father's bleeding and prone body, we can see the fight between father and son does not represent a binary choice. The conflict is not between good and evil, where Ruben must defeat his abhorrent father in order to usher in a new, more peaceful age. Rather, violence is a family trait and Ruben is very much part of the family. While he is not as brutal as Ira and uses violence for relatively better goals, Ruben's difference is a matter of degree, not kind. Therefore, unlike the texts in the last chapter, we are left without a White character whose violence guides the community toward healing.

Instead, shortly after the interaction in the cemetery, Ruben decides to go back and kill his father. This choice leads him to his childhood home, where Ira still lives. When Ruben arrives, Ira takes it in stride. He tells his son, "Am I really supposed to be scared a' you pointin' a gun at me? You couldn't kill me three days ago, boy. Somthin' supposed to be different now?" (77). The reference to three days suggests some sort of Biblical rebirth, and Ruben follows up his father's skepticism by demonstrating his newly born ability to commit real violence. First, he shoots the old man in the shoulder, then the kneecap, demanding answers about his mother who disappeared when Ruben was a child. Ira yells, "Arrgggh, you sonuva bitch! Shoot me like a fuckin' man!" (78). Ruben answers, "I'll shoot ya however the hell I like" (78). Here, we can see the two "manly" wills facing off, complete with a sexist reference to Ruben's being a "sonuva bitch."[6] The son, though, seems ready to fully inherit the violence that is his birthright. He prepares to kill Ira with a final bullet to the head and to assume his role as the Rath patriarch. However, Ira refuses to go down easily. He lunges at his son, punches him in the mouth, then smashes him across the face with a dirty pot from the sink. Ira takes the gun and stares down at Ruben, declaring, "You're a Rath all right through and fuckin' through" (82). As he looks at his prostrate boy, though, Ira seems to have a change of heart and a rebirth of his own. Instead of shooting the younger Rath, Ira gives him all the cash he has earned from his career as an assassin. He tells Ruben to take the money, to leave the South, and to start a new life somewhere far from their violent native land (84).

Ruben is understandably confused. He says, "Why didn't ya kill me? You were sure as hell goin' to the other day?" (85). Ira does not have much of an answer, but he expresses a hope that the violence will finally end with his change of heart and his son's flight from the South. In an earlier era, this moment of conversion and removal from a fallen community might have been enough to offer readers a sense of resolution. As we saw in the 1970s–1990s, there was a sense that progress could occur through an authentic change of heart and a decision to establish an identity as an outsider. But the novel does not end with Ira's gift to his son. Rather, as Aaron seems to understand and relays through the remaining narrative, inherited violence is deeply and unavoidably woven into the societal fabric and will not disappear through individual conversions or leaving behind the South. Instead, America's pervasive and all-encompassing commitment to self-advancement and protecting one's own interest leaves no one safe. In fact, Ira's gift itself is a continuation of this cycle. By taking the money born from violence and using it only to protect his own son, he does nothing to disrupt or challenge existing systems. The novel demonstrates the shortsightedness of Ira's strategy as Ruben goes to his girlfriend Lizzie, who is in labor with their child at the hospital. In the waiting room, the Polk gang riddles Ruben's body with bullets, murdering him before he can meet his child. Garney closes the scene by prominently drawing a toy sheep covered in blood (94). While we can applaud Ira's and Ruben's change of heart, like a sheep led to slaughter, Ruben's naive belief that he can simply walk away from his past leads to his death. What this suggests is that without combatting the problems from which he and his family have benefitted, Ruben cannot hope to escape the generational violence that will plague him wherever he goes. Merely deciding he no longer wants to associate with the Polks does not end their relationship or provide protection from the culture he and his family helped create. Instead, the Rath family (the reader's family) must account for their history and be willing to fight against the ingrained violence they perpetuated.

After hearing about his son, Ira starts a version of this fight. He uses his talents as an assassin to kill those he feels are responsible for Ruben's death, starting with the corrupt and weak sheriff. He then hunts down and murders the Polk gang, including several members of the Polk family. The violence is swift and gruesome, and the scenes where he kills these men are some of the most brutal in the book. Finally, some of the Polk gang try to kill Ira at his house, and during the ensuing gunfight, the Rath family home catches fire. Garney draws the scene so the screams of the men Ira kills seem to be coming from the burning house itself. In the almost literal death of the Rath family home, it is easy to imagine that Ira has finally managed to separate himself from the systems of violence with which he was previously aligned. However, the story does not end here either. Again, Aaron seems to recognize not only the impossibility of existing outside the problem, but he also rejects the framing we saw in the last chapter, where White men violently built healed communities through removing the South's worst elements. The sheriff, the Polk gang, and even the Rath's familial history are easy targets to condemn. Like we saw with Merle, Wesley, and Wormy, relatively enlightened White people are more than willing to point toward other White individuals or groups and label them the problem. What is harder (and the novel tries to accomplish this) is seeing beyond the surface and probing the roots of White supremacy. After the inferno and screaming house, the next page is black, interrupted only by a single white box, containing the words "Let's say grace" (110).

As readers turn past these words of prayer, they are transported to a jarringly different space. Juxtaposed against the naked violence and gore found in the preceding images, Garney draws a white columned plantation home, which looms large and tranquil in its agrarian setting. The next panel depicts a table full of food and drink. Seated at the table's head, readers find the speaker, a bearded and fatherly figure, who concludes his blessing, saying, "we Polks remain ever grateful for this and all the blessings yet to come. In Jesus' name we pray" (111). In these images and words, readers witness what has always upheld systems of violence in America. It is not some black-hatted, moustache-twisting villain. It is a family man sitting in the relative isolation and manufactured peace of the "big house." Like generations before him, the Polk patriarch has the luxury of pretending he is removed from the violence in his community. In fact, it is easy to imagine this man, as he sits and prays with his family, disdaining the murders carried out on his behalf. However, it is also clear he has enjoyed benefits derived from the bloodshed surrounding him. Mr. Polk, then, is characterized by his ability to separate his wealth and comfort from the violence his family has helped create. Like so many White people before him, including Ira after his "conversion," Mr. Polk is simply following the rules of consumption that dictate providing for one's own family or group, regardless of the cost, should be one's central goal. Therefore, as he serves his family what looks like a rich Thanksgiving feast, which evokes the legacy of Indigenous genocide, readers are again reminded how efforts to enrich a narrowly defined "us" often means more of those defined as "them" suffer and die.

Put plainly, Aaron and Garney seem to recognize the necessity of interrupting the false peacefulness that separates individuals from the violence they help produce. As readers turn the page past the food and serenity, that interruption arrives in the form of Ira Rath. He stands over the praying Mr. Polk with a gun aimed at his head. Garney does not have to draw what comes next. Readers are well-aware of Ira's ability to end lives. In going back to the plantation, which is home to so much racial violence in America, and in killing this man, Ira appears to have again finished his mission. It would be tempting to conclude the narrative here with a triumphant Ira defeating the novel's true villain. However, Aaron and Garney keep probing what stands between the nation's current environment and a more fully healed community. In the end, they do not allow readers to embrace a fantasy where violent White heroes overcome all odds and prevail. If they did stop here, the novel would simply be one more narrative recentering White people's colonial myth that their violence will eventually produce peace and happiness. Instead, the final pages reveal that Ira (and White people like him, who ascribe to his "might makes right" philosophy) must also be removed before progress can occur. In other words, if Ira's actions are to be truly redemptive and meaningful, they must also include a realization there is no future for his way of finding solutions. As Audre Lorde puts it, "the destruction of our sons" begins with that first lesson "that might makes right" (49). For most people in America, Lorde explains, we have been taught "to think in an either/or mode" where we must "kill or be killed, dominate or be dominated" (50). If Ira were to be left retaining his power at the end of the novel, *Men of Wrath* would simply be another text promoting this 'kill or be killed logic," wherein White people again demonstrate the false belief that their violence will ultimately make the world a better place.

What the authors finally depict, though, is that as long as White people look out into the world and see the problem as mainly located elsewhere, there will never be a true confrontation with the nation's evils. Viewing racial violence as primarily beyond the self, always underestimates inequity's true scope and encourages the kind of violence that seems to produce only more death and destruction. Instead, the text suggests there must be some recognition that the problem is internal as much as it is external. In other words, there must be a willingness to turn inward and to recognize how all of us, at some level, reproduce and further entrench the nation's "kill or be killed" colonial logic. After removing the Polk patriarch, Ira seems to recognize he has not yet succeeded in ending the cycles of violence plaguing his family. Back at the hospital, he tells Lizzie (who has just given birth to her child), "You know that boy's gone be a problem right. Fathers and sons. That's how it started. That's how it's passed down. That boy . . . it's *in* him whether you see it or not. He's the son of a Rath. He's always gonna be" (116–117). As Ira puts it, the family's violent history is something that is "in" them and there is little that can be done about this inheritance. Even his best efforts to go out and destroy the systems promoting injustice and bloodshed still do not provide a viable break in the societal pattern. So, as he lies on his deathbed consumed by the cancer that will kill him, he acknowledges there is no path forward if fathers and sons continue passing down power to one another.

The narrative, however, concludes with some hope. Lizzie responds to Ira's warning, saying, "Won't be no more Rath sons. Fathers neither. Not ever again" (117). Ira is stunned, and he can only say, "Well. I'll be damned. What's her name?" (117). With these words, the novel's violence and bloodshed finally end. Through the termination of the family's male line, Aaron indicates that for society to truly change there must not only be a reckoning with the plantation, but also there must be a major change carried out within the family itself. Indeed, for progress to truly occur, there must be something fundamentally different planted in the hole violence creates. Stopping old and failed ways of doing things is only the starting point. There must also be efforts to build systems that are deeply different from existing masculine fantasies, which have long-given White people license to dominate and destroy those they deem inferior or no longer useful. Aaron replaces this commitment to violence with the feminine. While it is unclear what exactly he means with this replacement, it is a clear refusal to reify traditional constructions of inherited White power. There is, then, in the novel's final moments a sharp departure from the patriarchal insistence on domination and control we saw in previous chapters. Unlike Rick Grimes and Leo King, for instance, who understood themselves as dictating not only the community's relationship with the past but also the projected future, Ira's death and replacement with the feminine illustrates a recognition that updating and sanitizing the narrative is not enough. To truly break cycles of inherited violence, there must also be a realignment of who stands at the center of the rebuilt community.

Men of Wrath's refusal to make peace with violence is articulated in even clearer terms in Cormac McCarthy's *The Road*. Similar to *The Walking Dead*, McCarthy's novel is set in a post-apocalyptic hellscape, where the world has suffered some devastating calamity. In *The Road* what is left are roving bands of cannibals and occasional communes with barriers and gates cutting off entry. In the wake of this societal destruction, an unnamed father and son journey south in pursuit of warmth and hope. However, while *The Road* resembles the texts in the last chapter, in that it "seems to be a response to an immediate and visceral fear of cataclysmic doom in the United States after the terrorist attacks on 9/11" (Cooper 221); it does not invest in the same violent reassertion of White male agency. Indeed, through the father and son's journey, readers again see what it means to confront and reject legacies of Whiteness that contend selfishness and violence are necessary for progress. Like *Men of Wrath*, *The Road* uses a commitment to self-preservation and family to illustrate what has gone wrong in the United States. *The Road* also brings us back to our discussion of White southern doctors and their role as potential healers.[7] Similar to Welty in "The Demonstrators," Hannah in *Ray*, and Percy in *The Second Coming*, McCarthy uses a southern doctor to interrogate what it means to prescribe a better future for the nation.[8] However, his physician is markedly different from the men we saw in the second chapter. Unlike those doctors, who seek some control over at least their interior environment, *The Road*'s physician is confronted with a world that has slipped beyond his reach and descended into literal cannibalism. Therefore, melancholic inaction (like Dr. Strickland), escaping into his own reality (like Ray, Will, and Allie), or just trying to fit in (like Dr. Duk and Dr. Battle) are largely unavailable courses of action. Instead, he exists in an environment stripped of civilization's veneer, which means he and his son must keep moving and searching for some alternative, viable future.

The doctor, though, fails in offering anything stable or lasting to his son, and this failure is ultimately bound up in his inability to fully understand what it means to create something new and different from what precedes the collapse. In other words, even when confronted with a world reduced to ruin, the father is unable to leave behind the logics of Whiteness that reproduce violence and make progress unavailable. In moving south, though, he sets up the possibility that his son will push past his inheritance and embrace something richer than a postmodern allegiance to individualized truth. As Linda Woodson explains, *The Road* offers its "post-postmodern position" through a "belief in the power of language to evoke that which is already understood at some deep level beyond language" (89, 96). Put perhaps more simply, instead of focusing on language's inherent divisiveness, which gives rise to the outsider's logic of dissensus, the novel illustrates language's potential role in elucidating something deep, shared, and lasting. Woodson points out that McCarthy accomplishes this, at least in part, by rejecting traditional "American road literature" (89). She explains, in the United States, road literature tends to trace the isolated subject escaping societal rules and cultural history, usually by heading to some frontier (88). Similar to what we saw in *The Walking Dead,* though, McCarthy rejects the idea that individuals can settle "new" lands somewhere beyond America's cultural imprint. In the novel, then, there is no metaphorical West available to reward White "cowboys" who believe they can carve out a space for themselves in a supposedly new environment.[9] Rather, what takes place in *The Road* is closer to what Christopher Lloyd articulates in *Rooting Memory, Rooting Place* (2015). He argues that the father and son's journey South represents a return "home" that takes seriously how "the grotesquerie and horror the man and boy witness" are tied to the novel's "regional surrounding" (141).

The Road, then, departs from *The Walking Dead,* "Dead Confederates," and *South of Broad,* which all imagine the South's history can either be forgotten or folded into an enlightened national narrative. Instead, McCarthy centers regional violence as a fundamental part of what has gone wrong in America. Moreover, there is no Merle, Wesley, or Wormy, whose defeat and dismissal would allow the father to "prove" his own innocence. Without this act of sloughing off racial guilt, McCarthy presents the region's violent legacies as key to understanding the communal breakdown readers witness. From the novel's very beginning, the narrative indicates if individuals are to reach some version of safety or healing, they must contend with a white, ancient predator that moves beneath the land. In *The Road*'s opening pages, the father describes a dream where his son leads him deep below the earth's surface. There, they find a monster that McCarthy likens to a spider, hiding and waiting

to devour its prey: "eyes dead white . . . Crouching there pale and naked and translucent, its alabaster bones cast up in shadow on the rocks
behind it" (2). In this otherworldly creature, we can begin to recognize
what menaces the world. As Lydia Cooper puts it, the monster serves as
a "recognition of Western society's complicity in its own destruction"
(221). Drawing from Jean Baudrillard's *The Spirit of Terrorism* (2002),
she argues the monster reveals "the American public's fear that the pursuit of political, global ascendency is in itself an act of violence whose
backlash will be both staggering in its magnitude and inexorable in its
execution" (221). However, Cooper links this monster to the darkness
in which it disappears rather than the whiteness that defines its body
(221). What gets left out of her analysis, then, is the way race specifically
plays into this image of American violence. The monster's disappearance
itself signals the way Whiteness has always benefitted from its ability to
remain invisible. Put simply, we see reflected in this alabaster monster,
which is marked by its blindness and aloneness, White people's commitment to selfish consumption and individualism, which defines the
nation's colonial past and haunts its present and future.

Taken alone, it might be easy to ignore the monster's whiteness and
to gloss over its symbolism. Like the father, we could "mistrust all of
that" and understand the dream as signifying nothing other than their
"peril" (18). The novel, however, invests deeply in the importance of
that which exists beyond words. McCarthy revisits the pale, unseen
forces haunting the travelers a few pages later. Still early in the novel,
the father again slips back into the realm of dreams. There, "his pale
bride came to him out of a green and leafy canopy. Her nipples pipe-
clayed and her rib bones painted white. She wore a dress of gauze and
her dark hair was carried up in combs of ivory combs of shell" (18). He
is haunted by "her smile, her downturned eyes," and when he awakes,
"it was snowing" (18). Again, we can see a lone figure dominated by
whiteness with "downturned," unseeing eyes. She is also linked to the
suffocated and frozen environment that surrounds the father and son
when they awaken. Like the creature in the opening pages, she represents another threat to their survival and to their journey. While she
is not physically menacing or trying to devour them in the traditional
sense, she is beckoning them toward an "eternal nothingness," a void

into which she has already surrendered. She emerges from a "green and leafy canopy" (17), and it would be so easy for them to stop and to follow her into that seemingly Edenic peace. Yet, it also seems clear that following her would mean giving up on any possibility of bringing change or healing to their environment.

Put plainly, the doctor's dreams exist on different ends of a spectrum: one encourages giving in to the consumption and predatory violence endemic to late capitalism and the other invites the safety of nothingness found in White people's postmodern retreat from engaging inherited realities. Together, they reveal the versions of Whiteness that seem available in the twenty-first century. They suggest individuals must either buy into the hierarchies born from dog-eat-dog capitalism or embrace a kind of nihilistic divorce from society. The father, though, is searching for a third option, one that can provide his son with safety and a future that contains at least some comfort and joy. In other words, he searches for a life that can bridge the gap between the fallen world and the safety he craves. However, he largely fails to build anything. The father's inability to construct something lasting and sustainable is largely tied to the fact he cannot perceive a world beyond violence or nothingness. Instead, he clings to the notion that he can maintain the innocence of nothingness while interacting with the fallen world. To that end, he manufactures a personally defined morality that allows them to claim they are the "good guys," all without ever truly challenging the facts of their existence or intervening on anyone's behalf.

In many ways, the father's belief in his own innocence while also rejecting societal responsibility aligns him with the White southern outsider. Like the post-1970s White characters in the first two chapters, he imagines his identity as being self-constructed and capable of existing beyond the larger, corrupt culture. As an imagined outsider, the doctor believes he is simply reacting to systems of power that render him helpless to do anything beyond care for his own offspring. In fact, the logic of the outsider almost necessitates a narrowly defined "us" that is positioned against a much larger and more powerful "them." Like we saw with Ray, it is this framework that allows individuals to feel innocent in their stasis because mobilizing means inevitable defeat. *The Road*'s doctor, though, does not simply reanimate the outsider logic.

Whereas those physicians demonstrated some hope in turning inward and healing the self or the localized community, the doctor in *The Road* admits he is not an agent of healing. Early in the novel they encounter a man who asks the father if he is a doctor and if he would he be willing to help an infirmed member of their group. Their interaction is full of mistrust and suspicion, and the father responds to the question about his profession, saying, "I am not anything" (64). A short while later, after the stranger seizes his son, the father shoots and kills the man. The father, in this denial of his profession, seems to understand that his position as an outsider renders him very close to the mother's position, as "not anything." However, he plunges forward, armed with his gun and the belief that even in his nothingness he can be a powerful source of good for his son.

In this brief and violent encounter, though, the father illustrates both the isolation and the logical end bound up in the outsider's retreat from community. First, in refusing the signification that marks him as a healer, he acknowledges that identity, like language, must be dialogical to be meaningful. In other words, without a larger community, he is indeed "not anything." Secondly, this withdrawal and constructed seclusion neither reduces the realities of his potential violence, nor his contribution to the world's kill or be killed mentality. Indeed, merely claiming nothingness (or building a liminal space of one's own making) does not serve as an interruption to the violence defining the larger society,[10] a violence which will inevitably intrude into one's life and demand allegiance. Because of this inevitable intrusion, the father's belief that he can be both an outsider and an agent of good for his son is ultimately doomed. Like we saw with Ira's cancer, regardless of the father's intentions, the world's violence seeps into his bloodstream and makes him sick. As Woodson puts it, he is "wounded and infected by that which is destroying the land" (226). Yet, despite the father's incessant coughing and growing weakness, he refuses to fully admit his nearness to the world's condition.

Ultimately, what the father's illness and eventual death show is how pronouncements of separation and individual goodness, like the father's insistence they are the "good guys," do little to provide distance from the environment's sickness. As the novel makes clear, what plagues the land will still be deadly, even if individuals claim separation from it. Again, like Ira, the father feels what is wrong with the world, and his immediate reaction is to use his remaining power to set things right for his son. As his wife tells him, "A person who has no one would be well advised to cobble together some passable ghost. Breathe it into being and coax it along with words of love. Offer it each phantom crumb and shield it from harm with your body" (57). Her belief in the necessity of laying down one's life for another is the kernel of hope at the novel's center. It is what keeps the father from succumbing to the beckoning, eternal nothingness and encourages him to continue even when things seem desperate. He grasps that human life without sacrifice and love is meaningless. Yet, the father is far too narrow in his views on who is worthy of that sacrifice. In other words, he fails to understand how his silence and his focus on only protecting his son dooms them all to a cold, barren world without the possibility of true community.

The father's failure to love broadly, at least in part, is born from his inability or unwillingness to understand America's history and how it informs their violent present. Instead, the father joins the White men from the last chapter in embracing an "us" versus "them" perspective, which allows him to maintain at least the illusion of his own goodness. According to the worldview he enacts, an alien and encroaching evil, rather than a personal selfishness, plagues the environment. The father's understanding of the world is shaped by looking outward and imagining the environment demands consistent readiness and opposition. As he explains to his son, "Maybe you should always be on the lookout. If trouble comes when you least expect it then maybe the thing to do is to always expect it" (160). There is a certain amount of realism in his outlook. It seems clear most people they meet on the road do have ill-intentions. However, his perspective is steeped in the same neoliberal, narrow logic that precludes any wide, communal interdependence. Put again, the father invests in the same flawed view of community we have already seen. It is a view closely linked to histories of colonialism and conquest, one that demands "our" needs and desires be met before any thought can be given to "them." Because of this insistence on their own safety and survival, the father refuses to trust anyone, and the goal remains singular and consistent: be on the lookout so that he and his son may live.

To be clear, moving away from individualism and toward communal answers is its own fraught project, full of failed and destructive attempts to organize around collective truth. The novel, though, is not naïve. It does not suggest we can reach some perfect version of truth or universal harmony. Instead, the truth the novel seems most intent on uncovering is the human ability not only to cannibalize one another, but also to justify that consumption. Therefore, whereas the texts in the previous chapter indicate the best pathway forward is to leave behind the nation's violent past as a guiding force, McCarthy seems to recognize the opposite is true. *The Road* demonstrates that any real progress starts with an honest recognition of one's relationship with the nation's violent history. What the travelers encounter when they head South, then, is not what the father hopes they will locate in the region. Rather than the warmth and comfort of his childhood, he finds the nation's crimes laid bare and exposed. Unlike what Chris Walsh argues, which is that "transnational capital exchange" is "completely absent from McCarthy's novel" (51), what readers find is that America, along with its southern region, has always been fixated on this kind of exchange. Put plainly, what they find is that the U.S. South has never offered anything fundamentally unique or different from the larger Western colonialist project. It is simply one more space where White people have traded human lives for profits. In fact, it is the unceasing monotony of this consumption that dominates their journey. Like generations of White people before him, though, the father resists recognizing his own participation in the violence he witnesses around him.

Perhaps the most telling example connecting the father to patterns of White consumption takes place against the backdrop of a planation's "big house." As in *Men of Wrath*, the plantation is used to reference the United States' long pattern of racial violence. The father and son, who have run out of food, approach a "tall and stately" edifice "with white doric columns across the front" (105). The large white columns indicate the home's plantation style, but McCarthy makes it clear a page later: "Chattel slaves had once trod those boards bearing food and drink on silver trays" (106). The juxtaposition of slavery and silver calls attention to how Black people were tortured so White families could live in opulence. He then adds to the home's historical framing, writing, "piled in a windrow in one corner of the room was a great heap" consisting of "Clothes and shoes" (107). In this image, which is reminiscent of the piles of clothes heaped outside gas chambers during the Holocaust, we again see how the events in *The Road* are tied to much larger narratives of racism and consumption.[11] Taken together, the evocation of slavery and the Holocaust signal to readers that the father and son are about to encounter the kind of cannibalism that has long existed amongst supposedly civilized White people.

While searching the house for food, the father comes across a locked trap door. Undeterred, he breaks the lock and enters the subterranean room. What he finds is deeply unsettling. McCarthy writes, "Huddled against the back wall were naked people, male and female, all trying to hide, shielding their faces with their hands. On the mattress lay a man with his legs gone to the hip and the stumps of them blackened and burnt. The smell was hideous" (110). Taking this all in, the father whispers, "Jesus," and "one by one they turned and blinked in the pitiful light. Help us, they whispered. Please help us" (110). The father responds, "Christ . . . Oh Christ," and he grabs his son, telling him to "hurry" (110). The father drops their lighter and they start to back toward the door. As they are leaving, "A bearded face appears blinking at the foot of the stairs. Please he called. Please" (110), but the father and son do not stop. They run. The scene is filled with the kind of horror that makes running appear to be the only option. Certainly, it would be asking a lot for them to risk their own lives in freeing the enslaved and half-devoured "huddled" masses. While an alliance formed between the father and those in the cellar might outnumber the approaching cannibals, neither their victory nor their escape would be guaranteed.

In their flight, though, McCarthy encapsulates what has always allowed evil to succeed. The man's unwillingness to risk what is most precious to him (his son's life) represents the "possessive investment" in Whiteness about which George Lipsitz writes. It is an investment that is exceedingly difficult to undo because White people's survival in the United States appears to rest on logics of consumption that the nation's racial history licenses. McCarthy fills the interaction with so much terror, running away seems the only natural and fitting reaction. However, in the repetition of the words "Jesus" and "Christ," we see another standard that could potentially offer something different from the continued patterns of violence undergirding the nation's past and present. Central to Christ's example is the idea that communal redemption rests on a willingness to sacrifice, even one's child, for a greater good. This is not to say the novel works as a kind of metaphorical altar call for Christianity or that it positions White men, like the father, as potential godlike saviors. Rather, McCarthy's evocation of Christ appears similar to how Slavoj Žižek characterizes the negation of self found in Christianity that could potentially provide a framework for moving past destructive elements of late capitalism and postmodern relativism.[12] In other words, McCarthy seems to understand while it may be relatively easy to imagine noble sacrifice in the abstract or to fantasize about being someone like Rick Grimes, who punches racists and declares a new post-racial age, true progress requires sacrificing one's own accrued advantages, even those advantages seeming to benefit loved ones. Like most people, the father decides his own child's safety and continued freedom is worth more than the lives of those already suffering. However, in his flight, he drops the lighter, the symbolic fire they have been claiming to carry, leaving it in a dark cell where men and women are housed as a food source.[13]

The symbolic importance of leaving the lighter behind is revisited a few pages later. After leaving the plantation, the son asks if they can have a fire to keep warm. However, they have nothing with which to start it. The boy then reflects on what he witnessed at the house, and asks, "They are going to eat them aren't they?" (127). The father answers, "Yes," and the boy declares, "And we couldn't help them because then they'd eat us too." The father, again, affirms his son's statement, saying, "Yes" (127), to which the boy repeats, "And that's why we couldn't help them" (127). Again, the father tells him, "Yes" (127). In this back and forth, the father and son reassure each other that protecting their own lives is unquestionably better than risking them for another group's survival. The lack of question marks in the latter half of the conversation drives home what must be repeated and believed if White people are to convince themselves of their own innocence. Indeed, it must be repeated and unquestioned that any action to help "them" means assured danger and devastation for "us." According to this framing, there is some retained morality located in their decision to help themselves while others suffer and die. As they sit shivering without a fire, though, McCarthy leaves readers with an image of the cold and lonely world such an outlook creates. Like we saw in *Men of Wrath,* this scene illustrates how turning inward and embracing individualistic advancement offers little real protection and ultimately leads to a bleak and dangerous environment for everyone.

As they move away from the plantation, the boy begins to understand how his father's individualistic worldview will never provide them with a communal and secure future. Rick and Jonathan Elmore explain, "What the boy sees more clearly than the father is that they are all hungry, they are all scared, they are all going to eventually die, and that ought to change how one lives at every moment," because "what is there to live for but a shared moment of a little less pain, a little more food, and a little community with other beings?" (145). The moment where his father turns his back on those most in need, though, seems to be an event that binds the father and son together rather than pulls them apart. At first, the boy seems willing to invest in a view of the world as a space with a clearly defined "us" and "them." However, as they continue to head south, we see the real point of divergence take place in a cotton field. There, in a place that is again closely tied to the nation's legacies of racial violence, the father and son find "a charred human infant headless and gutted and blackening on the spit" (198). The boy, upon seeing this horror, repeats, "I'm sorry . . . I'm sorry" (198). In the moment, it is unclear why exactly he is apologizing. However, after leaving the scene, the boy connects his apology to what he had said a few pages earlier, about "those people that got burned up" (200). What he is referencing is a brief interaction, where he had blamed some victims of a fire for their own deaths (191). The son's apology, then, is one that recognizes the link between individual internal callousness and the historic and still-present horrors they encounter on the road. Indeed, his apology is a recognition that the true nature of American capitalism is a devoured infant in a cotton field and what gives license to this predation is a world willing to meet atrocity with victim blaming or indifference.

After the encounter in the cotton field, the physical and ideological separation between father and son grows.[14] The journey south and the horrors they encounter on the way eventually, fully lead the father and son to different conclusions. For the father, it has all merely reaffirmed the worst aspects of humanity and justified his belief that they should always be on the lookout. He almost expects the emptiness they find at the southern shoreline. So, when they arrive, the barrenness confirms to him they are without any real hope, except in maybe blind luck. The father's journey, then, is one marked by very little growth, and at the end of the novel he succumbs to his sickness. In what are almost his final words, he reiterates to his son the philosophy that he has clung to throughout the novel. He says, "Keep going south. Do everything the way we did it . . . Keep the gun with you at all times. You need to find the good guys but you can't take any chances. No chances. Do you hear?" (278). However, almost immediately after the father's death, the son rejects this worldview. He takes a chance and offers his newly inherited gun, with all its phallic symbolism, to the first stranger he meets on the road.

What the son seems to understand is the impossibility of his father's command. He grasps that to find the "good guys" necessitates a willingness to put down the gun and to offer oneself up to the possibility of community. Allan Josephs may be right that *The Road* gives us some window into the divine or the transcendent, but it is not that "the divine becomes immanent in the love between the father and the boy" (144).[15] Instead, if there is a gesture toward hope in something bigger than the self, it is found in the boy's rejection of the father's model and a willingness to care about something more than physical comfort and survival. Like in *Men of Wrath*, we see a clear link between societal violence and an inherited logic that must be broken if any true healing is to occur. Again, Rick and Jonathan Elmore are helpful. They write: "The hope or lesson of *The Road*" is found through moving away from "the world represented by the father, the world of late industrial, patriarchal, capitalist individualism," which should be combined with "a change in our ethical comportment, a change that privileges community over goods and the relief of suffering over future-oriented calculations" (145–146). What is left out of their diagnosis, though, is the extent to which histories of racial violence are intertwined with the father's identity. Recognizing the father's connection to White supremacy, makes the change in "ethical comportment" they suggest, not a shift driven by altruism or even vague self-interest. Rather, it is a change that justice demands. In other words, after witnessing the plantation and the cotton field, along with the other horrors on the road, the boy realizes there is hope in humility and service rather than self-proclaimed innocence and self-interest. In this recognition, he moves away from most White people in the United States, who imagine their violent self-protection to be righteous and a necessary good. Instead, he risks his life in the hope that abandoning his father's example will have its own regenerative impact on the world. There may be some naivety in the boy's belief, but he also seems to recognize destroying patterns of White-authored selfishness may be the only antidote for a world so invested in violence and consumption.

Ultimately, both *Men of Wrath* and *The Road* do not offer neat or easy solutions. However, they do demonstrate that stasis or insisting on innocence should not be an option for their White characters. The novels also illustrate that investments in Whiteness are not easily abandoned in a world committed to narrow definitions of "us" and "them." Too much of what is consumed as thoughtful engagements on race, like the texts in the last chapter, suggest we can have a healed community through a slight shift in behavior, adopting a better narrative, or by rejecting only the South's ugliest elements. In contrast, *Men of Wrath* and *The Road* show the costs of such a worldview. They illuminate the false pretense that White people can claim innocence or can secure safe communities without radical change. They are also clear that the ruptures necessary for change must be both internal and external. There is always a temptation to believe that if we destroy only those more dangerous than ourselves, we can achieve peace. However, this view always falls short of actually bringing about change and usually merely introduces more suffering into the world. Instead, as these novels suggest, there must be a willingness to turn inward and to combat one's own commitments to colonial patterns of violence. This is always easier said than done. However, as these texts suggest, the stakes are high; and, in the end, fantasies of White innocence provide little protection from a cannibalistic reality that threatens us all.

Conclusion

Embracing Crosshatched Histories

At its heart, this book strives to illuminate strategies White people have used to imagine innocence. It also hopes to illustrate how clinging to these narratives and refusing to acknowledge guilt suspends or at least postpones any real fight for national or personal healing. As Ibram X. Kendi concludes in *Stamped from the Beginning* (2016), "when we fight for humanity, we are fighting for ourselves" (511). While the book is focused on southern men, I also hope it is clear the racial wounds produced by White people have never been isolated to a single sex or to certain parts of the national body. Colonial violence and anti-Blackness are an American sickness and a personal sickness. Without widespread, sustained efforts to uncover the roots and to combat the causes of the disease, we are all made worse and more susceptible to the violence it licenses. Kendi explains, "Racial reformers have customarily requested or demanded that Americans, particularly White Americans, sacrifice their own privileges for the betterment of Black people" (503). He argues, though, that "this strategy is based on one of the oldest myths of the modern era, a myth continuously produced and reproduced by racists and antiracists alike: that racism materially benefits the majority of White people, that White people would lose and not gain in the reconstruction of an antiracist America" (503). Yet, as we covered in the last chapter, the truth that White people would "gain" in an antiracist America cuts against the very foundational "us" and "them" logic upon which most White people have organized and built their lives.

Because of the perceived risk to this foundation, it is often difficult to convince White people what they would actually gain through honestly confronting America's racist history. It is difficult, in part, because if we are honest, at least in the short term, it seems most White people would likely not gain financially or socially through admitting and confronting their allegiances to anti-Blackness. More than that, an honest account would reframe restorative actions, not as altruism, but merely what justice demands. In fact, for most White people, truthfully admitting their relationship to inherited history would lead to an irreversible realization of their own guilt. This is why the White, male, southern outsider is such an appealing figure. He gives license for almost everyone to ignore their relationship with the systems they inevitably help maintain. As Baldwin puts it, "It has always been much easier (because it has always seemed safer) to give a name to the evil without than to locate the terror within" (Nothing 51). He goes on to explain how terrifying it can be to acknowledge "that the self one has sewn together with such effort is all dirty rags, is unusable, is gone" (51). Again, it is far less horrifying to imagine that one is mostly innocent and that any guilt one feels can be alleviated through being nicer to Black people or buying a copy of *White Fragility* from a Black-owned bookstore.

However, minimizing guilt into something that can be alleviated through small actions or gaining a Black friend's approval is a misunderstanding of the problem's scope. Indeed, an honest accounting of the past demands a transformation that reshapes the relationship between the self and the systems we inhabit. Baldwin hopes that realizing guilt and artifice will lead, "One day, perhaps, unimaginable generations hence," to the "knowledge that human beings are more important than real estate" (59). As he puts it, this truth must then "become the ruling principle of our lives" (59). Put plainly, what Baldwin suggests is that acknowledging guilt, or "the terror within," potentially leads to deep and important gains that could reorder how we think about our communities. In place of fear and violence, he argues we could perhaps gain a culture defined by love and generosity, where human life is finally understood as more important than individual profit. However, as he contends, White Americans continue to exhibit a "universal fear of love" (58), which has led even progressive White people to abandon any real effort to confront their own entrenched interests. As bell hooks so artfully explains, among progressives there is "a collective failure to acknowledge the needs of the spirit and an overdetermined emphasis on material concerns" (244). She argues, because of this deficit, "we desperately need an ethic of love to intervene" (244).

It might seem contradictory to talk about love and guilt in the same context. However, they are closely linked. The human response to harming those we love is to feel guilty and to not rest until the harmed party is materially and spiritually restored. Ultimately, a failure to admit guilt and a refusal to act in restoration are failures of love. Yet, as we have seen throughout this book, White people's most consistent response when faced with their own inherited reality is to embrace what hooks calls a "politics of domination," which preserves personal interests while offloading guilt onto someone else (244). As she puts it, "A culture of domination is anti-love. It requires violence to sustain itself" (246). We see this refusal to love mixed with domination and violence not only in easily identified reactionaries on the right, but also in a brand of progressive puritanism, which promotes a logic where innocence is proven through someone else's relative guilt. Truthfully, in progressive circles we often see very little of the selflessness and love about which hooks writes. Instead, there seems to be a deep fear of admitting personal guilt, at least the kind that would compel action from a place of humility and service. As hooks points out, "Without justice there can be no love" (Justice 30), and most White people seem far more interested in deferring blame than doing the difficult work of building just and loving communities.

In southern studies, we have also seen a desire to embrace a post-southern outlook that diminishes the region as a source of White people's guilt. To be clear, the field's focus on a postsouthern environment partially arises from an accurate assessment of how the North/nation uses the region to isolate America's racial sins away from a mythologized, liberal U.S. identity.[1] There is also much to be learned through putting the American South in broader international contexts.[2] However, there is another powerful, often implicit postsouthern argument that suggests we move past the South because continuing to talk and write about the region only promotes a form of guilt that will inevitably turn into shame or melancholy and arrest progress.[3] This fear of stasis, though, often rests on a false premise that whether or not White people should feel guilty is a matter of strategy rather than the natural and correct response to the facts of the nation's past and present. In other words, the question should not be if White people are guilty and, therefore, should feel that guilt. On that matter, the verdict seems clear.

Instead, the conversation should center on how that guilt is to be acknowledged and acted upon. Audre Lorde warns, "all too often, guilt is just another name for impotence, for defensiveness destructive of communication; it becomes a device to protect ignorance and the continuation of things the way they are, the ultimate protection for changelessness" (114). However, she goes on to explain that, at its most basic level, what people are feeling "is a response to one's own actions or lack of action." She then argues we should work to move past this definition of guilt through knowledge and restoration (114). However, if we understand knowledge and restorative action to be ongoing practices, then it also seems productive to become comfortable with the fact that locating new facets of our own guilt or implication in harmful systems will also be an ongoing and never complete process. Again, this does not simply mean feeling worse about the realities of our existence. Rather, it is merely encouragement to not hide or deny how each of us (in ways we recognize and in ways we still must learn) inevitably help maintain the violence that surrounds us. This realization, then, should lead to a generation of scholars who are not afraid to take on hard topics and are willing to act boldly to bring down damaging systems—even the ones we feel protect us and our families.

Natasha Trethewey's poem "Native Guard" helps us understand the potential power born from encountering a South that refuses White people their innocence while also pointing toward something beyond shame or melancholy. As Sarah Ford, Pearl McHaney, and Giorgia De Cenzo all point out, "Native Guard" works as a powerful reclamation that reintroduces not only forgotten history but also the past's impact on the present.[4] Ford explains, Trethewey uses her "haunting" poetry "to teach readers there is no safe barrier between past and present" (267). Because of the nearness between past and present, "Native Guard" suggests we learn something important by turning South and examining the stories and myths that come from the region. In the poem, Trethewey calls attention to Louisiana's Native Guard, which was the first African

American regiment to be formed in the Civil War. Throughout the conflict, these men fought protecting their homeland from Confederate soldiers and sympathizers. However, outside a few Civil War scholars, their role in the struggle had largely been forgotten. They are made invisible by the war's traditional narratives, which focus on stories of a good North and bad South or fictions of two disagreeing brothers disputing over something like states' rights.[5] As we saw in *The Dukes of Hazzard, In the Heat of the Night, Ray,* and "Dead Confederates," White people have long-tried to claim a version of the Civil War that could minimize Black people's presence because through such a framing the war is merely between competing brands of Whiteness, leaving only Whiteness as the possible victor.

"Native Guard," then, interrupts the obsession with Whiteness that usually dominates discussions of the Civil War and places a Black soldier at the center of the account. However, at the same time, the poem does not allow Whiteness the power of invisibility, which has long granted White people license to rewrite the past in a way that preserves their innocence. Instead, "Native Guard" works as a call to memory that can be used to center something other than Whiteness while also helping readers understand White supremacy's lasting impact on the nation. Below the title, Trethewey includes an inscription from Frederick Douglass, which reads, "If this war is to be forgotten, I ask in the name of all things sacred what shall men remember" (25). As De Cenzo puts it, "Trethewey, in her poem, regains possession of Douglass's challenge to America to 'never forget' its responsibilities" (31). Indeed, the poem starts with an encouragement to honestly assess the nation's violent past and to remember the Civil War in all its complexities and contradictions.

Following Douglass' call to remember the war, the poem then uses a series of diary entries to suggest the frame through which this memory should take place. Trethewey's choice to use the diary's form suggests that to truly remember the Civil War requires a wresting back of perspective. Diaries centering on White people's suffering or conquest have long-dominated popular accounts of the Civil War. In giving the diary a Black author, Trethewey again asks readers to rethink how they account for the past. Instead of relying on White-authored narratives, which prove changeful and always make room for White people's innocence, she offers an alternative perspective that can amend what is often omitted from the nation's history. As Trethewey's soldier puts it, "I now use ink/ to keep record, a closed book, not the lure/ of memory—flawed or changeful—that dulls the lash/ for the master, sharpens it for the slave" (11–14). In these closing lines to the first diary entry, the poem's speaker outlines the stakes for clearly remembering the past. As the lines contend, if we lose sight of history as a relatively "closed book" and let it become "changeful," we embrace an environment that "dulls the lash for the master" and "sharpens it for the slave." In other words, if we let history become merely a reflection of White people's views, like we saw throughout this book, they will almost certainly continue rewriting the story in a way that protects both their interests and their innocence. Indeed, it is this ability to change and mutate that allows for the fantasy that guilt is only an unnecessary and destructive emotion.

In the following journal entries, the soldier further describes what it would mean to break dangerous patterns of White-authored innocence and to honestly account for the past. First, he describes brutal realities the Native Guard endured as they worked for the Union Army. He recounts, they "haul burdens for the army no less heavy/ than before. I hear the colonel call it/ *ni**er work*. Half rations make our work familiar still" (21–23). In these lines, Trethewey resists old temptations of dumping racial injustice solely on the antebellum South and makes clear that, even as members of the Union army, Black people's work and treatment is "familiar still." The injustice persists because White people in both the North/nation and the South have always been operating within a similar framework that defends and protects White supremacy. Conditions wrought by this framework may shift and vary over time, but the work and treatment itself remains familiar. Again, like Chester Himes, who puts cotton in Harlem and challenges the good North/bad South binary, Trethewey refuses to allow White readers a sense that there are triumphant spaces in the United States, where they can find separation from the nation's racial history. Instead, there is a consistent, unchanging sense that everyone in the poem is impacted by "the same old stupid plan/ Of dog eat dog, of mighty crush the weak" that Langston Hughes identifies and condemns (363).

According to Trethewey's framing, it is impossible for anyone in

America to fully separate from the pain and injury born from White people's violence. Therefore, while "Native Guard" introduces and centers the Guard's heroism and makes clear that no version of American history is complete without what Baldwin calls "the monumental fact" of Black people's history ("No Name" 473), the poem also reflects that Whiteness is a factor that must be reckoned with if we are truly to tell America's story. She drives this truth home through the soldier's diary that is "near full/ with someone else's words." As the soldier writes, these White-authored words become "overlapped now, / crosshatched beneath" the Black soldier's own account (25–27). The soldier's reclaimed history, then, does not erase the old narrative. Rather, it is a palimpsest, where Black and White narratives overlap and create something new and different. What this means is that an honest narrative of American history cannot be one where stories of Black people's hardship and heroism exist alongside or separated from tales of White heroes and villains. This separation is key to the fantasy we saw in almost all the White-authored texts in this book. It is a fantasy rooted in the same "separate but equal" logics that have always slowed and damaged attempts at true equity. As we saw in *A Gathering of Old Men,* simply hearing Black voices (as one of many truths) does little to unsettle systems of White power, especially for those like Sugar Washington and Ford Reynolds who sit atop the existing power structures. Trethewey's poem, then, instead of isolating Blackness from Whiteness, illustrates how racial identity in America has always been intertwined and can never truly be separated. In other words, as Toni Morrison reminds readers in *Playing in the Dark,* there is no US narrative or history absent Black people and their lived experiences.[6]

To be clear, the poem's acknowledgment of intersection does not create false equivalency between Black and White ways of knowing. The crosshatched journal is not suggesting White-authored histories are equivalent to Black-authored corrections to that history. Rather, the poem demonstrates how in the United States we are all inevitably a part of someone else's story. There is no way to conceive of past or present identities without taking into account how individuals are products of overlapping and often contradictory histories. Remembering this reminds readers that White-authored violence does not cease to exist, even when new histories are written. Like we saw in the TV show *Roots,* White people have long-been willing to tolerate and even embrace stories of Black heroism and White villainy—as long as those stories offer a sense that most White people could easily separate themselves from the damning aspects of that imagined identity. According to this framing, White people could maintain accounts of their own personal innocence while condemning any number of other people as being the real problem. To counteract these manufactured histories, Trethewey's poem seeks to reframe the United States' past as something fixed and relatively stable, a narrative with multiple perspectives but all written in the same book. Ultimately, by inextricably connecting both Black and White histories into a single narrative, she both refuses to allow Whiteness its malleability and, at the same time, rejects versions of the past that are obsessed with White people's actions or inactions. Her poem, then, reminds readers that while individuals might maintain different perspectives and inhabit different positionalities, they are all inheriting a shared, violent American history.

In many ways, southern studies has long focused on this work of collapsing binaries, not only between North and South but also between Black and White. As Tara McPherson points out, those studying the region should shatter "the fixed binary logic of a lenticular vision" that separates Black and White ways of knowing (247). Or, as Patricia Yeager suggests, we should "dynamite the tracks separating an 'African American' from a 'southern' tradition" (32). What Trethewey makes clear, though, is that collapsing these binaries does not mean embracing a postsouthern environment that diminishes difference. In other words, the goal of realizing that the South is in the North and that Black and White narratives are related is not to promote some finished or fixed narrative where we arrive at a newly reconciled account of American history and literature. Instead, Trethewey uses the palimpsest or a crosshatched account of the past to illustrate how the nation's divisions can never sit easily with one another. Michele Janette explains, "As hermeneutic tool, the palimpsest illuminates complexities without requiring them to reconcile with one another. It asks us to dwell in the uncomfortable and sometimes jarring intellectual space of unreconciled complexity" (174). Indeed, "Native Guard" encourages readers to resist the urge of reconciliation and to instead embrace the complexity that admits difference alongside an irrevocable unity.

Whereas White people have long looked Southward and embraced narratives that could grant them a reconciled relationship with their inherited identity, the crosshatched account Trethewey delivers does not allow for the imagined peace of a wholly unified or separated account. Instead, it suggests that any attempt to truthfully acknowledge the nation's past must embrace what Audre Lorde calls the "threat of difference." As Lorde explains, White people too often misunderstand calls for "unity" as "a need for homogeneity" (Age 101). Put plainly, like Lorde, Trethewey suggests fighting for justice means becoming comfortable with difference, even as we acknowledge a common damage wrought by centuries of practiced White supremacy. Therefore, unlike Rick Grimes's "us and the dead" philosophy in *The Walking Dead* or Coach Jefferson's assertions that there is "No white. No black. No more" in Pat Conroy's *South of Broad,* Trethewey's framing suggests readers should recognize the lasting impact of practiced White supremacy while still working toward healing and progress.

We see the complex balance between unity and difference more clearly in the next stanza, when Trethewey again revisits the symbol of the crosshatched diary. She writes about a "dark man" who takes off his shirt to show "scars, crosshatched/ like the lines in this journal, on his back" (50–51). In drawing a connection between the man's scars and the journal, readers again see why they must hold the two unreconciled histories together as one image. First, they must bear witness to the scarring and wounds that investments in White supremacy have wrought. Unlike most of the White-authored texts in this book that are quick to try and move past damaging histories, Trethewey's poem suggests those wounds are a necessary part of the story and cannot easily be shed. Second, readers should also recognize that the scars, while they are part of the man, do not define him. He is not a degraded subject of pity; he is a soldier fighting for both his freedom and for the United States' future. To take either the scars or the man alone would mean to deny a vital piece of the larger American reality. As the poem frames it, if we are truly to reckon with the United States' racial history and move toward a unified fight for progress, we must be able to see the nation as a place bearing the guilt of White supremacy yet enduring full of possibilities beyond that violence.

Trethewey then concludes her poem by locating hope in a truthful account of the nation's past and present. The final entry comes after the Civil War's end. Trethewey writes, "These are things which must be accounted for" (127). She then evokes the image of the exiled native and reminds readers of the acts of violence carried out against Black people during and after the War. Trethewey adds, "Beneath the battlefields, green again, / the dead molder—a scaffolding of bone/ we tread upon, forgetting" (138–140). The bones beneath the seemingly peaceful greenery build a platform upon which the forgetting can take place. "Native Guard" then calls upon readers to account for these forgotten bodies. Yet, as we have seen throughout this project, White people most often refuse to see much beyond an unperturbed pasture. To remedy this sense of denial, the poem's final lines declare, "Truth be told" (140). On one hand, this line acknowledges the poem's truth—that White Americans, rather than facing the realities of their history, prefer "forgetting" and treading upon the dead. On the other hand, the line is also a call for truth-telling. In this appeal, the poem compels readers to interrogate the nation's past and to be honest about links between the violence they uncover and their own sense of an innocent landscape.

Often the prospect for honest reflection and truth telling seems hopeless. The winning 2016 campaign slogan of "Make America Great Again," the violent backlash against gains made by the Black Lives Matter movement, and the panic over Critical Race Theory, all represent the worst impulses of White people wanting to preserve narratives of their own innocence. Moreover, the comforting lure of denial and narrow definitions of "us" and "them" are not confined to any one party or group. It is always easier to embrace someone else's guilt than to admit one's own personal failures. However, I am also reminded that art is a powerful resource, capable of bringing about transformation. The narratives we consume, teach, discuss, and use to inform our perspectives have real power to provide "a map to guide us on our journey to love," as hooks puts it (Clarity 14). Authors and artists also seem to be responding to a national cry for community and shared belief. Whether or not these metamodern impulses will lead to healing or further division and violence remains to be seen. Yet, it appears the nation stands at a cross-road. One familiar path again leads to White people denying their guilt, "forgetting" in an effort to maintain their interests. The other, fainter one, leads toward a transformed spirit that acknowledges the dangers of White innocence and encourages revolutionary, restorative justice.

This project takes seriously Jennifer Rae Greeson's and Scott Romine's call to move away from defining what southern studies "is," and instead to begin asking, "what does southern studies *do?*" (3). It seems to me if southern studies is indeed to "do" important work, it is imperative that those invested in its texts work to broaden and illuminate the path that acknowledges and works against the damage done by imagined White innocence. As we have seen, though, there is a strong and consistent desire amongst most White people to keep the bodies buried that might expose their guilt. Whether that separation from guilt is imagined as communal or as individual, White people have found ways to look toward "Dixie" and to see their own innocence. However, as Trethewey demonstrates and we saw illustrated in the third and final chapters, looking South can also be a powerful tool for framing communal identity. If the South is to be a space that promotes healing, though, it means embracing a view of the region as an unreconciled narrative that proves both links to guilt and, at the same time, endless possibilities for restoration and progress.

Notes

Introduction

1. Throughout this project, I capitalize the word White to draw distinctions between white people, who merely share the phenotype of "white" skin, and White people, who are those benefitting from centuries of practiced racial violence. There is obviously a great deal of overlap between the capitalized and uncapitalized versions of this word. However, I think in most instances we are better served by an understanding of Whiteness that extends beyond the color of one's skin.

2. The term North/nation is borrowed from Jennifer Rae Greeson's *Our South*, which she uses to refer to the regions outside the South that aligned themselves with a supposedly liberal non-southern identity. As she puts it, for the nation, "'North' serves as center and norm, while 'South' stands as deviation, in need of intervention and reform from without" (12).

3. While in the following chapters I primarily focus on a Black/White binary to help illuminate the contours of White people's imagined innocence, dynamics of race and power in the United States have always existed beyond this binary. For instance, Eric Gary Anderson's *American Indian Literature and the Southwest: Contexts and Dispositions* (University of Texas Press, 1999); Melanie Benson Taylor's *Reconstructing the Native South: American Indian Literature and the Lost Cause* (University of Georgia Press, 2011); and Gina Caison's *Red States: Indigeneity, Settler Colonialism, and Southern Studies* (University of Georgia Press, 2018), all clearly demonstrate productive ways to think about the South and racial violence as it relates to Native Americans. Therefore, while White people's reaction to what Toni Morrison calls "a dark, abiding, signing, Africanist presence" looms large in this book (5), it should be understood that it is not the only "presence" driving White people to construct narratives of their own innocence. The White southern outsider is such a powerful tool for White people because it frees individuals from feeling connected to inherited racial violence, regardless of where that violence originated or against whom it is directed. Therefore, much of what this book argues about constructions of postmodern White southern innocence can be applied beyond the binary on which the following chapters focus.

4. For an examination of outsiders in early American literature, see Karen Weyler, *Empowering Words: Outsiders and Authorship in Early America* (University of Georgia Press,

2013); and for an exploration of twentieth century authors, see Grace Elizabeth Hale, *A Nation of Outsiders: How the White Middle Class Fell in Love with Rebellion in Postwar America* (Oxford University Press, 2011).

5. For more on the fracture and dissensus that leads to increased individualism in the 1960s and 1970s see, Daniel T. Rodgers, *Age of Fracture* (Belknap Press of Harvard University Press, 2011); Bruce J. Schulman, *The Seventies: The Great Shift in American Culture, Society, and Politics* (Da Capo Press, 2008); and Robert D. Putnam, *Bowling Alone: The Collapse and Revival of American Community* (Touchstone, 2000).

6. As John Neff, Jarod Roll, and Anne Twitty explain, "the monument since its inception promoted four basic ideals: first, it extolled the heroism of Confederate soldiers and identified Confederate defeat as the product of Union advantages in manpower and materials rather than their martial superiority; second, it declared that states' rights—rather than the preservation of slavery, which they insisted was a benevolent institution in any case—had been the noble principle upon which the Confederacy was based; third, it proclaimed Reconstruction a failed experiment in racial equality that was vindictively foisted upon white southerners by a victorious Union; and fourth, it asserted that southern whites possessed a unique identity that gave the Confederacy enduring cultural power despite its defeat" (1). https://history.olemiss.edu/wp-content/uploads/sites/6/2017/08/A-Brief-Historical -Contextualization-of-the-Confederate-Monument-at-the-University-of-Mississippi.pdf

7. For more on this need for a change in spirit, see bell hooks's *Outlaw Culture: Resisting Representations* (Routledge, 1994) and more specifically her essay "Love as the Practice of Freedom."

8. The quoted portions come from David Roediger, *The Wages of Whiteness: Race and the Making the American Working Class* (Verso, 2007).

9. Although we come to very different conclusions on what the response to confronting the southern past should look like, for more on White melancholia, see Jon Smith, *Finding Purple America: The South and the Purpose of American Cultural Studies* (University of Georgia Press, 2013).

10. For more on guilt as a productive emotion, see P. S. Greenspan, *Practical Guilt: Moral Dilemmas, Emotions, and Social Norms* (Oxford University Press, 1995).

1. Desiring Dixie

1. For more on the decline of the "big three," which takes place during the 1980s–1990s, see, Douglas Blanks Hindman, and Kenneth Wiegand, "The Big Three's Prime-Time Decline: A Technological and Social Context," *Journal of Broadcasting & Electronic Media* vol. 52, no. 1 (2008): 119–135.

2. To support their conclusions about the dual intimacy and collectivity of television, Hinrichsen, Caison, and Rountree draw from Milly Buonanno, *The Age of Television: Experiences and Theories* (Intellect Books, 2008); Rober C. Allan and Annette Hill, eds., *The Television Studies Reader* (Routledge, 2004); and Raymond Williams, *Television: Technology and Cultural Form* (Routledge, 2003).

3. Michael Kreyling locates aspects of the postsouthern earlier in facets of Faulkner's later work, but his treatment of Faulkner, while valuable, still avoids the framing I am discussing in this chapter that directly places motivations for the post South on growing realizations of White national guilt. For more on Kreyling's treatment of Faulkner, see his essay "Fee Fie Faux Faulkner: Parody and Postmodernism in Southern Literature" in *The Southern Review* vol. 29, no. 1 (winter 1993): 197–211.

4. I am thinking here of Michael Kreyling, *Inventing Southern Literature* (University Press of Mississippi, 1998); Martyn Bone, *The Postsouthern Sense of Place in Contemporary Fiction* (Louisiana State University Press, 2014); and Scott Romine, *The Real South: Southern Narrative in the Age of Cultural Reproduction* (Louisiana State University Press, 2008); as well as Romine's influential article "Where Is Southern Literature? The Practice of Place in a Postsouthern Age" in *Critical Survey* vol. 12, no. 1 (2000): 5–27.

5. For more on new southern studies and the dangers of obsessing over the White South, see Smith's *Finding Purple America* and Patricia Yeager's *Dirt and Desire: Reconstructing Southern Women's Writing, 1930–1990* (University of Chicago Press, 2000).

6. See Houston A. Baker and K. Merinda Simmons, eds., *The Trouble with Post-Blackness,* (Columbia University Press, 2017).

7. I agree with a great deal of Phoebe Bronstein's argument in her excellent article "Comic Relief: *The Andy Griffith Show*, White southern Sheriffs, and Regional Rehabilitation" in *Camera Obscura* vol. 30, no. 2 (2015): 124–154. However, whereas Bronstein positions *The Andy Griffith Show*'s framing as being largely an attempt to "appease" both the North and South (128), I argue the show's "rehabilitation" of the South reveals a deeply held desire for White innocence that extends to both regions. In other words, the show is not trying to navigate a tightrope of national difference to deliver something both regions would find acceptable. Instead, it is speaking directly to the investments in White supremacy that bind together the two regions. In appealing to this shared narrative, the show provides White people throughout the nation with a powerful and enjoyable fantasy of their own collective innocence and goodness that is rooted in long-held accounts of American exceptionalism.

8. *The Danny Thomas Show* was originally titled *Make Room for Daddy* and ran under that name for its first three seasons.

9. Ultimately, Sara K. Eskridge and I come to somewhat similar conclusions regarding the function of rural television, in that it effectively promotes Black erasure, but we largely differ in how the South aids White people in this erasure. Whereas she argues television shows of the 1960s "demonstrate that the South was an entity unto itself that lived by a divergent and unchangeable set of values different from those of the nation as a whole" (147); I argue these shows demonstrate the opposite—in that they show a deep connection between the regions. See "Rural Comedy and the 'Foreign' South" in *Small-Screen,* edited by Lisa Hinrichsen, Stephanie Rountree, and Gina Caison (Louisiana State University Press, 2017): 133–149.

10. For a similar example of how southerners used supposed innocence narratives of national history to escape a damning Confederate past, see Stephanie E. Yuhl's *A Golden Haze of Memory: The Making of Historic Charleston* (University of North Carolina Press, 2005).

11. Andy's mention of "Indians" here is a powerful reminder that for most of the nation's history, White people have viewed the slaughter of Indigenous people and the theft of their land as non-controversial and part of a proud past. For more on the South's relationship with Indigenous people, see Caison's *Red States*.

12. See "Opie's Piano Lesson," season 7, episode 26. Bronstein's "Comic Relief" also offers a similar assessment, arguing Flip Conroy's character helped viewers "envision a color-blind contemporary Southern world" (143).

13. For more on Andy Griffith's career after *The Andy Griffith Show*, see Daniel de Visé's *Andy and Don: The Making of a Friendship and a Classic American TV Show* (Simon and Shuster, 2015).

14. The "rural purge," which could also be termed a southern purge, is a term used to reference the 1970–1971 cancellation of shows that either were set in the country or were thought to appeal to rural audiences, mainly carried out by CBS. Shows, such as *Green Acres, The Beverly Hillbillies, Hee-Haw, Mayberry RFD,* and *The Virginian,* all were cancelled at the end of the 1971 season.

15. For more on Fred Silverman and the rural purge, see Cynthia Littleton, "Fred Silverman Helped Shape Modern Television," *Variety* 347.1 (2020).

16. For more on the postmodern outsider's typical features see Hale's *Nation of Outsiders*.

17. For more on Rorty's use of "knowingness," see *Achieving Our Country: Leftist Thought in Twentieth-Century America* (Harvard University Press, 1998).

18. For more on the way *The Andy Griffith Show* was incorporated into *Matlock,* see de Visé's *Andy and Don*.

19. Gy Waldron, the show's creator, made this link between Lee and the Duke boys even clearer, as the car was originally to be named "Traveler" after Robert E. Lee's horse, which would essentially transfer the relationship between Lee and his horse to the boys and their car. Fears that audiences would not get the reference, though, led the creators to name the car after Lee. See David Hofstede, *The Dukes of Hazzard: The Unofficial Companion* (St. Martin's Griffin, 2005), 55.

20. We see another particularly clear example of how the flag is linked to White ahistoricism later in the pilot episode. In the scene, the Duke boys call together friends to help thwart Boss Hogg's efforts to destroy a local orphanage. The group includes Black and White southerners, who are shown huddled together around the Dukes' car using the roof with its battle flag as a kind of table around which they congregate. In the shot, we see an image of a supposedly unified, multicultural South aligned against the corruption embodied by Hazzard's police and J. D. Hogg with the flag working as a symbol of unity bringing Black and White southerners together.

21. Carrol O'Connor also expressed fear that his character might be construed as another racist. Fred Silverman recounts, O'Connor "was worried that after Archie Bunker he might be construed as doing another bigot role and then we sat down and realized he wasn't doing Archie again. I think the chief is much more liberal in his point of view, much

more open to change than Archie." See Ivor Davis, "Deep South as Hot as Ever for Two Cops," in *The Globe and Mail,* 5 Mar. 1988.

22. The action of the pilot is split over two episodes that both aired on the same night.

23. For more on how White people manipulate Martin Luther King Jr.'s sentiments in his "I Have a Dream" speech, see Gary Younge, "The Misremembering of 'I Have a Dream,'" *The Nation* (15 Jan. 2016), https://www.thenation.com/article/archive/misre membering-i-have-dream/.

24. Viewers first see the painting of Robert E. Lee to set up a contrast with the self-serving mayor Jim Findlay. Lee's portrait sits behind Gillespie's desk, and in the initial view of it, the painting is shot at a low angle, forcing viewers to look up at Lee as he gazes nobly out into the distance. The camera then moves down to form a connection between the General and a tired William Gillespie, who is smoking his pipe and looking over case files. After resting on Gillespie, the shot then rotates around so we can see a cup on his desk holding an American flag alongside a Confederate one. The paradoxical marriage of the two flags on his desk combined with the portrait, again effectively strips the secession from its historical connections to chattel slavery and rebellion. Instead, we see the Confederate iconography linked to a noble police chief, who is doing everything in his power to bring peace and healing to his community.

25. Even in shows like *Dallas* (1978–1991), *St. Elsewhere* (1982–1988), and *Hill Street Blues* (1982–1988), which present characters with some social or institutional power, the primary heroes are still mostly framed as outsiders who do not conform to communal expectations.

2. Switching the Patient

1. For a more complete treatment of this term, see Charles Taylor's *A Secular Age,* (Belknap of Harvard University Press, 2009), or the introduction.

2. Here, as in chapter 1, I use "post-southern" to indicate a move past the racial guilt that long defined the "South" as a separate space in the national imaginary.

3. James Baldwin writes that White people when they look into their past, see "an appallingly oppressive and bloody history, known all over the world. What they see is a disastrous, continuing, present, condition which menaces them, and for which they bear an inescapable responsibility. But since, in the main, they seem to lack the energy to change this condition, they would rather not be reminded of it" (722). In other words, when White people see the truth of their past, they find ways not to be reminded of that past. See Baldwin, "The Devil Finds Work," *Collected Essays: Notes of a Native Son, Nobody Knows My Name, The Fire Next Time, No Name in the Street, The Devil Finds Work, Other Essays* (Library of America, 1998): 515–521.

4. For more on the debate around the "post-southern," see chapter 1 or Martyn Bone's explanation of the term and its history in "Postsouthern" in *Keywords for Southern Studies,* edited by Scott Romine and Jennifer Rae Greeson (University of Georgia Press, 2016): 340–353.

5. Some of the ideas in this section overlap with my article "Learning to Listen: The Way a Society Speaks in Eudora Welty's 'Where Is the Voice Coming From?' and 'The Demonstrators'" in *Eudora Welty Review* 8.1 (2016): 109–122.

6. We see this threat to the larger culture further demonstrated through the threat to Marcia Pope, whose survival is called into question in the story's closing lines.

7. For more on Benjamin's treatment of melancholy, see, *The Origin of German Tragic Drama*, trans. John Osborne (Verso, 1977).

8. See Bronstein's "Comic Relief" for more on how *The Andy Griffith Show* responds to racial tensions in America.

9. For more on this period of literature and its celebration of working-class southern Whiteness, see Zachary J. Lechner's *The South of the Mind: American Imaginings of White Southernness, 1960–1980* (University of Georgia Press, 2018).

10. I use "nonracist" here to reference Ibram X. Kendi's use of the word in *How to Be an Antiracist* (Vintage, 2019). He argues, "There is no such thing as a nonracist . . . every community in every nation is producing or sustaining either racial inequity or equity between racial groups" (18).

11. For more on this opposition toward addressing racism through government action, see Robert D. Putnam and Shaylyn Romney Garrett, *The Upswing: How We Came Together a Century Ago and How We Can Do It Again* (Swift Press, 2021); Schulman, *The Seventies*; and Michael Omi and Howard Winant, *Racial Formation in the United States: From the 1960s to the 1990s* (Routledge, 2021).

12. Even though Allie has to work her way back into a sense of identity to become capable of action, Percy casts her as being made better by her initial loss of a historically based sense of self. In fact, without her memory, she is framed as a pure being living in an Edenic garden (she lives in a greenhouse), where she flips the Biblical narrative of Eve and helps lead Will to a sense of freedom and peace.

13. For more on Fredric Jameson's use of "schizophrenia," see *Postmodernism, or the Cultural Logic of Late Capitalism* (Verso: 1991).

14. Percy said "The world is already destroyed. The world is already dead." in an interview with Peggy Castex in "An Interview with Walker Percy" in *More Conversations with Walker Percy*, edited by Lewis A. Lawson and Victor A. Kramer (University Press of Mississippi, 1993) 58.

15. Percy explained to Jo Gulledge, going "out of bounds" is an important part of Allie and Will finding the peace they achieve at the end of the novel (307). In other words, they must go beyond what their community will tolerate and embrace their own version of identity outside the boundaries set for them. See Gulledge, "The Reentry Option: An Interview with Walker Percy" in *Conversations with Walker Percy*, edited by Lewis A. Lawson and Victor Anthony Kramer (Oxford: University Press of Mississippi, 1985).

16. Hannah goes on to admit he is overgeneralizing when he calls everyone who makes it into *Southern Living* "awful people." See Barry Hannah and John Griffin Jones, *Conversations with Barry Hannah*, edited by James G. Thomas (University of Mississippi Press,13).

17. The rainbow flag made its first major public appearance in association with gay pride in 1978, two years before the publication of *Ray*, at the San Francisco Gay Freedom Day Parade. See Gilbert Baker, *Rainbow Warrior: My Life in Color* (Chicago Review Press, 2019).

3. Seeing the Lynching Ropes

1. For more on the importance of recognizing a relationship between individuals and a collective racial history, see Christina Sharpe's *In the Wake: On Blackness and Being* (Duke University Press, 2016), which I also cover at more length in chapter 5.

2. I do not mean to suggest, here, that this push back against histories of erasure is something that only started in the 1960s. African American authors understood long before postmodernism that White-authored versions of history were a fiction, and they have long used literature to call attention to these false national narratives. Texts like Frederick Douglass's *The Heroic Slave* (1852) or James Weldon Johnson's *Autobiography of an Ex-Colored Man* (1912), are two early examples of countless narratives in which Black authors call attention to the fact that people of color were being left out of the nation's accepted "histories."

3. Isabel Wilkerson powerfully captures the realities of the Great Migration in her book *The Warmth of Other Suns: The Epic Story of America's Great Migration* (Penguin Random House, 2010). She also offers more context as to why and how many Black southerners left the region.

4. In the *Narrative of the Life of Frederick Douglass* (1845), Douglass explains that the songs sung in the fields should not be taken as proof of the enslaved people's happiness (13–15).

5. One of the few instances of interracial harmony in the novel occurs at a jazz club where Black and White patrons dance together, "guided by the talking of the jazz" (34). The music works as a metaphorical guide, showing listeners how to move beyond the absurdity of racism that dominates the rest of the novel. As the scene builds, "two saxes [start] swapping fours with the rhythm always in the back," and Grave Digger Jones says, "Listen to that . . . Somewhere in that jungle is the solution to the world" (33). After taking in the music for a moment, Coffin Ed replies, "if only we could find it" (33). The "it" is not clearly defined and could mean either the missing money or "the solution to the world," but Grave Digger Jones follows this statement by pointing to the language of Jazz as having the ability to unlock any "solution" they seek. He says, "If we could read that language, man, we could solve all the crimes in the world" (33–34). For Himes's characters, this music born from African American collaboration in the South and mixed with the growing expressiveness allowed in the North contains the power to lead both Blacks and Whites to a better place. The problem, however, is that there are always those who work against hearing that kind of music, and as Grave Digger Jones concludes, "Life could be great but there are hoodlums abroad" (34). See Chester B. Himes, *Cotton Comes to Harlem* (Vintage, 1988).

6. As Sven Beckert points out in his 2014 book *Empire of Cotton: A Global History* (Knopf, 2014) cotton production from the slave South laid the groundwork for the United

States' status as an economic power. Himes, by literally mixing cotton and cash together in the space of the novel, makes clear the long historical legacy of using black bodies to enrich the nation.

7. For more on the cultural upheaval of the seventies that led to the "outsider" character see Schulman, *The Seventies*; Putnam, *Bowling Alone*; Hale, *A Nation of Outsiders*; and Thomas Borstelmann, *The 1970s: A New Global History from Civil Rights to Economic Inequality* (Princeton University Press, 2012).

8. For more on how Gaines is framed as a "traditional" author, see Jeffrey J. Folks's "Ernest Gaines and the New South," *The Southern Literary Journal*, vol. 24, no. 1 (1991): 32–46. We can also see this emphasis on placing Gaines alongside "traditional" White southern writers in the way he is so often put in conversation with William Faulkner, as an inheritor and respondent to Faulkner's writing. We can see examples of this framing in David Lionel Smith's chapter "Bloodlines and Patriarchs: *Of Love and Dust* and Its Revision of Faulkner," *Critical Reflections on the Fiction of Ernest J. Gaines*, edited by David C. Estes (University of Georgia Press, 1994) and Michel Fabre's "Bayonne or the Yoknapatawpha of Ernest Gaines," *Callaloo*, no. 3 (1978): 110–124.

9. Hobson writes that their relationship gives "support to the argument that Bear Bryant and his recruitment of black athletes did more for race relations in the Deep South than any politician could ever do—or to put it another way, if you couldn't legislate morality, you could bring it about on a football field." See Hobson, *The Southern Rage to Explain* (Louisiana State University Press, 1983), 100. Matthew Teutsch also suggests, "Athletes and sports make repeated appearances as inspiration and possible saviors of the community" in Gaines's work, and Gil and Cal's relationship, in particular, "provides a template for race relations in the post-civil rights South" (178). While Taylor Hagood points out that football, more generally, on TV points to a superficial change that suggests "moral and social problems can be rectified quickly and easily" (284), he uses Gil's and Cal's relationship as suggesting "recuperative capabilities of the football South(s)." See Teutsch, "'Mr. Joe Louis, Help Me': Sports in the Fiction of Ernest J. Gaines," *MELUS: Multi-Ethnic Literature of the United States*, vol. 42, no. 3 (2017): 285.

10. In Gaines's *A Gathering of Old Men* (Vintage, 1983) we see another example of how Cal and Gil's projected unity primarily benefits White people when Gil leaves his father's house. His friend Russ reminds him that playing football on television is what is best for the Cajun community. Russ says, "There isn't a thing you can do here tonight," but "Tomorrow you can do something for yourself, and for all the rest of us—play the best game you ever played. Luke Will [the leading voice to kill Mathu] and his kind don't want to see you and Pepper in that backfield tomorrow . . . Many would hate it. But the Game is going to be seen on TV by millions, and more of them will be pulling for you and Pepper than pulling against you" (150). When Gil pushes back, saying he is only concerned about his family's future, Russ tells him again that the best thing he can do for them is to become an All-American. Noticeably, though, all the novel's African American characters are left off Russ's list of people who will benefit from Salt and Pepper's projected unity. The focus remains on

how playing the game will cast an image of post-racial accord that will benefit Gil's family and perhaps a larger national audience wishing to consume an easy, post-racial narrative.

11. My argument runs counter to Reynolds Price, who describes the scene as an "oddly comic trial of both vigilantes and blacks" that "achieves a surprising but just resolution of the tragic events" (15) and Maria Hebert-Leiter's argument that the novel "ends with a significant reversal of tradition when all the men responsible, including the Black men, are freed because the guilty parties were killed in the shooting commotion, erasing the lynching ritual's power over this particular community and making African Americans and white Louisianians equal in the eyes of the law" (114).

12. Ford and Washington are both national names (Henry Ford and George Washington). On the other hand, Reynolds and Sugar point toward the R. J. Reynolds Company and the crop grown in Bayonne, both of which are connected to the South. The joining of these names seems to signal a marriage between the region and nation under a universal commitment to capitalism that maintains the racial status quo.

13. Komunyakaa writes, the man who threatens the son is the "pick-up man from Bogalusa Dry Cleaners" who leans "against his van, with an armload/ Of her Sunday dresses" (27–29).

4. Searching for Innocence

1. For more on post-postmodernism or metamodernism see, Robert L. McLaughlin, "Post-Postmodern Discontent: Contemporary Fiction and The Social World," *Symploke* vol. 12, no. 1 (2004): 53; Mary K. Holland, *Succeeding Postmodernism: Language and Humanism in Contemporary American Literature* (Bloomsbury, 2014); Marjorie Perloff et al., "The Birth, Death, and Rebirth of Postmodernism," The Chronicle of Higher Education, 14 June 2009. Luke Turner, "Metamodernism: A Brief Introduction," *Notes on Metamodernism*, 12 Jan. 2015. Linda Hutcheon, *The Politics of Postmodernism* (Routledge, 2002); and Timotheus Vermeulen and Robin van den Akker, "Notes on Metamodernism," *Journal of Aesthetics and Culture*, vol. 2, no. 1 (2010).

2. "Dead Confederates" was originally published in the 2008 edition of *Shenandoah* before it was collected in Ron Rash's *Burning Bright: Stories* (Echo, 2010).

3. The comics are written by Robert Kirkman. Tony Moore did the art for the first six issues. Then, Charlie Adlard took over, and Adlard has drawn the subsequent issues.

4. Erik T. Kasper and Troy A. Kozma's "No Arts, No Letters, No Society, and Which Is Worst of All, Zombies: *The Walking Dead* and Hobbesian Politics," *The Journal of Popular Culture*, vol. 52, no. 3 (2019) also looks back to argue *The Walking Dead* promotes a Hobbesian view of politics, which demands personal freedoms be exchanged for government protection.

5. Crèvecoeur's *Letters from an American Farmer and Sketches of Eighteenth-Century America* (Penguin Classics, 1981) likens the southern city of Charleston to "Lima," situating the region outside the America about which he writes (166). He also argues that people living on the western frontier are "no better than carnivorous animals" (72).

6. For more on Rash and the Shelton Laurel Massacre, see Zackary Vernon, "The Role of Witness: Ron Rash's Peculiarly Historical Consciousness," *The South Carolina Review,* vol. 42, no. 2 (2010): 19–24.

7. We see a similar instance of racial tensions being defused through a personal connection in a later scene that takes place in California during the 1980s in Pat Conroy's *South of Broad* (Nan A. Talese, 2009). At first, the scene, which features a Black man named Macklin Jones trying to rob Sheba, is charged with racial anger. However, when they recognize each other as fellow Charlestonians, the anger quickly fades; they begin to joke with one another; and Macklin agrees to help them find Trevor (254–259).

5. Building on New Foundations

1. The year 2015 is when Jason Aaron and Ron Garney's *Men of Wrath* (Icon, 2015) collected edition came out, which is what I use for this chapter. The first of the original five issues was published in 2014, and the series continued into 2015.

2. I am also thinking here of the texts in the last chapter as well as popular novels such as Sue Monk Kidd's *The Secret Life of Bees* (Penguin, 2003), Hillary Jordan's *Mudbound* (Algonquin, 2009), and Kathryn Stockett's *The Help* (Penguin, 2009), all of which position the problem of Whiteness as something that can be absolved through an association with Blackness.

3. This idea that racial violence is deeply embedded in almost all facets of American identity is demonstrated throughout the work done in Critical Race Theory, including Derrick Bell's foundational *Faces at the Bottom of the Well: The Permanence of Racism* (Basic Book, 1992) and Richard Delgado and Jean Stefancic's *Critical Race Theory: An Introduction* (New York University Press, 1995).

4. John Jurgensen, "Hollywood's Favorite Cowboy," *Wall Street Journal* (13 Nov. 2009), https://hendrix.idm.oclc.org/login?url=https://www.proquest.com/newspapers/holly-woods-favorite-cowboy/docview/399070032/se-2?accountid=11371.

5. Aaron, here, is most likely assuming his readers are largely White and male. As Frances Gateward and John Jennings point out, a great many comics are centered around "a white-male-dominated power fantasy" (5). It makes some sense, then, White men would be the primary audience attracted to comic books that, at least on the cover, seem to be playing into this fantasy. Also, it seems like a somewhat safe assumption that the vast majority of people choosing to read a comic book centered on the life of a southern White man with a gun would be White and male—similar to those attracted to "Grit Lit," which is a genre which the graphic novel seems to fit (Vernon). However, the general call that "we" are all part of the family, speaks to the pervasive impact of White supremacy and violence on English-speaking readers more generally, which extends inclusion in the family to a much wider audience. See Aaron and Garney, *Men of Wrath.*

6. Later we learn that Ruben's mother killed herself because she could not live any longer with Ira and his commitment to violence (86).

7. For more on how *The Road* is a southern text, see Christopher Lloyd's chapter "The Road Home: Southern Narratives of Return" in *Rooting Memory, Rooting Place: Regionalism in the Twenty-First-Century American South* (Palgrave MacMillan, 2015).

8. It is never clearly expressed that the father character is a doctor, but his knowledge of human anatomy suggests he has this vocation in the pre-apocalypse world (64).

9. Here, I am arguing the opposite of Chris Walsh's contention in "The Post-Southern Sense of Place in *The Road*" in *The Cormac McCarthy Journal*, vol. 6 (2008) that the novel's depiction of the South "re-habilitates the myth of the frontier in the American literary imagination" (53).

10. For more on how White people frame the viability of inhabiting liminal spaces, see Smith's *Finding Purple America*.

11. We again see this acknowledgment of larger patterns of colonial consumption later in the novel, as the father finds a Spanish coin alongside arrowheads in a plowed field. Again, in this scene, we witness the agrarian fantasies of the farm or plantation intermixed with reminders of racial violence and Indigenous genocide (203–204).

12. For more on Žižek's position, see Slavoj Žižek and John Milbank, *The Monstrosity of Christ: Paradox or Dialect* (MIT Press, 2009).

13. Throughout the novel, the son and father repeat that they are "carrying the fire" (70, 109, 238), meaning they are the ones carrying the hope for civilization's future.

14. We see him moving further away not long after this scene as he goes out to find food for his ailing father (278–280). As he collects supplies, readers witness the switching of the roles between father and son beginning to be established.

15. Lydia Cooper's "Cormac McCarthy's *The Road* as Apocalyptic Grail Narrative," in *Studies in the Novel*, vol. 43, no. 2 (summer 2011), also points to the boy as what offers hope for humanity, as he embodies the hope of the "grail," but she too seems to focus on the boy as a manifestation of the father's love, writing "The father's love for his son becomes the boy's longing for his father and for community with others" (234). D. Marcel DeCoste's "'A Thing That Even Death Cannot Undo': The Operation of the Theological Virtues in Cormac McCarthy's *The Road*,'" *Religion & Literature*, vol. 44, no. 2 (2012): 67–91, makes a similar argument, pointing toward selfless love as being the novel's most important message. Yet, he too points to the father as the model for the son's version of this love.

Conclusion

1. See Leigh Anne Duck, *The Nation's Region: Southern Modernism, Segregation, and U.S. Nationalism* (University of Georgia Press, 2006); Jennifer Rae Greeson, *Our South: Geographic Fantasy and the Rise of National Literature* (Harvard University Press, 2010); and Houston A. Baker, Jr., and Dana D. Nelson, "Preface: Violence, the Body and 'The South,'" *American Literature*, vol. 73, no. 2 (2001): 231–44.

2. See Bone, *The Postsouthern Sense of Place in Contemporary Fiction*.

3. See Smith, *Finding Purple America*.

4. Giorgia De Cenzo, "Natasha Trethewey: The Native Guard of Southern History," *South Atlantic Review*, vol. 73, no. 1, *Southern Atlantic Review*, vol. 73, no. 1 (2008): 20–49; Sarah Ford, "Claiming the Property of History in Natasha Trethewey's Native Guard," *Mississippi Quarterly*, vol. 70/71, no. 3 (2017): 251–270; Pearl Amelia McHaney, "Natasha Trethewey's Triptych: The Bodies of History in Bellocq's Ophelia, Native Guard, and Thrall," *Southern Quarterly*, vol. 50, no. 4 (summer 2013): 153–172.

5. For more on legacies of Civil War memory, see Gary W. Gallagher's *Causes Won, Lost, and Forgotten* (University of North Carolina Press, 2008).

6. See Toni Morrison, *Playing in the Dark: Whiteness and the Literary Imagination* (Harvard University Press, 1992).

Works Cited

Aaron, Jason, and Ron Garney. *Men of Wrath*. Icon, 2015.

Allan, Robert C., and Annette Hill, eds. *The Television Studies Reader*. Routledge, 2004.

Anderson, Benedict. *Imagined Communities*. Verso Books, 1983.

Anderson, Carol. *White Rage: The Unspoken Truth of Our Racial Divide*. Bloomsbury, 2016.

Anderson, Eric Gary. *American Indian Literature and the Southwest: Contexts and Dispositions*. University of Texas Press, 1999.

Applebome, Peter. *Dixie Rising: How the South Is Shaping American Values, Politics, and Culture*. Harcourt Brace, 1997.

Arendt, Hannah. *The Human Condition*. 2nd ed. University of Chicago Press, 2013.

Babb, Valerie Melissa. *Ernest Gaines*. Twayne, 1991.

Baker, Gilbert. *Rainbow Warrior: My Life in Color*. Chicago Review Press, 2019.

Baker, Houston A., Jr., and Dana D. Nelson. "Preface: Violence, the Body and 'The South.'" *American Literature*, vol. 73, no. 2, 2001, pp. 231–44.

Baker, Houston A., and K. Merinda Simmons, editors. *The Trouble with Post-Blackness*. Columbia University Press, 2017.

Baldwin, James. "The Devil Finds Work." *Collected Essays: Notes of a Native Son, Nobody Knows My Name, The Fire next Time, No Name in the Street, The Devil Finds Work, Other Essays*. Library of America, 1998, pp. 515–521.

———. "No Name in The Street." *The Price of the Ticket: Collected Nonfiction 1948–1985*. St. Martin's Press, 1985, pp. 449–556.

———. "On Being 'White' . . . and Other Lies (1984)." *Black on White: Black Writers on What It Means to Be White*, edited by David R. Roediger. Schocken Books, 1999, pp. 177–180.

————. "The White Man's Guilt." *Black on White: Black Writers on What It Means to Be White,* compiled by David R. Roediger. Schocken Books, 1999, pp. 320–326.

Barrett, James Lee. "Pilot Part One." *In the Heat of the Night,* season 1, episode 2, NBC, 6 Mar. 1988.

————. "Pilot Part Two." *In the Heat of the Night,* season 1, episode 2, NBC, 6 Mar. 1988.

Baudrillard, Jean. *Simulacra and Simulation.* Translated by Sheila Faria Glaser. University of Michigan Press, 2014.

————. *The Spirit of Terrorism and Other Essays.* Translated by Chris Turner. Verso, 2012.

Beckert, Sven. *Empire of Cotton: A Global History.* Alfred A. Knopf, 2014.

Beidler, Philip D. *American Literature and the Experience of Vietnam.* University of Georgia Press, 1982.

Bell, Derrick. *Faces at the Bottom of the Well: The Permanence of Racism.* Basic Books, 1992.

Belsches, Alan T. "Life over Death: The Use of Memory in Walker Percy's The Second Coming." *Southern Quarterly,* vol. 23, no. 4, summer 1985, pp. 37–47.

Benjamin, Walter, *The Origin of German Tragic Drama,* translated by John Osborne. Verso, 1977.

Berry, Wendell. *The Hidden Wound.* North Point Press, 1989.

Blinn, William, et al. *Roots.* Warner Bros. Entertainment, 2011.

Bone, Martyn. *The Postsouthern Sense of Place in Contemporary Fiction.* Louisiana State University Press, 2014.

Bonilla-Silva, Eduardo. *Racism Without Racists: Color-Blind Racism and the Persistence of Racial Inequality in the United States.* 2nd ed. Rowman & Littlefield Publishers, 2006.

Borstelmann, Thomas. *The 1970s: A New Global History from Civil Rights to Economic Inequality.* Princeton University Press, 2012.

Boulton, Andrew. "The Popular Geopolitical Wor(1)Ds of Post-9/11 Country Music." *Popular Music and Society,* vol. 31, no. 3, July 2008, pp. 373–387.

Bronstein, Phoebe. "Comic Relief: The Andy Griffith Show, White Southern Sheriffs, and Regional Rehabilitation." *Camera Obscura,* no. 89, 2015, pp. 124–154

Brown, Wendy. "Resisting Left Melancholy." *boundary 2,* vol. 26, no. 3, 1999, pp. 19–27.

Buonanno, Milly. *The Age of Television: Experiences and Theories.* Intellect Books, 2008.

Caison, Gina. *Red States: Indigeneity, Settler Colonialism, and Southern Studies.* University of Georgia Press, 2020.

Cavallaro, Rosanna. "Chester Himes's Cotton Comes to Harlem." *Law & Literature,* vol. 19, no. 1, 2007, pp. 103–137.

"Civil Rights Memorial Mississippi." *Visit Oxford MS,* 27 Sept. 2019, https://visitoxfordms.com/attractions/civil-rights-monument/.

Clark, Keith. "Re-(W)righting Black Male Subjectivity: The Communal Poetics of Ernest Gaines's *A Gathering of Old Men.*" *Callaloo,* vol. 22, no. 1, Jan. 1999, pp. 195–207.

Cobb, James C. *Away Down South: A History of Southern Identity.* Oxford University Press, 2007.

———. *Redefining Southern Culture: Mind and Identity in the Modern South.* University of Georgia Press, 1999.

Conroy, Pat. *South of Broad.* Nan A. Talese, 2009.

Cooper, Lydia. "Cormac McCarthy's *The Road* as Apocalyptic Grail Narrative." *Studies in the Novel,* vol. 43, no. 2, summer 2011, pp. 218–236.

Crèvecoeur, J. Hector St John De. *Letters from an American Farmer and Sketches of Eighteenth-Century America.* Penguin Classics, 1981.

The Danny Thomas Show, season 7, episode 20. Originally aired 15 Feb. 1960 on CBS. Dir. Sheldon Leonard. Writ. Arthur Stander.

Darabont, Frank. "Days Gone By." *The Walking Dead,* season 1, episode 1, AMC, 31 Oct. 2010.

———. "Guts." *The Walking Dead,* season 1, episode 1, AMC, 7 Nov. 2010.

Davis, Ivor. "Deep South as Hot as Ever for Two Cops." Review of *In the Heat of the Night. The Globe and Mail,* 5 Mar. 1988.

Davis, Thadious M. *Southscapes: Geographies of Race, Region, and Literature.* University of North Carolina Press, 2014.

De Cenzo, Giorgia. "Natasha Trethewey: The Native Guard of Southern History." *South Atlantic Review,* vol. 73, no. 1, 2008, pp. 20–49

DeCoste, D. Marcel. "'A Thing That Even Death Cannot Undo': The Operation of the Theological Virtues in Cormac McCarthy's *The Road.*'" *Religion & Literature,* vol. 44, no. 2, 2012, pp. 67–91.

Delgado, Richard, and Jean Stefancic. *Critical Race Theory: An Introduction.* New York University Press, 1995.

Desmond, John F. *Walker Percy's Search for Community.* University of Georgia Press, 2004.

Dischinger, Matthew. "The Walking Dead's Postsouthern Crypts." *Small-Screen Souths: Region, Identity, and the Cultural Politics of Television,* edited by Lisa

Hinrichsen, Stephanie Rountree, and Gina Caison. Louisiana State University, 2017, pp. 259–276.

"Discrimination and Racial Inequality." *Pew Research Center's Social & Demographic Trends Project*. Pew Research Center, 31 Dec. 2019, www.pewsocial trends.org/2016/06/27/3-discrimination-and-racial-inequality/.

Douglass, Frederick. *Narrative of the Life of Frederick Douglass*. Unabridged Edition, Dover Publications, 1995.

Duck, Leigh Anne. *The Nation's Region: Southern Modernism, Segregation, and U.S. Nationalism*. University of Georgia Press, 2006.

The Dukes of Hazzard. Perf. John Schneider, Tom Wopat, Catherine Bach, and Denver Pyle. CBS, 1979–1982.

Durrant, Sam. *Postcolonial Narrative and the Work of Mourning: J.M. Coetzee, Wilson Harris, and Toni Morrison*. Albany, State University of New York Press, 2004.

Egerton, John. *The Americanization of Dixie: The Southernization of America*. Harper's Magazine Press, 1974.

Elliott, Carl, and John Lantos, eds. *The Last Physician: Walker Percy and the Moral Life of Medicine*. Duke University Press, 2012.

Ellison, Ralph. *Shadow and Act*. New American Library. 1964

Elmore, Rick, and Jonathan Elmore. "'You Can Stay Here with Your Papa and Die or You Can Go with Me': The Ethical Imperative of The Road." *The Cormac McCarthy Journal*, vol. 16, no. 2, Oct. 2018, pp. 133–48.

Eskridge, Sara K. "Rural Comedy and the 'Foreign' South." *Small-Screen Souths Region, Identity, and the Cultural Politics of Television*, edited by Lisa Hinrichsen, Stephanie Rountree, and Gina Caison. Louisiana State University Press, 2017, pp. 133–149.

Fabre, Michel. "Bayonne or the Yoknapatawpha of Ernest Gaines." *Callaloo*, no. 3, 1978, pp. 110–124.

Faulkner, William. *Intruder in the Dust*. Vintage, 2015.

Fellman, Michael. *The Making of Robert E. Lee*. Random House, 2000.

Flanagan, James. "Deconstructing Mayberry: Utopia and Racial Diversity in the Andy Griffith Show." *Continuum*, vol. 23, no. 3, 2009, pp. 307–319.

Folks, Jeffrey J. "Ernest Gaines and the New South." *The Southern Literary Journal*, vol. 24, no. 1, 1991, pp. 32–46.

Ford, Sarah. "Claiming the Property of History in Natasha Trethewey's Native Guard." *The Mississippi Quarterly*, vol. 70/71, no. 3, 2017, pp. 251–270.

Frankenberg, Ruth. "Mirage of an Unmarked Whiteness." *The Making and Unmaking of Whiteness*, edited by Birgit Brander Rasmussen. Duke University Press, 2001, pp 72–96.

Gaines, Ernest J. *A Gathering of Old Men*. First Vintage Contemporary ed., Vintage Books, 1983.

Gaines, Ernest J., and Mary Ellen Doyle. "A MELUS Interview: Ernest J. Gaines. 'Other Things to Write About.'" *MELUS: Multi-Ethnic Literature of the United States*, no. 2, 1984, pp. 59–81.

Gaines, Ernest J., Marcia Gaudet, and Carl Wooton. "Fiction into Film." *Porch Talk with Ernest Gaines: Conversations on the Writer's Craft*. Louisiana State University Press, 1990, pp. 87–104.

Gaines, Ernest J., Elsa Saeta, and Izora Skinner. "Interview with Ernest Gaines," *Conversations with Ernest Gaines*. Edited by John Lowe. University Press of Mississippi, 1995, pp 241–52.

Gallagher, Gary W. *Causes Won, Lost, and Forgotten: How Hollywood and Popular Art Shape What We Know about the Civil War*. University of North Carolina Press, 2008.

Gateward, Frances K., and John Jennings, "The Sweeter the Christmas." *The Blacker the Ink: Constructions of Black Identity in Comics and Sequential Art*. Edited by Frances K. Gateward and John Jennings. Rutgers University Press, 2015, pp. 1–15.

Gencarella, Stephen Olbrys. "Thunder without Rain: Fascist Masculinity in AMC's The Walking Dead." *Horror Studies*, vol. 7, no. 1, 2016, pp. 125–146.

Gitlin, Todd. "Prime Time Ideology: The Hegemonic Process in Television Entertainment." *Television: The Critical View*, edited by Horace Newcombe. Sixth Edition. Oxford University Press, 2000, pp. 574–594.

Greeson, Jennifer Rae. *Our South: Geographic Fantasy and the Rise of National Literature*. Harvard University Press, 2010.

Greeson, Jennifer Rae, and Scott Romine. "Introduction." *Keywords for Southern Studies*, edited by Scott Romine and Jennifer Rae Greeson. University of Georgia Press, 2016, pp. 1–5.

Griffith, D. W., et al. *The Birth of a Nation*.

Guinn, Matthew. *After Southern Modernism: Fiction of the Contemporary South*. University Press of Mississippi, 2006.

Haddox, Thomas F. "Elizabeth Spencer, the White Civil Rights Novel, and the Postsouthern." *Modern Language Quarterly*, vol. 65, no. 4, 2004, pp. 561–581.

Hagood, Taylor. "Football, the South, and the Spatiality of Television." *Small-Screen Souths: Region, Identity, and the Cultural Politics of Television*, edited by Lisa Hinrichsen, Stephanie Rountree, and Gina Caison. Louisiana State University Press, 2017, pp. 277–293.

Hale, Grace Elizabeth. *A Nation of Outsiders: How the White Middle Class Fell in Love with Rebellion in Postwar America*. Oxford University Press, 2011.

Hannah, Barry. *Ray*. Penguin Books, 1980.

Hannah, Barry, and John Griffin Jones. "Barry Hannah." *Conversations with Barry Hannah,* edited by James G. Thomas. University Press of Mississippi, 2016, pp. 3–31.

Hannah, Barry, Larry McCaffery, and Sinda Gregory. "An Interview with Barry Hannah." *Conversations with Barry Hannah,* edited by James G. Thomas. University Press of Mississippi, 2016, pp. 68–82.

Hannah, Barry, and R. Van Arsdall. "The Spirit Will Win Through: An Interview with Barry Hannah." *Conversations with Barry Hannah,* edited by James G. Thomas. University Press of Mississippi, 2016, pp. 42–67.

Hargrove, Dean. "Diary of a Perfect Murder." *Matlock,* season 1, episode 1, NBC, 3 Mar. 1986.

Harris, Trudier. *The Scary Mason-Dixon Line: African American Writers and the South.* Louisiana State University Press, 2009.

———. *Summer Snow: Reflections from a Black Daughter of the South.* Beacon, 2003.

Harrison, Suzan. "Racial Content Espied: Modernist Politics, Textuality, and Race in Eudora Welty's 'The Demonstrators.'" *Eudora Welty and Politics: Did the Writer Crusade?* edited by Harriet Pollack and Suzanne Marrs. Louisiana State University Press, 2001, pp. 89–108.

Hebert-Leiter, Maria. "A Breed between: Racial Mediation in the Fiction of Ernest Gaines." *MELUS: Multi-Ethnic Literature of the United States,* vol. 31, no. 2, 2006, pp. 95–117.

Hentz, Caroline Lee. *The Planter's Northern Bride.* Kessinger Publishing, 2010

Himes, Chester B. *Cotton Comes to Harlem.* Vintage, 1988.

———. *My Life of Absurdity: The Autobiography of Chester Himes.* Thunder's Mouth Press, 1998.

Himes, Chester B., Michel Fabre, and Robert E. Skinner. *Conversations with Chester Himes: Literary Conversations Series.* University Press of Mississippi, 1995.

Hindman, Douglas Blanks, and Kenneth Wiegand. "The Big Three's Prime-Time Decline: A Technological and Social Context." *Journal of Broadcasting & Electronic Media,* vol. 52, no. 1, 2008, pp. 119–135.

Hinrichsen, Lisa, et al. "Introduction: The Televisual South." *Small-Screen Souths: Region, Identity, and the Cultural Politics of Television,* edited by Lisa Hinrichsen, Stephanie Rountree, and Gina Caison. Louisiana State University Press, 2017, pp. 1–23.

Ho, Helen K. "The Model Minority in the Zombie Apocalypse: Asian-American Manhood on AMC's *The Walking Dead*." *The Journal of Popular Culture,* vol. 49, no. 1, 2016, pp. 57–76.

Hobson, Fred C. *The Southern Writer in the Postmodern World*. University of Georgia Press, 1991.

———. *Tell about the South: The Southern Rage to Explain*. Louisiana State University Press, 1983.

Hofstede, David. *The Dukes of Hazzard: The Unofficial Companion*. St. Martin's Griffin 2005.

Holland, Mary K. *Succeeding Postmodernism: Language and Humanism in Contemporary American Literature*. Bloomsbury, 2014.

hooks, bell. "Clarity: Give Love Words." *All about Love: New Visions*. William Morrow, an Imprint of Harper Collins Publishers, 2001, pp. 1–14.

———. "Justice: Childhood Love Lessons." *All about Love: New Visions*. William Morrow, an Imprint of Harper Collins Publishers, 2001, pp. 15–30.

———. *Outlaw Culture: Resisting Representations*. Routledge, 1994.

———. "Postmodern Blackness." *Postmodern Debates*, edited by Simon Malpas. Palgrave, 2001, pp. 128–135.

"The Horse Trader." *The Andy Griffith Show*, written by Jack Elinson, et al., season 1, episode 14, CBS, 9 Jan. 1961.

Hughes, Langston. "Let America be America Again." *The Collected Poems of Langston Hughes*. Vintage Classics, 1995, pp. 189–191.

Hutcheon, Linda. *The Politics of Postmodernism*. Routledge, 2002.

Jacks, Robert L., et al., directors. *The Waltons*. Warner Home Video, 2018.

Jackson, Alan. "Where Were You (When the World Stopped Turning)." Arista Nashville, 2001.

Jameson, Fredric. *Postmodernism, or the Cultural Logic of Late Capitalism*. Verso, 1991.

Janette, Michele. "'Distorting Overlaps': Identity as Palimpsest in *Bitter in the Mouth*." *MELUS: Thick Historical and Cultural Contexts for the Study of Multi-Ethnic Literary Texts*, vol. 39, no. 3, fall 2014. Oxford University Press, pp. 19–27.

Jennings, Waylon. "Theme from the Dukes of Hazzard (Good Ol' Boys)." Playlist: The Very Best of Waylon Jennings. RLG Legacy, 2008.

Jones, LeRoi. *Blues People: Negro Music in White America*. Morrow, 1963.

Josephs, Allen. "The Quest for God in the Road." *The Cambridge Companion to Cormac McCarthy*, edited by Steven Frye. Cambridge University Press, 2013.

Jurgensen, John. "Hollywood's Favorite Cowboy." *The Wall Street Journal*. Dow Jones & Company, 20 Nov. 2009, https://www.wsj.com/articles/SB10001424052748704576204574529703577274572.

Kane, Patricia, and Doris Y. Wilkinson. "Survival Strategies: Black Women in Ollie Miss and Cotton Comes to Harlem." *Critique: Studies in Contemporary Fiction*, vol. 16, no. 1, Oct. 1974, pp. 101–109.

Kasper, Eric T., and Troy A. Kozma. "No Arts, No Letters, No Society, and Which Is Worst of All, Zombies: The Walking Dead and Hobbesian Politics." *The Journal of Popular Culture*, vol. 52, no. 3, 2019, pp. 542–563.

Keith, Toby. "Courtesy of the Red, White and Blue (The Angry American)." *Unleashed*, Dreamworks Nashville, 2002.

Kendi, Ibram X. "The Hopefulness and Hopelessness of 1619." *The Atlantic*. Atlantic Media Company, 20 Aug. 2019, www.theatlantic.com/ideas /archive/2019/08/historical-significance-1619/596365/.

Kendi, Ibram X. *How to Be an Antiracist*. Vintage, 2019.

———. *Stamped from the Beginning: The Definitive History of Racist Ideas in America*. Bold Type Books, 2016.

King, Martin Luther, Jr. *Where Do We Go from Here: Chaos or Community?* Harper & Row, 1967.

Komunyakaa, Yusef. *Magic City*. Wesleyan University Press, 1992.

Kreyling, Michael. "Fee Fie Faux Faulkner: Parody and Postmodernism in Southern Literature." *The Southern Review*, vol. 29, no. 1, winter 1993.

———. *Inventing Southern Literature*. University Press of Mississippi, 1998.

Lambert, Raphaël. "The Conservative Dispositions of Roots." *Transition*, vol. 122, no. 1, 2017, pp. 98–112.

Leach, Laurie F. "Roots and the Trope of the Good Slaveholder." *Slavery & Abolition*, vol. 40, no. 2, 2018, pp. 361–379.

Lechner, Zachary J. *The South of the Mind: American Imaginings of White Southernness, 1960–1980*. University of Georgia Press, 2018.

Lipsitz, George. *The Possessive Investment in Whiteness: How White People Profit from Identity Politics*. Temple University Press, 1998.

Littleton, Cynthia. "Fred Silverman Helped Shape Modern Television." *Variety*, 347.1, 2020.

Lloyd, Christopher. *Rooting Memory, Rooting Place: Regionalism in the Twenty-First-Century American South*. Palgrave Macmillan, 2015.

Lorde, Audre. "Age, Race, Class and Sex: Women Redefining Difference." *Your Silence Will Not Protect You*. Silver Press, 2017, pp. 94–106.

———. "The Uses of Anger: Women Responding to Racism." *Your Silence Will Not Protect You*. Silver Press, 2017, pp. 107–118.

Lumumba, Ebony O. "Demonstrations of Life: Signifying for Social Justice in Eudora Welty's 'The Demonstrators.'" *New Essays on Eudora Welty, Class, and Race*, edited by Harriet Pollack. University Press of Mississippi, 2020, pp. 171–188.

Majeres, Kevin D. "The Doctor and the 'Delta Factor': Walker Percy and the Dilemma of Modern Medicine." *Perspectives in Biology and Medicine,* vol. 45, no. 4, 2002, pp. 579–592.

Mallet, Gina. "Griffith Leaves Mayberry for Matlock." *Chatelaine,* vol. 60, no. 1, 1987, pp. 14.

Matlock. Perf. Andy Griffith, Linda Purl, Kene Holliday. NBC, ABC, 1986–1995.

McCarthy, Cormac. *The Road.* Vintage International, 2006.

McHaney, Pearl Amelia. "Natasha Trethewey's Triptych: The Bodies of History in *Bellocq's Ophelia, Native Guard,* and *Thrall.*" Southern *Quarterly,* vol. 50, no, 4, summer 2013, pp. 153–172, 224.

McLaughlin, Robert L. "Post-Postmodern Discontent: Contemporary Fiction and the Social World." *Symploke,* vol. 12, no. 1, 2004, pp. 53–68.

McPherson, Tara. *Reconstructing Dixie: Race, Gender, and Nostalgia in the Imagined South.* Duke University Press, 2003.

MELUS: Multi-Ethnic Literature of the United States, vol. 39, no. 3, 2014, pp. 155–177.

Miller, Cynthia J. "'So This Zombie Walks into a Bar . . .': The Living, the Undead, and the Western Saloon." *Undead in the West: Vampires, Zombies, Mummies and Ghosts on the Cinematic Frontier,* edited by Cynthia J. Miller and A. Bowdoin Van Riper. Scarecrow Press, 2012, pp. 3–18.

Miller, Donna S. "Relentless Crime Threatens Heat's Credibility." Review of *In the Heat of the Night, Chatelaine,* vol. 62, no. 24, Apr. 1989.

Mitchell, W. J. T. *Iconology: Image, Text, Ideology.* University of Chicago Press, 1986.

Morrison, Toni. *Playing in the Dark: Whiteness and the Literary Imagination.* Harvard University Press, 1992.

———. "Unspeakable Things Unspoken: The Afro-American Presence in American Literature." *Michigan Quarterly Review,* vol. 28, no. 1, winter 1989, pp. 1–34.

MSNBC. "Blaming President Donald Trump Is Too Easy: This Is Us. | Deadline | MSNBC." Lean Forward. *YouTube,* YouTube, 5 Aug. 2019, https://www.youtube.com/watch?v=QKiBoAPdxTo. Accessed 19 Jan. 2022.

———. "Eddie Glaude: It's Easy To Place It All On Donald Trump's Shoulders. This Is Us. | Deadline | MSNBC" Lean Forward. *YouTube,* YouTube, 5 Aug. 2019, https://www.youtube.com/watch?v=S2SF34Bg4_k. Accessed 19 Jan. 2022.

Murray, William. "Learning to Listen: The Way a Society Speaks in Eudora Welty's 'Where Is the Voice Coming From?' and 'The Demonstrators.'" *Eudora Welty Review* vol. 8, no. 1, 2016, pp. 109–122.

Nealon, Jeffrey T. *Post-Postmodernism: or, The Cultural Logic of Just-in-Time Capitalism.* Stanford University Press, 2012.

Nealon, Jeffrey T., and Susan Searls Giroux. *The Theory Toolbox: Critical Concepts for the Humanities, Arts, and Social Sciences.* Rowman & Littlefield, 2012.

Neff, John, Jarod Roll, and Anne Twitty. "A Brief Historical Contextualization of the Confederate Monument at the University of Mississippi." University of Mississippi, https://history.olemiss.edu/wp-content/uploads/sites/6/2017/08/A-Brief-Historical-Contextualization-of-the-Confederate-Monument-at-the-University-of-Mississippi.pdf.

Nietzsche, Friedrich Wilhelm. *Beyond Good and Evil.* Gateway Editions; distributed by H. Regnery Co., 1955.

O'Connor, John J. "Review/Television; For 'Heat of Night,' A New Life." *The New York Times,* April 5, 1988, Tuesday, Late City Final Edition.

Painter, Nell Irvin. *The History of White People.* W. W. Norton, 2010.

Pearson, Michael. "Language and Love in Walker Percy's *The Second Coming.*" *The Southern Literary Journal,* vol. 20, no. 1, 1987, pp. 89–100.

Percy, Walker. *The Second Coming.* Farrar, Straus, Giroux, 1980.

Percy, Walker, and Zoltan Abadi-Nagy. "The Art of Fiction XCVII: Walker Percy." *More Conversations with Walker Percy,* edited by Lewis A. Lawson and Victor A. Kramer. University Press of Mississippi, 1993, pp. 134–155.

Percy, Walker, and Peggy Castex. "An Interview with Walker Percy." *More Conversations with Walker Percy,* edited by Lewis A. Lawson and Victor A. Kramer. University Press of Mississippi, 1993, pp. 44–58.

Percy, Walker, and Jo Gulledge. "The Reentry Option: An Interview with Walker Percy." *Conversations with Walker Percy,* edited by Lewis A. Lawson and Victor Anthony Kramer. University Press of Mississippi, 1985, pp. 284–308.

Percy, Walker, and Marc Kirkeby. "Percy: He Can See Clearly Now." *Conversations with Walker Percy,* edited by Lewis A. Lawson and Victor Anthony Kramer. University Press of Mississippi, 1985, pp. 190–198.

Percy, Walker, and Robin Leary. "Surviving His Own Bad Habits: An Interview with Walker Percy." *More Conversations with Walker Percy,* edited by Lewis A. Lawson and Victor A. Kramer. University Press of Mississippi, 1993, pp. 59–65.

Percy, Walker, and William Starr. "Interview." *More Conversations with Walker Percy,* edited by Lewis A. Lawson and Victor A. Kramer. University Press of Mississippi, 1993, pp. 36–43.

Perloff, Marjorie, et al. "The Birth, Death, and Rebirth of Postmodernism." *The Chronicle of Higher Education,* 14 June 2019.

Perry, Imani. *South to America: A Journey below the Mason-Dixon to Understand the Soul of a Nation.* ECCO, an Imprint of Harper Collins Publishers, 2022.

Price, Reynolds. "A Louisiana Pagent of Calamity." *The New York Times,* 30 Oct. 1983, p. 15.

Putnam, Robert D. *Bowling Alone: The Collapse and Revival of American Community.* Touchstone, 2000.

Putnam, Robert D., and Shaylyn Romney Garrett. *The Upswing: How We Came Together a Century Ago and How We Can Do It Again.* Swift Press, 2021.

Rash, Ron. "Dead Confederates." *Something Rich and Strange: Selected Stories.* Harper Collins, 2014.

Rasmussen, Birgit Brander, editor. *The Making and Unmaking of Whiteness.* Duke University Press, 2001.

Rodgers, Daniel T. *Age of Fracture.* Belknap Press of Harvard University Press, 2011.

Rodogno, Raffaele. "Shame and Guilt in Restorative Justice." *Psychology, Public Policy, and Law,* 14, pp. 142–176.

Roediger, David R. *The Wages of Whiteness: Race and the Making of the American Working Class.* Verso, 2007.

Romine, Scott. *The Real South: Southern Narrative in the Age of Cultural Reproduction.* Louisiana State University Press, 2008.

———. "Where Is Southern Literature? The Practice of Place in a Postsouthern Age." *Critical Survey,* vol. 12, no. 1, 2000, pp. 5–27.

Rorty, Richard. *Achieving Our Country: Leftist Thought in Twentieth-Century America.* Harvard University Press, 1998.

Ross, Thomas. "Innocence and Affirmative Action." *Vanderbilt Law Review,* vol. 43, no. 2, Mar. 1990, pp. 297–304.

Sallis, James. *Chester Himes: A Life.* Walker & Co., 2002.

Schulman, Bruce J. *The Seventies: The Great Shift in American Culture, Society, and Politics.* Da Capo Press, 2008.

Seib, Kenneth. "'Sabers, Gentlemen, Sabers': The J.E.B. Stuart Stories of Barry Hannah." *The Mississippi Quarterly,* vol. 45, no. 1, 1991, pp. 41–52.

Seltzer, Catherine. *Understanding Pat Conroy.* University of South Carolina Press, 2015.

Sharpe, Christina. *In the Wake: On Blackness and Being.* Duke University Press, 2016.

Simpson, Lewis P. *The Brazen Face of History: Studies in the Literary Consciousness in America.* University of Georgia Press, 1997.

Sirota, David. *Back to Our Future: How the 1980s Explain the World We Live in Now—Our Culture, Our Politics, Our Everything.* Ballantine Books, 2011.

Smith, David Lionel. "Bloodlines and Patriarchs: *Of Love and Dust* and Its Revision of Faulkner." *Critical Reflections on the Fiction of Ernest J. Gaines*, edited by David C. Estes. University of Georgia Press, 1994.

Smith, Jon. *Finding Purple America: The South and the Future of American Cultural Studies*. University of Georgia Press, 2013.

Spikes, Michael P. "What's in a Name? A Reading of Barry Hannah's 'Ray.'" *The Mississippi Quarterly*, vol. 42, no. 1, 1988, pp. 69–82.

Sugg, Katherine. "The Walking Dead: Late Liberalism and Masculine Subjection in Apocalypse Fictions." *Journal of American Studies*, vol. 49, no. 4, 2015, pp. 793–811.

Taylor, Charles. *The Ethics of Authenticity*. Harvard University Press, 1999.

———. *A Secular Age*. Belknap of Harvard University Press, 2007.

Taylor, Kristine. "Untimely Subjects: White Trash and the Making of Racial Innocence in the Postwar South." *American Quarterly*, vol. 67, no. 1, 2015, pp. 55–79.

Taylor, L. Jerome. "The Movement to Selfhood." *Renascence*, vol. 44, no. 3, 1992, pp. 163–174.

Taylor, Melanie, Benson. *Reconstructing the Native South: American Indian Literature and the Lost Cause*. University of Georgia Press, 2011.

Tenga, Angel, and Jonathan Bassett. "'You Kill or You Die, or You Die and You Kill': Meaning and Violence in AMC's the *Walking Dead*." *The Journal of Popular Culture*, vol. 49, no. 6, 2016, pp. 1280–1300.

Teutsch, Matthew. "'Mr. Joe Louis, Help Me': Sports in the Fiction of Ernest J. Gaines." *MELUS: Multi-Ethnic Literature of the United States*, vol. 42, no. 3, 2017, pp. 176–200.

Thomas, James G., editor. *Conversations with Barry Hannah*. University Press of Mississippi, 2016.

Torres, Sasha. *Black, White, and in Color: Television, Policing, and Black Civil Rights*. Princeton University Press, 2003.

Townsend, Leo, and Pauline Townsend. "Opie's Piano Lesson." *The Andy Griffith Show*, season 7, episode 26, CBS, 13 Mar. 1967.

Trethewey, Natasha. *Native Guard*. Mariner Books, 2007.

Troy, Gil. *Morning in America: How Ronald Reagan Invented the 1980s*. Princeton University Press, 2007.

Tucker, Terrence T. "(Re)Claiming Legacy in the Post-Civil Rights South in Richard Wright's 'Down by the Riverside' and Ernest Gaines's *A Gathering of Old Men*." *The Southern Literary Journal*, vol. 43, no. 2, 2011, pp. 105–24.

Turner, Luke. "Metamodernism: A Brief Introduction." *Notes on Metamodernism*, January 12, 2015, http://www.metamodernism.com/2015/01/12/metamodernism-a-brief-introduction.

"University Sets Oct. 1 Dedication for Civil Rights Monument." *Newswise*, 22 Sept. 2006, http://www.newswise.com/articles/university-sets-oct-1-dedication -for-civil-rights-monument.

Vaughan, Don Rodney. "Why the Andy Griffith Show Is Important to Popular Cultural Studies." *The Journal of Popular Culture*, vol. 38, no. 2, 2004, pp. 397–423.

Vermeulen, Timotheus, and Robin Van den Akker. "Notes on Metamodernism." *Journal of Aesthetics & Culture*, vol. 2, no. 1, 2010.

Vernon, Zackary. "The Role of Witness: Ron Rash's Peculiarly Historical Consciousness." *The South Carolina Review*, vol. 42, no. 2, 2010, pp. 19–24.

———. "Romanticizing the Rough South." *Southern Cultures*, vol. 22, no. 3, fall 2016, pp. 77–94.

Visé, Daniel De. *Andy and Don: The Making of a Friendship and a Classic American TV Show*. Simon & Schuster, 2015.

Waldron, Gy. "One Armed Bandits." *The Dukes of Hazard*, season 1, episode 1, CBS, 26 Jan. 1979.

Wallace, David Foster. *A Supposedly Fun Thing I'll Never Do Again: Essays and Arguments*. Little, Brown, 1997.

Walsh, Chris. "The Post-Southern Sense of Place in *The Road*." *The Cormac McCarthy Journal*, vol. 6, 2008, pp. 48–54.

Watts, Amy. "South of Broad." *Library Journal*, vol. 134, no. 12, July 2009, p. 80.

Waugh, Patricia. "Introduction." *Postmodernism: A Reader*, edited by Patricia Waugh. Arnold, 1996, pp. 1–10.

Welty, Eudora. "The Demonstrators." *Eudora Welty: Stories, Essays, & Memoir*. Library of America, 1998.

Werning, David Hugh. "The Creeper Scene in Walker Percy's *The Second Coming*." *Renascence*, vol. 54, no. 4, 2002, pp. 247–257.

Weyler, Karen. *Empowering Words: Outsiders and Authorship in Early America*. University of Georgia Press, 2013.

Whedon, John. "Andy Discovers America." *The Andy Griffith Show*, season 3, episode 23, CBS, 4 Mar. 1963.

Wiebe, Joseph R. "Race, Place, and Radical Remembering in Wendell Berry's *Andy Catlett*." *Early Travels, Literature and Theology*, vol. 32, no. 3, pp. 340–356.

Wilkerson, Isabel. *The Warmth of Other Suns: The Epic Story of America's Great Migration*. Penguin Random House, 2010.

Williams, Linda. *Playing the Race Card: Melodramas of Black and White from Uncle Tom to O. J. Simpson*. Princeton University Press, 2002.

Williams, Raymond. *Television: Technology and Cultural Form*. Routledge, 2003.

Winant, Howard. "White Racial Projects." *The Making and Unmaking of Whiteness,* edited by Birgit Brander Rasmussen. Duke University Press, 2001, pp. 97–112.

Woodson, Linda. "Mapping *The Road* in Post-Postmodernism." *The Cormac McCarthy Journal,* vol. 6, 2008, 87–97.

Woodward, C. Vann. *The Burden of Southern History.* Louisiana State University Press, 1960.

Wright, Richard. *Black Boy.* Anniversary Edition; Harper Perennial Modern Classics, 2007.

X, Malcolm, and Alex Haley. *The Autobiography of Malcolm X: with the Assistance of Alex Haley.* Ballantine Books, 1973.

Yeager, Patricia. *Dirt and Desire: Reconstructing Southern Women's Writing, 1930–1990.* University of Chicago Press, 2000.

Younge, Gary. "The Misremembering of 'I Have a Dream.'" *The Nation,* 15 Jan. 2016, https://www.thenation.com/article/archive/misremembering-i-have-dream/.

Yuhl, Stephanie E. *A Golden Haze of Memory: The Making of Historic Charleston.* University of North Carolina Press, 2005.

Žižek, Slavoj, and John Milbank. *The Monstrosity of Christ: Paradox or Dialectic?* MIT Press, 2009.

Index

Printed in the USA
CPSIA information can be obtained
at www.ICGtesting.com
CBHW021318280324
6002CB00002B/16

9 780807 181553